Desserts

by
THE EDITORS OF TIME-LIFE BOOKS

TIME-LIFE BOOKS·AMSTERDAM

TIME-LIFE INTERNATIONAL
EUROPEAN EDITOR: Kit van Tulleken
Design Director: Louis Klein
Photography Director: Pamela Marke
Chief of Research: Vanessa Kramer
Text Director: Simon Rigge (acting)
Chief of Design: Graham Davis
Chief Sub-Editor: Ilse Gray

THE GOOD COOK
Series Editor: Windsor Chorlton
Series Co-ordinator: Liz Timothy

Editorial Staff for *Desserts*
Text Editor: Alan Lothian
Anthology Editor: Liz Clasen
Staff Writers: Gillian Boucher, Jay Ferguson,
Mary Harron, Norman Kolpas
Designer: Rick Bowring
Researcher: Alexandra Carlier
Sub-Editors: Nicoletta Flessati, Katie Lloyd
Permissions Researcher: Mary-Claire Hailey
Assistant Designer: Mary Staples
Design Assistant: Cherry Doyle
Editorial Assistant: Molly Sutherland

EDITORIAL PRODUCTION FOR THE SERIES
Production Editor: Ellen Brush
Quality Control: Douglas Whitworth
Traffic Co-ordinators: Pat Boag, Joanne Holland
Picture Co-ordinator: Philip Garner
Art Department: Julia West
Editorial Department: Anetha Besidonne,
Debra Dick, Margaret Hall

TIME
LIFE
BOOKS

WORLD WAR II
THE SEAFARERS
THE GOOD COOK
THE TIME-LIFE ENCYCLOPAEDIA OF GARDENING
HUMAN BEHAVIOUR
THE GREAT CITIES
THE ART OF SEWING
THE OLD WEST
THE WORLD'S WILD PLACES
THE EMERGENCE OF MAN
LIFE LIBRARY OF PHOTOGRAPHY
THIS FABULOUS CENTURY
FOODS OF THE WORLD
TIME-LIFE LIBRARY OF ART
GREAT AGES OF MAN
LIFE SCIENCE LIBRARY
LIFE NATURE LIBRARY
YOUNG READERS LIBRARY
LIFE WORLD LIBRARY
THE TIME-LIFE BOOK OF BOATING
TECHNIQUES OF PHOTOGRAPHY
LIFE AT WAR
LIFE GOES TO THE MOVIES
BEST OF LIFE

Cover: Whole blackberries and a blackberry purée
decorate a *flamri* (*page 54*)—a moulded soufflé pudding
made from semolina. To present this fragile pudding in a
double-tier form, the *flamri* was cooked in two separate
moulds, and one was turned out on top of the other.

THE CHIEF CONSULTANT:
Richard Olney, an American, has lived and worked since 1951
in France, where he is a highly regarded authority on food and
wine. A regular contributor to the influential journals *Cuisine et
Vins de France* and *La Revue du Vin de France,* he has also
written numerous articles for other gastronomic magazines in
France and the United States, and is the author of *The French
Menu Cookbook* and the award-winning *Simple French
Food.* He has directed cooking courses in France and the
United States and is a member of several distinguished gas-
tronomic societies, including *La Confrérie des Chevaliers du
Tastevin, La Commanderie du Bontemps de Médoc et des
Graves* and *Les Amitiés Gastronomiques Internationales.*

SPECIAL CONSULTANT:
Jeremiah Tower is an eminent American *restaurateur* who lived for many years in
Europe and is a member of *La Commanderie du Bontemps de Médoc et des Graves*
and *La Jurade de Saint-Émilion.* He has been largely responsible for the step-by-step
photographic sequences in this volume and has worked closely with the other consultants on the anthology selections.

THE PHOTOGRAPHERS:
Alan Duns was born in 1943 in the north of England and studied at the Ealing School of
Photography. He specializes in food photography and has undertaken many advertising assignments. His work has appeared in major British publications.
Tom Belshaw was born near London and started his working career in films. He now
has his own studio in London. He specializes in food and still-life photography,
undertaking both editorial and advertising assignments.

THE INTERNATIONAL CONSULTANTS:
Great Britain: *Jane Grigson* was born in Gloucester and brought up in the north of
England. She is a graduate of Cambridge University. Her first book on food, *Charcu-
terie and French Pork Cookery,* was published in 1967; since then, she has published a
number of cookery books, including *Good Things, English Food* and *The Mushroom
Feast.* She became cookery correspondent for the colour magazine of the London
Observer in 1968. *Alan Davidson* is the author of *Fish and Fish Dishes of Laos,
Mediterranean Seafood* and *North Atlantic Seafood.* He is writing *The Oxford Com-
panion to Food,* to be published by the Oxford University Press. **France:** *Michel
Lemonnier* was born in Normandy. He began contributing to the magazine *Cuisine et
Vins de France* in 1960, and also writes for several other important French food and
wine periodicals. The co-founder and vice-president of the society *Les Amitiés Gastronomiques Internationales,* he is a frequent lecturer on wine and vineyards, and a
member of most of the vinicultural confraternities in France. **Germany:** *Jochen Kuchen-
becker* trained as a chef, but worked for 10 years as a food photographer in many
European countries before opening his own restaurant in Hamburg. *Anne Brakemeier,*
who also lives in Hamburg, has published articles on food and cooking in many
German periodicals. She is the co-author of three cookery books. **The Netherlands:**
Hugh Jans, a resident of Amsterdam, has been translating cookery books and articles
for more than 25 years. He has also published two books of his own, *Bistro Koken* and
Koken in Casserole, and his recipes are published in many Dutch magazines.
The United States: *Carol Cutler,* a resident of Washington, DC, is the author of *Haute
Cuisine for Your Heart's Delight* and the award-winning *The Six-Minute Soufflé and
Other Culinary Delights.* A contributing editor of both *International Food and Wine* and
Working Woman magazines, she frequently lectures about food and gives demonstra-
tions of cooking techniques. *Shirley Sarvis,* a freelance food writer and consultant in San
Francisco, is the author and co-author of a dozen cookery books. *José Wilson* moved
to the United States from England in 1951. The food editor of *House and Garden*
magazine for 15 years, she has written many books on food and interior decoration,
including *American Cooking: the Eastern Heartland* in TIME-LIFE Books' *Foods of the
World* series and, with Arthur Leaman, *The Complete Food Catalog.*

Valuable help was given in the preparation of this volume by the following members of
TIME-LIFE Books: *Michèle le Baube, Cecile Dogniez, Maria Vincenza Aloisi, Joséphine
du Brusle* (Paris); *Jeanne Buys* (Amsterdam); *Hans-Heinrich Wellmann, Gertraud
Bellon* (Hamburg); *Bona Schmid, Maria Teresa Marenco* (Milan).

CONTENTS

Ending a Meal with Grace and Flavour

All good food affords pleasure; desserts are devised for pleasure alone. At the end of the meal, when appetites are largely satisfied, the dessert restores the palate and hints at sensuous luxury. Even Mrs. Beeton, the 19th-century culinary encyclopaedist and a woman not much given to figures of speech, was moved by the subject. In *The Book of Household Management*, she wrote, almost grudgingly: "If there be any poetry at all in meals, or the process of feeding, there is poetry in the dessert".

How to compose such "poetry" is the subject of this book. At their simplest, desserts need not involve more than choosing ripe, perfect fruit and presenting it unadorned. Other, more elaborate, desserts may require the application of many techniques—pounding or sieving, beating or churning, baking or freezing—and these are fully covered in the chapters that follow. But whatever the degree of complexity, all desserts demand attention to detail, whether in removing the pith from an orange peel or in carefully separating eggs for a custard. Happily, the ingredients themselves are seldom elaborate. A few eggs, cream, chocolate or some fresh fruit are almost all that is required to produce an exquisite layered Bavarian cream; with some semolina from the store cupboard, you can create the soufflé pudding shown on the cover.

Sugar, of course, is present in practically any meal-ending creation. Most human beings have an irrepressible appetite for sweet things, and desserts exist to indulge it. Indeed, the development of the modern idea of desserts is inseparable from the increasing availability—and hence popularity—of sugar. Although sugar was widely used in India by the 5th century B.C., it was a rare delicacy elsewhere, imported in small quantities and so highly priced that it was known as "white gold". Honey was the main sweetener in European cookery until the 15th century. Moorish conquerors gradually spread the cultivation of sugar cane from the east through North Africa into Sicily and Spain, but supplies of sugar in Europe only increased dramatically when the Spaniards colonized the Caribbean from the 16th century onwards and introduced plantations there.

Even "white gold" was not the pure, evenly granulated sucrose we know today. Until the beginning of this century sugar came in the form of rock-hard loaves. Heavy iron tongs were needed to break up the loaves, after which the sugar had to be pounded in a mortar to make a powder. Refining methods were crude: cooks who wanted pure sugar cooked a syrup and then clarified it by lengthy skimming to remove impurities.

Although the modern cook is spared such chores by today's refineries, it is still necessary to transform sugar into syrups and caramel at home. For this reason you will find a guide on page 8 to all the syrups commonly used in dessert cookery, and an explanation of the eccentric terminology often used to describe them.

Egg whites, too, are another dessert essential that has engendered mysterious descriptions and murky advice. Despite hints to the contrary, making a voluminous, stable foam is not a matter of luck, magic, or the phases of the moon: on page 14, you will discover how proper equipment, correctly cared for, and adroit whisking will yield the sort of foam you require. Once you have mastered these basic beating skills, you will find no difficulty in making any of the scores of desserts that depend on egg whites for their leavening. On the same pages, a step-by-step photographic sequence shows you how to recognize the stages through which the beaten whites will pass—and indicates the optimum stage for different types of dessert. To make a perfect soufflé or a mousse, for example, (*page 50 and 52*) the whites must be soft enough to blend easily with a flavouring; they should be beaten only until they form gently drooping peaks. Meringues (*page 46*) need no such blending; to make them firm and almost weightless, the whites must be beaten until they are very stiff.

Any list of key ingredients necessarily includes gelatine, for it allows you to set a dessert in an attractive mould, then turn it out for serving. Gelantine can also give added body to mousses or cold soufflés, but in every instance it must be used with care: too much, and the dessert is tough and rubbery, too little and the dessert collapses. Page 16 shows how to use ordinary commercial gelatine, whether it has come in leaf or powder form, and, using traditional methods, how to prepare gelatine yourself, starting with calf's feet—source of the finest and purest gelatine of all.

Immediately following these guides to the use of essential ingredients are chapters dealing with the basic categories of dessert cookery—among them fruit desserts, crêpes and fritters and frozen desserts. On these pages are demonstrated the fundamental techniques of dessert cookery, from the preparation of fruit for a salad to the making of a smooth, pouring custard. The final chapter in this section of the book combines and extends the varous techniques explained earlier to encompass such classic creations as charlotte russe and dramatic constructions such as a basket of meringue filled with fruit and ice cream.

The second half of the book comprises an international anthology of dessert recipes, chosen from the best ever published. Some recipes call for precision: it would be unwise to stray too far from the proportions and timings given in a recipe for a fruit jelly or a soufflé, for example. But other recipes—for trifle, fruit compotes or ice cream, perhaps—can be adapted endlessly. Within the

guidelines spelled out in the first half of the book, and aided by the inspiration provided by the recipe anthology in the second half, the possibilities for creativity and experiment are limited only by your imagination.

Desserts in the menu

Although people have eaten various kinds of sweet dishes since earliest times, the notion of a separate sweet course, served at the end of a meal, is a relatively modern idea. As late as the 14th century, as one recorded Parisian menu reveals, a French banquet might feature frumenty—a kind of sweet grain porridge—as well as fruit jellies and fritters, set alongside haunches of venison and platters of lampreys and sturgeon: the guests helped themselves haphazardly to whatever they fancied. The history of some of today's desserts reflects an erstwhile lack of clearly differentiated food categories. *Blanc-manger*, a Bavarian cream made with almond milk, gelatine and whipped cream (*page 44*) was once a sweetened concoction of pounded chicken breast and almonds. (The name *blanc-manger* aptly describes both versions: it translates as "something white to eat").

One reason for the indiscriminate mingling of sweet and savoury dishes—to modern tastes, almost in the manner of a children's party—was undoubtedly ostentation. A table crowded with as many different dishes as it would bear made an impressive display. At the same time, because sweetenings (and the spices that often went with them) were costly, a host who served sweet dishes at every opportunity left his guests in no doubt that he was a man of means.

Even when low-priced sugar became widely available, the separation of the dessert into the final course of a meal took time. Cooks and their employers alike were reluctant to abandon the grandiose table settings they had grown up with, and it was not until the middle of the 19th century that the idea of presenting foods in the order in which they should be eaten, so that each course in turn was replaced with a subsequent course, won full acceptance. But once *service à la russe*—as the innovation was called—had been adopted, it rapidly became the norm throughout the Western world.

Diners welcomed the new system, since they were at last able to eat all their food while it was still at the correct temperature. Cooks benefited because their creations would be enjoyed at their best. At the same time, cooks had the pleasant challenge of developing a new and demanding art form: the menu. Dish succeeded well-chosen dish in a carefully calculated sequence

that imposed a kind of rhythm, a developing play of diminuendo and crescendo on the palate. And the dessert completed the work.

Presentation and selection

Because of its culminating position in the menu, the dessert must complement, and even compete with, all that has gone before it. In order to tempt the appetites of guests at the conclusion of a long meal, the dessert presentation should be exciting and attractive. Indeed, the art of dessert cookery is very much the art of temptation. In the past, dessert presentations owed as much to architecture as to cookery; the Victorians favoured enormous, multi-tiered centrepieces, vast and fantastical assemblies decorated with spun sugar and often gold leaf.

Few diners today would be impressed by such creations. In fact, their very size often made them a poor way of appreciating them as food. Immense jellies, for example, would only support their own weight if they contained so much gelatine that the dessert's texture was almost chewy. Nevertheless, although the trend is towards relative simplicity, modern cooks still enjoy making displays that demonstrate the beauty of their materials, and since the materials for desserts are so varied and often so eye-catching, decorative presentation remains as attainable as ever.

Fruit desserts are a case in point. An impeccable fruit salad (*page 22*) needs a minimum of preparation to radiate freshness. Fruit purées, combined with whipped cream or beaten with egg white (*page 26*) provide desserts of refreshing simplicity. And fruit also can be served to more formal effect: poached fruit, for example, can lend itself to a mesmerizing interplay of pattern and colour (*page 84*).

But no dessert should be considered outside the context of the meal in which it is to be served. What constitutes a perfect conclusion obviously depends upon the preceding courses. Except at feast times, the heartiest of desserts—the steamed puddings (*page 58*)—generally conclude the simplest meals, perhaps no more than a bowl of meaty soup as the main course. Rich, main dishes call for light and simple desserts, such as a water ice. Conversely, a menu may build up, through dishes of increasing complexity, to a lavish—but never ponderous—finale.

In a single menu you should try to avoid the repetition of flavours and textures. If you have a main course with a fruit element—duck with orange, for example—you should not include the same fruit in the dessert, and you should never serve more than one rich, egg-bound sauce in the course of a meal. Colour is almost as important: a series of creamy-white courses concluded by a similarly coloured dessert is likely to be dull, no

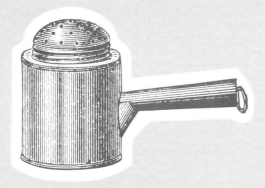

matter how successful each individual dish may be. But there are few hard and fast rules for menu construction, and within the bounds of these commonsense restrictions you are free to experiment as much as you please.

Wine and desserts

The potential relationship of desserts to wine, both as an ingredient and as an accompaniment, is richer and more intricate than many people imagine.

The simplest transformation of wine into an integral part of a dessert consists in merely pouring it over fresh fruit—especially strawberries. Wherever grapes are grown for wine, the onset of the strawberry season launches a delightful ritual for vintners and their families; every day, at least one meal is finished with the presentation of a huge bowl of strawberries. Occasionally the berries in the bowl are sprinkled with sugar and doused in advance with a bottle of red wine, but, most often, the wine glasses containing the last red wine drunk during the meal are filled with strawberries by each person at table, sugared to taste—some prefer not to sugar them—and the strawberries are lightly crushed with a spoon so that the perfumes may intermingle for a moment before being savoured. The qualities of both ingredients are sharpened and thrown into relief by the presence of the other. The strawberries' clean taste is accented and the wine suddenly takes on a new life and freshness.

Strawberries are not the only fruit to bring about such a transformation; peaches, either white or yellow, may be treated in the same way with similar success. Champagne also is often poured over strawberries or peaches. Such use is a particularly attractive possibility for an old champagne, its sparkle on the wane. But champagne's happiest dessert synthesis is probably reached when a dribble of vigorously sparkling wine is poured over a sensuously mushy ice that itself contains champagne, such as the one demonstrated on page 70.

When wine becomes a cooking medium, its character is progressively altered, depending on the degree to which the wine is heated and the length of time that it is cooked. A *sabayon* sauce (*page 39*) might stand as an example of the milder end of the spectrum of treatments: the assemblage of ingredients is merely heated without ever approaching the boiling point. *Sabayon* sauces are often made from undistinguished white wines buttressed by a flavouring agent such as lemon or orange rind and, often, a liqueur of some sort. The result is honourable but, since the wine used in this kind of preparation retains its own charac-

ter, a cook should consider the option of eliminating the extra flavourings and using instead a particularly fine wine that may render that sauce unique.

Longer cooking can change a wine beyond recognition. The syrup drawn from pears cooked in red wine (*recipe, page 100*) is a marvel of sumptuousness, but due to a prolonged simmering, no trace of the wine's original character remains; hence, an honest rustic wine with a good depth of colour is a logical choice. And whereas pouring a noble first growth over fresh strawberries exalts both wine and fruit, poaching your pears in that same wine is tantamount to vinicide.

For some time, the drinking of sweet wines has been unfashionable, in part, no doubt, because they once were habitually served with extraordinarily sweet or rich confections that only clashed with them. In truth, they can be supremely pleasurable especially if allied with a suitable dessert. Despite the French tradition of serving champagne with desserts, it is practically impossible to ally a dry wine and a sweet dessert successfully. For the marriage to be a happy one, the dessert must be less sweet than the wine, since a dessert that is noticeably sweeter will make even the finest of accompanying wines seem thin and acid. It is also best to assume that the dessert should be less cold than the wine (the champagne ice with champagne poured over is a wonderful, but unusual, exception). The dessert should also exclude chocolate, which is one of the most effective of all wine-killers; and acid fruits should enter into the dessert's composition only with the greatest of discretion.

The kind of apple described by the English as an eating apple and by the French as a cooking apple is, in its many dessert guises, an ideal complement to a great sweet wine. Sliced, sautéed in butter, wrapped in hot crêpes, lightly sprinkled with sugar and rapidly glazed beneath a grill or in a hot oven, apples constitute a traditional and brilliant accompaniment to a fine sauternes or an exquisite Trockenbeerenauslese. Pear desserts also lend themselves well to wine accompaniments, as do all nuts and, most particularly, almonds. Bavarian creams (*page 44*) are good with sweet wines; one of the most beautiful and complex of tasting experiences may be a *blanc-manger*, made with almond milk that includes a hint of bitter almond savoured in conjunction with an old sauternes. The typically penetrating depth and vibrant fruit of such a wine, offset by the veiled background of delicate bitterness, the sweetness never flat or cloying, interweave perfectly with the flavours of the dessert. Such an alliance makes a great dessert greater still.

Sugar: a Multi-Purpose Foundation

The common element linking virtually all desserts is sugar. It may be sprinkled over fruit, for example, or beaten into egg yolks for a custard. But in many desserts, sugar is first dissolved and cooked in water to make a syrup that will blend quickly and thoroughly with the other ingredients.

Syrup can be used in a multiplicity of ways: as a poaching liquid for fruit (*page 34*), for instance, or combined with egg yolks in some ice creams. And a concentrated syrup produces caramel.

The traditional pan for syrup-making is of unlined copper, which conducts heat extremely well; it will not react chemically with the sugar. Sugar and water are heated together and then boiled (*box, below*). The sugar must be thoroughly dissolved by stirring over low heat before the syrup is brought to the boil; any undissolved sugar could cause the syrup to crystallize as it boils. Once the syrup has reached the boil, stirring can also bring about crystallization.

The density of the syrup—that is, the proportion of sugar to water—must be tailored to the requirements of the dessert. A light syrup, for example, serves as a dressing for a fruit salad; water ice or a parfait would require a syrup with more body. If you want to prepare a syrup in advance and keep it in the refrigerator for later dessert-making, a heavy, so-called "stock" syrup is the most useful: it can be diluted to whatever strength you want.

In the upper part of the chart opposite are shown the proportions of sugar and water that—with identical cooking time, counted from the moment the mixture begins to boil—will yield the various syrups most useful in dessert cookery. As a convenient—but antiquated—shorthand, cookery writers sometimes describe the sugar content of syrups in terms of the readings the syrups would give on a saccharometer—an instrument for measuring a syrup's density that is calibrated in Baumé degrees. Nowadays, saccharometers are scarce; but if you come across a recipe that calls, say, for a 22° syrup, you can use the chart to translate the figure into proportions of sugar and water.

The syrups in the lower part of the chart—which play a smaller part in most dessert cookery—are much more concentrated, ranging up to a sugar content of 100 per cent. To make them, a different technique is necessary. The sugar is dissolved in a minimum of water, and this small quantity of water is then evaporated by rapid boiling. The properties of the syrup change rapidly as the water boils away, and careful timing is important to obtain the syrup you require. Once all the water has evaporated, only molten sugar is left; after a few seconds, it starts to change colour and become caramel.

For concentrated syrups, the most accurate way of checking what stage the sugar has reached is to take a temperature reading of the boiling syrup; sugar has a higher boiling point than water, so the higher the concentration of sugar, the hotter the syrup will be. Use a sugar thermometer (*Step 2, below*), capable of recording such high temperatures.

If you have no sugar thermometer, you can use the syrup's consistency and, finally, its colour (*box, below right*) as an indication of its progress.

Making Syrup and Caramel

1 Removing crystals. Put the required amounts of sugar and water (*chart, opposite page*) into a pan. Stir gently over low heat to dissolve the sugar. With a pastry brush dipped in hot water, dissolve any sugar crystals that have collected on the sides of the pan.

2 Boiling the syrup. When the sugar has dissolved, stop stirring and increase the heat. Warm a sugar thermometer in a bowl of hot water to lessen the shock of contact with the hot syrup, and place it in the syrup. Boil the syrup rapidly for the time indicated in the chart, or until the thermometer registers the required temperature.

A Guide to Syrup Proportions and Densities

Product	Uses	Sugar	Water	Boiling Time	Temperature	Baumé Density	Yield
Light syrup	A light dressing for fruit salads.	500g 1 lb	90 cl 1½ pints	1 min	102°C approx 215°F	17°	1.25 litres 2 pints
Medium syrup	A heavier dressing for fruit salads, and a poaching liquid for fruits.	500g 1 lb	60 cl 1 pint	1 min	102°C approx 215°F	22°	90 cl 1½ pints
Medium/heavy syrup	A poaching liquid for tart fruits; suitable for thinning and sweetening fruit purées, and preparing water ices and parfaits.	500g 1 lb	50 cl ¾ pint	1 min	102°C approx 215°F	28°	80 cl 1¼ pints
Heavy stock syrup	A heavy syrup that can be stored and diluted as required. Also used in some water ices and parfaits.	500g 1lb	30 cl ½ pint	1 min	104°C approx 220°F	32°	60 cl 1 pint
Sugar at small thread stage	A highly concentrated syrup called for in some ice cream recipes.	500g 1 lb	4 tbsp	20 secs	102°C 215°F	38°	30 cl 10-12 fl oz
Sugar at hard crack stage	Used for glazing fruits, and for making decorative spun threads, in the same way as caramel.	500g 1 lb	4 tbsp	5 mins	157°C 315°F	—	30 cl 10 fl oz
Caramel	Used for glazing fruit, for making decorative spun threads, for lining moulds, and as a flavouring.	500g 1 lb	4 tbsp	6 mins	173°C 345°F	—	30 cl 10 fl oz

Testing a Syrup's Progress

The small thread stage. After about 20 seconds' boiling, stand the pan in cold water to stop further cooking. Let some of the syrup dribble from a spoon: if the syrup falls in a fine, short thread, it has reached the small thread stage (*above*).

The hard crack stage. After the syrup has boiled for 4 to 5 minutes, stand the pan in cold water. Drop a little syrup into cold water. With your fingers, lift out the solidified lump and bend it. If it snaps apart cleanly (*above*), it has reached the hard crack stage.

The caramel stage. Boil the syrup until it begins to colour. Put a spoonful on a white plate; the caramel should be a rich amber shade (*above*). Remove the pan immediately from the heat, and place it in cold water for a few seconds. Overcooked caramel has a bitter taste.

Edible Embellishments of Every Hue

Most smooth, evenly coloured desserts can be made more tempting with a judicious touch of decoration. Contrasting colour is sometimes provided by flower petals or a sprig of leaves—but a decoration that can be eaten as well as admired adds more to a dessert. Intrinsically decorative foods, such as nuts (*page 12*) and fruits—can be used plain or glazed.

Immersing small whole fruits and slices of larger, firm fruits in melted sugar (*below*) coats them with a shiny, transparent film that dries to a crisp casing. Poaching finely cut citrus peel in syrup (*opposite page, above*) then rolling them in sugar, gives the peel a crunchy crust. Both garnishes suit fruit purées and puddings.

Threads of caramel, spun from a spoon and allowed to harden in a criss-cross pattern (*right*), form a shining amber lattice. Use it on ice cream or other cold desserts; warm desserts would melt it.

By pouring melted chocolate on to a flat surface and scraping it with a knife (*opposite page, below*), you can make flaky scrolls to garnish almost any dessert, especially one based on chocolate.

Golden Wisps of Caramel

Making caramel wisps. Prepare some caramel (*page 8*). Use a spoon to dribble it in a thin stream on to an oiled baking tray. Move the spoon over the tray to make a delicate criss-cross tracery (*above, left*). Allow the caramel to cool and harden. Lift it from the tray with your fingers or a small spatula (*above, right*).

Coating Fruit with a Syrup Glaze

Glazing fruit. Wash the fruit and leave it to dry on a rack; then dip the fruit— here, strawberries, grapes and cape gooseberries—into sugar cooked to the hard-crack stage (*page 8*). To dip stemmed fruit, such as grapes, hold them by the stem or loop the stems of a small bunch through the prongs of a fork. Impale other whole fruit, or fruit slices, one at a time, on a skewer. Dip the fruit in the syrup, then hold it over the pan until excess syrup has drained off. Cool the fruit on a rack.

Preparing a Citrus Peel Garnish

1 **Preparing citrus peel.** Wash the fruit—here, an orange and a lemon. Peel the fruit as thinly as possible with a sharp knife. Trim away any bitter white pith so that only the rind itself is left.

2 **Cutting the peel.** With a sharp knife, slice the peel lengthwise into thin strips—each one about half the width of a matchstick. For the most professional effect, try to keep the thickness of the strips as even as possible.

3 **Cooking the strips.** Boil the strips in light syrup for about 5 minutes. Use a fork to lift the strips out of the syrup and set them on a plate to cool. If you like, roll the cooled strips in a tray which has been sprinkled with castor sugar.

Creating Chocolate Scrolls

1 **Pouring the chocolate.** Put dark chocolate into a heavy saucepan and melt it by standing the pan over hot water. When the chocolate has melted, pour it on to a flat, hard surface—a marble slab, as here, or a baking tray.

2 **Spreading the chocolate.** With a palette knife, quickly spread out the warm chocolate to the thickness of card. Smooth the surface of the chocolate as evenly as possible.

3 **Forming the scrolls.** Working away from yourself, gently push a sharp-bladed knife along the work surface, holding it with both hands and keeping the blade at a 45° angle to the surface. The chocolate should roll up into scrolls; if it hardens too much and starts to powder, warm the blade in hot water.

Nuts: a Resource for Flavour and Decoration

Whether whole or ground, roasted or caramelized, nuts are an indispensible part of dessert cookery. Nuts make integral flavourings for creams and ice creams, stuffings for fruit and crêpes and decorations for a large number of other desserts.

The first step in the preparation of nuts is to shell them, usually a simple task that requires only an efficient nutcracker. Inside their shells, nuts are further enclosed by a thin, bitter skin that is often removed. Almonds and pistachios are easily skinned by blanching in boiling water (*below, left*) which loosens the skin and lets it slip off. The nuts are then dried out in the oven. Blanching does not loosen the skin of hazelnuts and brazil nuts so effectively, but 15 minutes' roasting in a moderate oven makes the skin of these nuts flaky and simple to rub off.

To rid nuts of their skin when blanching or after roasting, either peel them with your fingers or roll the nuts briskly in a towel—a method especially effective with small, rounded nuts (*box, opposite page, above left*).

Coconuts need special treatment. Before breaking one open, drain it of its milky liquid by piercing it with a skewer through all three of the soft indentations—or "eyes"—in its husk. Pour off the liquid. Use the back of a large cleaver to break the nut open—a sharp tap about one-third of the way from the end opposite the "eyes" will crack it open along a weak seam. Peel away and then grate or chop the coconut's white flesh.

Used as decorations, nuts can provide a contrast of texture as well as an embellishment. As a garnish, use whole nuts dipped in thick syrup (*page 8*); add chopped or slivered nuts to stuffings for baked fruit (*page 28*) or use them as toppings. Follow the chopping technique demonstrated here (*box, far right*). To sliver almonds, prise the two halves of the nut apart, place each half flat-side down and cut it lengthwise into five or six pieces. You can give chopped or splintered nuts extra flavour and colour by roasting them in a moderate oven, 180°C (350°F or Mark 4) for about 5 minutes.

Nuts that have been ground, pounded or grated release aromatic oils and make excellent flavourings. Ground almonds, for example, can be mixed with sugar to make versatile sweet pastes; ground hazelnuts are sometimes incorporated in a basic meringue mixture (*page 46*). You can pound the nuts in a mortar and pestle (*below*) or an electric food processor.

To make delicately scented nut milks to flavour custards (*page 38*) or Bavarian creams (*page 45*), pounded almonds, or grated coconut, are infused in milk or water (*opposite page, below right*).

Almonds—with or without their skins, and sometimes lightly roasted—are the basis of praline (*opposite page, below*), made by cooking the almonds with caramelized sugar and letting them harden into a brittle slab. Praline can be broken up coarsely for toppings or ground to a powder to flavour soufflés and ice creams.

Blanching and Peeling Tight-Skinned Nuts

1 **Softening the skins.** Put shelled nuts—here, almonds—into a pan of boiling water and parboil them. After a minute or so, remove a sample nut: if its skin slips off easily, the nuts are ready. Drain them.

2 **Removing the skins.** With your fingers, peel the loosened skins from the nuts. Drop almonds in cold water to keep them white. To dry the nuts, so that they keep longer, spread them on a baking tray in an oven preheated to 170°C (325°F or Mark 3) for about 5 minutes.

Pulverizing in a Mortar

Pounding the nuts. Put skinned nuts—here, almonds—in a mortar; to prevent the nuts from spilling over as you work, do not fill the mortar to more than a third of its depth. Using a pestle, pound and grind the nuts until they are reduced to the desired consistency.

Peeling Loose-Skinned Nuts

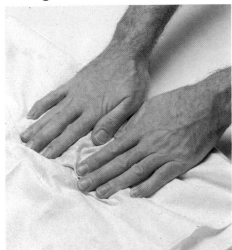 

1 **Loosening the hulls.** Lay a clean towel on a work surface. Wrap parboiled or roasted nuts—here, parboiled pistachios—in the towel. Using the palms of your hands, roll the nuts in the towel.

2 **Peeling the nuts.** After a minute or two of rolling, unwrap the nuts. Most of them will have shed their skins; if any skins cling stubbornly to the nuts, remove them by hand, since repeated rolling will damage the nuts.

Chopping Nuts

Rocking the knife blade. Put a pile of peeled nuts—here, hazelnuts—on a chopping board. Position the blade of a large knife above the pile, resting the fingers of your free hand on its tip. Using the tip as a pivot, move the blade in a rocking motion; chop slowly at first so that the nuts do not jump off the board.

Preparing Praline

1 **Caramelizing the almonds.** Put equal quantities of peeled almonds and sugar in a heavy pan. Cook over a very low heat, stirring constantly. When the sugar turns pale amber, tip the mixture on to an oiled marble slab or baking tray (*above*) and spread it out with a spatula.

2 **Crushing the praline.** Leave the praline to cool until it forms a solid mass. Put the praline in a plastic bag and, using a rolling pin, crush the praline to the desired degree of fineness. The bag will prevent the small pieces of praline from spreading out across the work surface.

Making a Nut Milk

Straining the milk. Infuse pounded almonds or, as here, grated coconut in scalded milk or boiling water for 1 hour. Strain the infused nut milk through a muslin-lined sieve. Squeeze the coconut in the muslin and add its juice to the milk.

Egg Whites: a Foundation Built with Air

When raw egg whites are beaten, air is trapped in the mixture in the form of bubbles. These air pockets become smaller and more numerous as the beating continues, expanding the volume of the whites and progressively stiffening them. The precise extent to which the whites should be beaten depends on how you intend to use them: egg whites beaten to soft peaks (*Step 3, below*) will support soufflés and mousses (*pages 50–53*), while for meringues (*page 46*) the whites must reach the firm peak stage (*Step 4, below*).

Such desserts literally stand or fall on the volume and stability of the beaten whites. These qualities in turn depend on the eggs themselves, on your choice of equipment and its cleanliness, and on the proficiency with which you carry out the beating process.

Fat is the great enemy of beaten egg whites; the slightest trace will prevent them mounting fully. Since egg yolk is rich in fat, you must separate yolk from white with care (*Step 1, below*). If a yolk breaks and leaks into the white, you may be able to remove the yolk with a spoon; but, as a precaution, crack each egg individually over a small bowl before adding the white to the mixing bowl. This way, any mishap will affect only one egg.

Many dishes, such as custards (*page 38*) and ice creams (*page 72*) require egg yolks but not whites. When preparing such dishes, separate yolks from whites with the usual care. The surplus whites can then be stored, tightly covered, in the refrigerator for 4 to 5 days, and used when required. Let them return to room temperature before beating them: chilled whites mount less successfully.

Utensils must be as free of fat as the egg whites themselves. Before use, wash both bowl and whisk carefully in hot, soapy water, then rinse them well in water mixed with a squeeze of lemon juice. Dry the equipment thoroughly with a clean cloth before adding the whites.

For beating egg whites, use a bowl that will not absorb grease easily—glass, porcelain or stainless steel rather than plastic. The best bowls of all are made of unlined copper; a chemical reaction between the metal and the egg whites strengthens the walls of the whisk-created air bubbles. The resulting foam is stable, even when mixed with other ingredients; it therefore gives better results in such desserts as meringues and soufflés. However, another chemical reaction will discolour the whites if you leave them in the bowl for more than 15 minutes or so.

Since even the slightest tarnish on a copper bowl would interfere with the reaction that strengthens the egg whites, the inside of the bowl needs special cleaning before each use (*box, right*).

The size and shape of the bowl also affect the results. The bowl should be large enough to allow room for vigorous whisking. Its interior surface should be hemispherical, as a flat-bottomed bowl would obstruct the action of the whisk.

A balloon whisk is the ideal tool for beating the whites; its wire loops quickly force air into the egg. If you can, choose a whisk with a wooden handle, which is

Whisking to the Perfect Peak

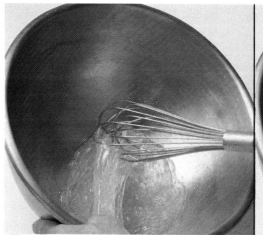
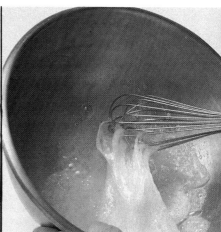

1 **Separating the eggs.** Crack each egg shell on the side of a small bowl; pull away half of the shell, leaving the yolk in the other half, and let the white drip into the bowl (*above*). Gently pass the yolk back and forth between the two halves until all the white has dripped into the bowl. Transfer the white to a larger bowl.

2 **Beating the whites.** When you have added all the whites to the beating bowl add a pinch of salt, which helps the whites to mount. Using a wire whisk, beat slowly and gently at first with a regular, figure-of-eight motion (*above, left*). When the clear whites begin to change to a frothy foam (*above, centre*), whisk with greater speed. When they begin to form into a uniformly fine, creamy foam (*above, right*), beat them rapidly with a circular motion that lifts the whites and incorporates air.

easy to grip and comfortable to work with.

Once you start to whisk the egg whites, you should continue without stopping until they are ready; any prolonged pause may cause the whites to subside or to separate into watery liquid and lumps—a process known as graining.

Work with the bowl positioned at arm's length; in this way, you can move the whisk rhythmically, the arm's movement coming easily from your shoulder without straining your forearm or wrist.

Although electric mixers beat whites quickly and effortlessly, they do not give the best results; the whites expand less than those beaten by hand because the machine's blades do not pass continuously through the whole body of the whites. And if you use an electric mixer, it is more difficult to judge the change in the consistency of the whites as they mount. The difference between whites that are almost ready to use and those that are beaten to just the right point (*Steps 3 and 4*) is a matter of only a few turns of the whisk; a few turns too many may convert perfect whites into a dry and inelastic mass.

Cleaning a Copper Bowl

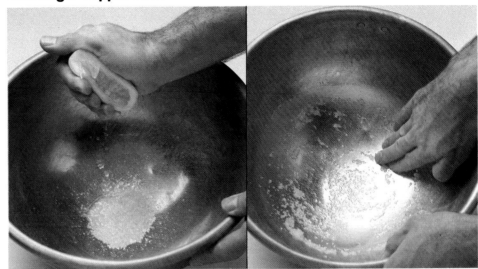

Scouring with salt and lemon juice. Put about two teaspoons of fine salt into the bowl and add the juice of half a lemon, as here, or a tablespoon of vinegar. Using your fingers, or a soft cloth, rub the salty, acid solution thoroughly around the bowl. Rinse the bowl well with hot water and dry it with a clean cloth.

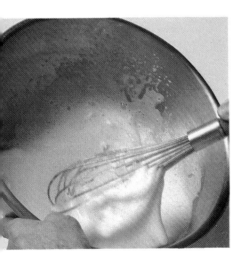

3 **Testing for soft peaks.** As soon as the whites offer a definite resistance to beating, lift up some of the white with the whisk. If it forms a soft, slightly drooping peak (*above*), it is firm enough for a soufflé or a mousse.

4 **Testing for firm peaks.** To reach the degree of stiffness required for meringues, beat the egg whites for a few seconds more, then test them again. When the whites stand up in stiff, pointed peaks, you can begin to beat in sugar to make meringue (*page 46*).□

Gelatine: a Transfiguring Element

Gelatine is a fundamental element in many cold, moulded desserts. It is the basis of translucent jellies flavoured with wine or fruit juice and it is also used to set Bavarian creams, mousses and fruit purées (*recipes, pages 115-118*).

For desserts in which gelatine is a principal ingredient—such as the fruit jelly on page 24—the purest setting agent, with the most delicate flavour and the richest body, is the gelatine extracted from calf's feet (*right; recipe, page 166*).

As a general guide, 3 to 4 calf's feet simmered in 2.5 litres (4 pints) of water will yield 1 litre (1¾ pints) of firm jelly that will set as much as 90 cl (1½ pints) of aditional liquid. However, a few refinements are needed to prepare the calf's foot jelly for use in a dessert. First, it must be allowed to cool, so that fat can be removed with ease. Then the jelly is reheated and, to neutralize any trace of meatiness, it is sweetened and lightly flavoured with spices and citrus rinds. Finally the jelly must be clarified—simmered with beaten egg whites and egg shells—and strained through a cloth. Minute solid particles in the jelly adhere to the cooked egg whites and shells and are trapped in the cloth. The clear liquid that remains will set to a jelly—a base to which wine or fruit juice can then be added.

For desserts such as Bavarian creams (*page 44*), commercially produced leaf or powdered gelatine (*box, below right*) makes a suitable setting agent. Not only is the amount of gelatine required small, because the dessert is partly supported by its content of cooked eggs or whipped cream, but the consistency of a calf's foot jelly would be masked by the cream. Powdered gelatine is quick and simple to use; leaf gelatine requires a preliminary soaking for up to 30 minutes.

Brands of gelatine differ slightly in setting strength. If the manufacturers indicate how much to use, follow their instructions. If not, use 15 g (½ oz) of gelatine—usually 4 sheets of leaf gelatine—to set about 60 cl (1 pint) of liquid to a consistency that can support its own weight. If you do not intend to unmould the dessert, you can reduce these quantities of gelatine by about one-third.

1 Splitting the calf's feet. If your butcher has not already soaked the calf's feet, immerse them in cold water for several hours to remove any blood, then rinse them well. Cut each foot in half at the end of its long bone and split the front of the foot in two. To keep the cut-up feet white, place them in a bowl of cold water while you prepare the others.

2 Removing the scum. Put the calf's feet in a saucepan and cover them with fresh cold water. Parboil the feet for 5 to 6 minutes. Drain and rinse the feet. Put them in a clean pan and add cold water to cover them well. Bring to the boil and simmer very gently, with the lid just ajar, for at least 7 hours. Skim with a ladle occasionally to remove scum (*above*).

Dealing with Leaf and Powdered Gelatine

Dissolving leaf gelatine. Place the sheets of gelatine in a bowl of cold water (*above*) and leave them to soak. When the leaves are supple, remove them and put them in a small, heavy pan with a little water. Set the pan over low heat until the gelatine has dissolved and the liquid in the pan is clear.

Dissolving powdered gelatine. For each 15 g (½ oz) of gelatine, put 3 tablespoons of very hot but not boiling water into a small bowl and sprinkle the powder on to it. The gelatine will swell and begin to dissolve. To complete the dissolving process, stand the bowl in a pan of hot water over a low heat for about 3 minutes.

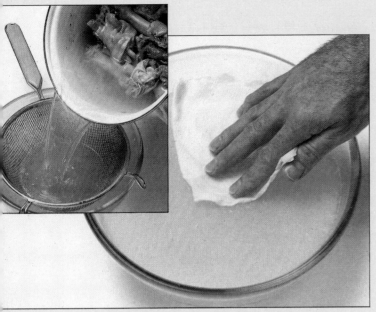

3 **Degreasing the jelly.** Strain the liquid through a sieve into a bowl (*above, left*), and put it in a refrigerator overnight to set. Discard the calf's feet. Remove the jelly from the refrigerator and scrape off any fat with a spoon. If any small globules of fat remain, mop them up with a towel wrung out in hot water.

4 **Clarifying the jelly.** In a large saucepan, heat the jelly gently until it melts. Add the basic flavourings: orange and lemon juice and rind, spices and sugar (*above, left*). In a large mixing bowl, beat egg whites with a little white wine until soft peaks form. Add the mixture, together with the crushed egg shells to the liquid jelly. Whisk over medium heat until a thick head of froth forms (*above, right*). Stop whisking and allow the jelly to come to the boil. Lower the heat and maintain the barest simmer for 15 minutes.

5 **Straining the jelly.** Suspend a jelly bag from a stand set over a bowl; you can improvise a stand from an upturned chair. Ladle the liquid jelly into the bag (*left*) and let it drip into the bowl. If necessary, repeat the process until the liquid in the bowl is clear. Chill the liquid until the jelly sets (*below*).☐

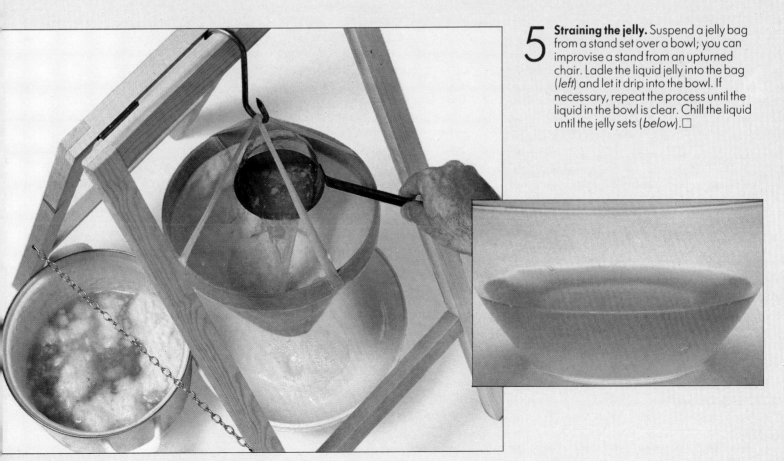

1
Fruit
Revelations of Colour and Taste

A dressing of raspberry purée completes a fresh fruit salad cupped in the shell of a pineapple. Whole strawberries and sliced kiwi fruit have been combined with chunks of pineapple flesh; crushed ice packed around the shell keeps the salad cool and adds an inviting sparkle to the dessert's presentation.

The best preparation for any food is one which does most justice to its essential flavour, and since ripe, perfect fruit needs little work on the cook's part, many fresh fruit desserts provide a maximum reward for a minimum of labour. Rinsing or peeling, sprinkling with sugar and wine or a little liqueur is enough to produce superb desserts, served cool but not so cold that the fruit's perfume and flavour are diminished. Fresh strawberries in a glass of good wine, for example, make a dessert that is as exquisite as it is radically simple. And, of course, you can combine a variety of fruits in salads (*opposite page and page 22*)—with an eye to complementary colours as well as flavours and textures.

Cooked fruit desserts range from the comforting earthiness of stuffed baked apples (*page 28*) to the elegance of poached compotes (*page 34*). Puréed fruit blended with whipped cream becomes a fruit fool (*page 26*); beaten with egg whites it makes a feather-light huff (*page 27*); encased in bread and baked, fruit purées form pudding-like charlottes (*page 32*).

Before deciding what fruit dessert to make, determine what is available in the market. Whenever possible, buy fruits that are in season; not only do they have more flavour, but abundance will make for lower prices.

Learn the signs of ripeness. A rich colour is the most obvious guide: mature apricots have a golden tinge, ripe gooseberries are tawny or pinkish. Softness and fragrance are other useful signs. A ripe pineapple has a sweet scent and its base yields to light pressure. Similarly, a fully ripe melon is scented and slightly softened at one end; it feels hollow when weighed in the hand or tapped.

Most species of fruit are available in many varieties; different varieties of the same fruit suit different purposes. Crisp, sweet apples are best for a fruit salad, for example, while a mealy type, which will not disintegrate with cooking, is more suited to baking or puréeing. Varieties of pear with succulent, sweet flesh are ideal for eating fresh but can only withstand brief cooking; other varieties are by nature hard, and perfect for baking or lengthy poaching in wine. Buy and taste as many varieties of every kind of fruit as you can; experience is the best teacher, and acquiring the experience is a pleasure, not a chore.

Readying Fruit for Eating and Cooking

Although it is no hardship for a diner to peel his own apple or banana at the table, fruits destined for salads, garnishes or cooked deserts need advance preparation. Special techniques for dealing with various fruits, from the everyday orange to the exotic mango, are demonstrated here.

The aim of these techniques is to free the flesh of all tough, inedible parts—but the by-products should not be wasted. Catch and save the juice that drips out as the fruit is manipulated; extract the flavour from edible peels—such as those of peaches or pears—by briefly poaching them in syrup.

For the freshest flavour and colour, leave the peeling and slicing until the last possible moment. Use stainless steel knives, since carbon steel gives a metallic taste to acid foods. Once cut, some fruits—peaches, apples and pears, for example—discolour rapidly in the air: immerse them immediately in lemon juice and water, or in syrup, or rub them with a lemon quarter.

Dividing up a Pineapple

1 **Peeling the pineapple.** Cut off the top of a pineapple and trim the base of the fruit. Stand the pineapple on a cutting board and push a fork into its top. Grasp the fork firmly to steady the fruit and slice off the skin in vertical strips. With the tip of a small knife, remove any spikes of skin in the pineapple (*above*).

2 **Removing the core.** Position a knife just to one side of the central core and slice vertically through the pineapple. In the piece of pineapple containing the core, make a second vertical cut, at 90 degrees to the first. Cut away the core from the remaining third section and reserve it to help to flavour a syrup. Cut the three sections of flesh into chunks.

Carving Perfect Orange Segments

1 **Peeling the oranges.** While rotating an orange slowly in the hand, use a small, sharp knife to slice away the peel of the fruit in a continuous spiral. If you like, cut the rind as thinly as possible from the pith and use it to flavour a syrup or to decorate a dessert (*page 10*).

2 **Slicing the oranges.** To separate each segment of orange flesh from the membrane that encloses it, cut down both sides of the segment between the flesh and the membrane. Slice the oranges over a dish to collect any juices.

3 **Squeezing out the juice.** When you have cut out all the segments, squeeze what remains of the oranges over the dish to extract all the juice. Serve the juice with the orange segments or reserve it to use as a flavouring for syrup.

Preparing a Soft-Fleshed Mango

1 Peeling the mango. To peel a ripe mango without damaging its soft flesh, secure one end of the fruit on the prongs of a fork. Slit the skin lengthwise to divide it into four sections. Grip the skin between your thumb and the flat of the knife and peel away each strip (*above*). Discard the skin.

2 Slicing the mango. Split the mango lengthwise and, working towards yourself, cut around the stone. Remove and discard the stone. Slice the mango for a fruit salad (*page 22*), or press it through a nylon sieve to make a purée.

Removing Stubborn Skins

Peeling a nectarine. Pour very hot water over tight-skinned fruit; after a few seconds, drain and cover with cold water. Remove the skin in strips: nicking it with a knife, hold a flap of skin between thumb and knife and pull it towards you.

Keeping Currants Intact

Stemming redcurrants. Place the stem of a small spray of redcurrants between the prongs of a fork. Pull gently on the stem (*above*). The berries will drop away intact and unbruised. Include them in salads, either raw or poached briefly.

Scooping out a Papaya

Removing the seeds. A papaya is a mass of soft flesh enclosing a pocket of small seeds. Using a paring knife, peel the papaya in lengthwise strips (*Step 1, above*). Discard the skin. Cut the fruit in half and remove the seeds with a spoon. To serve the papaya halves, sprinkle them with a little sugar and lemon juice; slice the halves thinly for a fruit salad.

Opening Passion Fruit

Scooping out the pulp. Slice off the tops of the passion fruit. Use a spoon to scoop the pulp and edible seeds into a bowl. Discard the shell-like skins. Add the pulp and seeds to a fruit salad, or use them as a sauce—poured over ice cream, for example (*page 73*).

Peeling Kiwi Fruit

Removing the skin. Use your fingernails (or a small, sharp knife) to peel away the rough brown skin from the kiwi fruit. Discard the skin; slice the bright green flesh and include it in a fruit salad.

Fruit Salads—Exotic or Simple

Fruit salads are among the simplest and most refreshing of desserts. Presented in clear glass bowls, or in decorative serving containers fashioned from the fruit itself, they can also be among the most eye-catching. Individual portions can be served in large orange and grapefruit shells (*recipe, page 92*), or in the Ogen melon halves shown here (*right*). Larger fruits, such as pineapple (*page 18*) and watermelon (*below, right*), can be hollowed out to make roomy baskets that will hold several servings of salad.

The choice of fruit for a salad is governed by the availability of ingredients as well as by personal taste. Always select ripe, perfect fruit and take advantage of seasonal produce—pears, tangerines and apples in winter, for example; berries and other soft fruits in summer. To keep the flavour of each fruit distinct, include no more than four or five different fruits in each assemblage. Here, a combination of kiwi fruit, papaya, mango and passion fruit is presented in the melon halves; in the watermelon basket, orange segments, pitted cherries and peeled grapes are mixed with the watermelon's own flesh.

To keep the colour of the fruit bright, leave peeling and slicing (*page 20*) until the last moment and add a dash of lime or lemon juice. A pinch of salt will help bring out the natural flavours. A sprinkling of sugar with a little wine, spirits—especially rum or brandy—or a fruit liqueur will complement the natural flavours. Grand Marnier, for example, goes well with a citrus fruit salad, pear liqueur with pears and kirsch with almost everything. A fruit purée or a light syrup (*page 8*), in which fruit or edible fruit peels have been poached, make ideal sauces. Use these additional elements alone, or experiment to find the combination that suits your palate—and your ingredients—best.

A Tropical Salad in a Melon Shell

1 **Cutting the melon.** Remove the stalk from the melon and score around the fruit's circumference with a small knife. Use this mark as a guideline to cut a zig-zag pattern around the centre of the melon (*top*). Gently prise apart the two halves of the fruit (*bottom*). Trim a thin slice from the bottom of each melon half to give it a secure base.

2 **Removing the seeds.** Use a metal spoon to remove the seeds and the seed membrane from each melon half. Before you discard them, press the seeds lightly in a strainer and save the juice. If you like, use a knife or melon ball cutter to remove some or all of the fruit: you can include it in the salad or purée it and include it in a water ice (*page 70*).

Carving a Natural Basket

1 **Designing the basket.** Tie a piece of string around the centre of the melon to indicate the rim for the basket. With a sharp knife, score two arcs on either side of the stem to outline the handle for the basket. Cut vertically and horizontally along the guidelines (*above*). Cut through to the centre of the melon, but do not cut along the base of the handle.

2 **Making the handle.** Remove the two wedges of melon on either side of the handle and reserve them. With a gentle sawing action, cut the flesh from the underside of the handle close to the skin, and along the base of the arc (*above*).

3 **Adding the syrup.** Make a light syrup (*page 8*); for extra flavour and colour you can use a syrup in which fruits—here, redcurrants—have been poached (*page 34*). While the syrup cools, prepare the fruit (*page 20*)—in this case a mixture of tropical fruits. Place the fruit pieces in a mixing bowl and pour over the cooled syrup (*above*).

4 **Mixing the salad.** Sprinkle a little lime or lemon juice over the salad and add a pinch of salt. Mix the fruit and syrup together by hand; hand-mixing the salad coats each piece evenly with syrup without damaging the fragile fruit.

5 **Serving the salad.** Carefully spoon the tropical fruit salad into each melon half (*above*) and place the halves on individual plates. Chill the filled melons for up to 2 hours before serving them.□

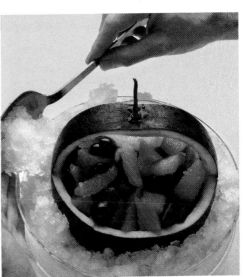

3 **Completing the basket.** Support the base of the melon with one hand and gently ease the flesh from under the handle. Cut downwards around the inside rim of the basket and scoop out the flesh with a spoon.

4 **Preparing the fruit.** Cut the flesh from the melon wedges and discard the rinds. Remove the seeds from the melon with the point of your knife (*above*). Cut the flesh into bite-sized pieces. Prepare the other fruits to be included—in this case, oranges, cherries and black grapes. Place them in a bowl with the melon.

5 **Filling the basket.** Add a pinch of salt and a sprinkling of sugar and lime juice. Mix the fruit by hand (*Step 4, above*) and arrange it in the basket. Place the basket in a bowl half filled with crushed ice. Spoon more crushed ice around the basket (*above*) and chill the fruit for about 15 minutes before serving.□

Creating a Pure and Shimmering Jelly

Turned out from a handsome, fluted mould, a fruit jelly combines an imposing appearance with a lightness that is welcome at the end of a rich meal. The translucent jelly in this demonstration is based on calf's foot gelatine (*page 16*), mixed with fresh orange juice; the additional juice of a single lemon helps bring out the flavour of the fruit (*recipe, page 103*). Lime or grapefruit juice can be substituted for the orange juice, but without the addition of lemon.

To extract the juice from the citrus fruits, use a lemon squeezer, and to make the jelly as clear as possible, strain the juice through a sieve lined with muslin.

If you are using calf's foot gelatine, simply melt it gently over low heat and combine it with a little less than its own volume of fruit juice. Add sugar if necessary—calf's foot gelatine is usually sweetened during its preparation—then pour it into the mould to set. If you are using commercial gelatine (*box, page 16*)—the manufacturers' instructions will tell you the proportions to use—the dessert may need to be sweetened. Combine the gelatine—after soaking—with water and sugar, and stir over low heat until both the gelatine and sugar have dissolved.

Make sure that the quantity of flavoured jelly is enough to fill your mould; if the dessert has to slide more than about 1 cm (½ inch) when it is turned out of the mould, it may be damaged by its impact with the serving plate.

The jelly will need about 4 hours in the refrigerator to set; cover it, to prevent it from being contaminated with other flavours. If necessary, it will keep for a day or two, but it will lose its fresh fruit flavour.

The unmoulding itself is simple. Melt the jelly's outermost surface by dipping the mould for a second in hot water: the jelly will slip out freely when the mould is turned over. Take care not to prolong the immersion, lest the jelly's contours melt and become blurred.

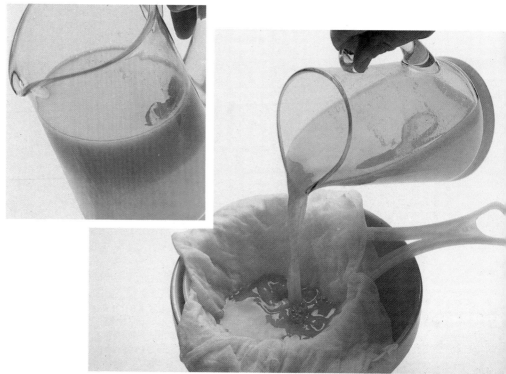

1 **Preparing the flavouring.** Squeeze the juice from a lemon and several oranges. Let the juice stand for 30 minutes, then pour it through a sieve lined with 2 layers of dampened muslin. The waiting time allows fragments of pulp to gather in a layer at the top of the juice (*inset*); the thick layer collects in the muslin and itself assists the straining process.

2 **Flavouring the jelly.** Gently heat calf's foot gelatine until it has barely melted. Measure the volume of the orange juice—you should have almost half as much as you need to fill the mould. Pour slightly more than the same volume of liquid gelatine into a bowl and mix in the juice. If you do not have enough liquid to fill the mould, add more liquid gelatine.

3 **Setting the jelly.** To accelerate the setting process, stand the bowl of jelly in a larger bowl of crushed ice. Stir the jelly constantly until it just begins to thicken, then ladle the jelly into a chilled mould. Refrigerate the jelly for at least 4 hours. Check its solidity by tilting the mould: when the jelly stays firm as the mould is tilted, it is ready to be turned out.

4 **Unmoulding on to a plate.** Run the tip of a knife around the inside rim of the mould, then dip the entire mould briefly in warm water to loosen the jelly. Invert a plate over the mould. Hold the mould firmly against the plate, and smartly turn over mould and plate together. Lift the mould away from the jelly.

5 **Decorating and serving.** If immersing the mould has melted the jelly slightly, return it to the refrigerator to firm. Garnish the jelly with fresh fruit—here, orange segments stripped of pith and membrane (*page 20*).□

Fruit Purées: Features and Flavourings

Fruit purées are one of the key elements in dessert cookery—as flavourings in ice creams and moulded puddings and as sauces for almost any dessert. Purées also make refreshing dishes in themselves, exemplified by the fool and the huff, the quaintly named but classically simple English desserts shown here.

How you prepare the purée depends not only on the use for which you intend it, but also on the kind of fruit you have and the texture you desire (box, below). Rhubarb is used for the fool demonstrated on the right, and gooseberries for the huff on the opposite page, below (recipes, pages 95-96); both these fruits are cooked, then coarsely puréed in a food mill.

To make a fool, the rhubarb is fluffed out with whipped cream; for the huff, the gooseberry purée is beaten into a snowy mass with egg whites and a sugar syrup—which helps stabilize the foamy egg whites. A huff can be made from raw or cooked fruit purée, but the best candidates for fools are fruits with enough acidity to balance the cream's richness.

Mellowing a Purée with Cream

1 Cooking the rhubarb. Discard the rhubarb leaves. Cut the stalks into 5 cm (2 inch) pieces. Put the pieces in a heavy saucepan with about half their weight of soft brown sugar and a knob of butter. Stir the rhubarb and sugar over a low heat until they are well mixed. Cover the pan and continue to cook the mixture until the fruit is tender—20 to 30 minutes.

2 Puréeing the rhubarb. To ensure the firm texture of the finished dessert, pour the cooked rhubarb into a colander and allow excess liquid to drain off. Using a food mill set over a bowl, purée the drained rhubarb, a few ladlefuls at a time. Set aside and allow to cool.

Choosing the Best Puréeing Method

Pressing raw raspberries through a nylon sieve

Forcing cooked apple through a drum sieve

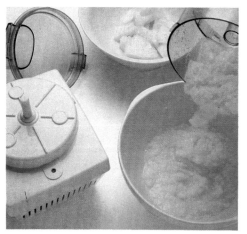

Fragmenting pineapple in a food processor

Fruits, such as ripe raspberries or bananas, that are soft enough to push through a sieve can be puréed raw. Use a nylon sieve for acidic fruits, since metal imparts an unpleasant taste.

Most fruits, however, must first be cooked to soften their fibres. To avoid making a watery purée, cook the fruit with no more than a knob of butter or a spoonful of water. Any liquid that the fruit releases should be strained off; if you like, reduce the liquid and return it to the fruit. The fruit can then be passed through a food mill (Step 2, above)—or, for a finer texture, sieved. Use a drum sieve to deal with large quantities of fruit. To make the very stiff purée required for some moulded desserts, cook the purée for at least 15 minutes, stirring continuously, until it is very firm.

Pineapple is too fibrous to purée smoothly, even cooked. To reduce it to pulp, purée it raw in an electric processor for a few seconds.

3 **Adding the cream.** Beat double cream until it forms soft peaks. Stir the purée into the cream, until the two ingredients are thoroughly blended. Taste for sweetness and add more sugar if necessary. Spoon the rhubarb fool into individual glasses; serve accompanied by sweet biscuits—such as almond shortcake wedges (*right*). The fool will keep in the refrigerator for several days. □

Lightening with Egg Whites

1 **Mixing fruit purée and egg whites.** Put whole gooseberries in a pan with a little sugar and just enough water to cover the base of the pan; cook, covered, over a low heat for 20 to 30 minutes until the fruit is soft. Strain off any liquid. Purée the fruit in a food mill, then let it cool. Lightly beat egg whites until they are opaque. Add the purée to the whites.

2 **Whisking the mixture.** *Make a small thread sugar syrup* (*page 8*) and allow it to cool. Whisk the gooseberry purée and egg whites mixture until it forms soft peaks. Gradually pour the syrup into the mixture, whisking continuously to blend in the liquid evenly.

3 **Serving the huff.** Continue whisking until the huff is almost white and stands up in firm peaks. Serve it immediately in individual glasses or in a glass bowl and accompany it with sweet biscuits or wafers (*above*). If left to stand, the huff will slowly subside; further whisking will restore its lightness. □

Whole Fruit, Stuffed and Baked

Baked fruits make fragrant and warming desserts: cooked gently, with just enough liquid or butter to moisten them, the fruits become tender without the flavour dissipating. Whole apples are used here (*recipe, page 98*), but the same technique can be applied to such diverse fruits as peaches, pears and bananas.

Most fruits—peaches and pears, for example—are peeled before they are cooked. To preserve their colour, rub them all over with lemon juice. If you do leave the skin on, you must prepare it so that the fruit does not burn when the flesh expands during cooking. Either partially peel the fruit, as here, or make a shallow cut round the fruit's circumference. Coring or stoning the fruit is optional: apples are usually cored before baking, but the stones of peaches and apricots will cause the diner little trouble, and can be removed or not as you please.

The bonus gained from coring or stoning is the cavity in the fruit's centre, which makes a container for a flavouring or stuffing. Here, the apples are filled with a paste of butter and sugar, scented with orange peel. Other possible stuffing ingredients include chopped nuts, dried fruits, spices such as cinnamon or nutmeg, and crushed sweet biscuits—macaroons, for example.

To guard against drying out, and to prevent the fruit from sticking to the bottom of the baking dish, cook the fruit with a little liquid—wine, a liqueur or orange juice, for example—and baste it at intervals. As the cooking progresses, the fruit itself may release additional liquid, and any butter used in the stuffing will melt. The resulting rich syrup glazes the fruit and serves as a sauce: if you want to soak up some of the syrup, bake the fruit standing on slices of bread or brioche.

1 Coring the apples. Wash some apples—either a tart or a sweet variety can be used. To core each apple, use an apple corer or hold the apple steady on a work surface and insert a small, sharp knife near the core and half way through the apple. Work round the half core, then pull it out and discard it. Turn the apple over and repeat.

2 Peeling the apples. Peel about 5 cm (2 inches) of skin from the top of each apple. To prevent the apples from discolouring, rub their peeled surfaces with a cut lemon and squeeze lemon juice into their hollow centres.

3 Cutting out bread rounds. For each apple, cut a 1 cm (½ inch) slice of bread—preferably from a loaf that is 1 to 2 days old. Remove the crusts, put each apple on a slice of bread, and cut the bread into circles of about the same diameter as the apples (*above*). If the bread is fresh, put the prepared rounds in a hot oven for 5 minutes to dry and firm them.

4 **Preparing the stuffing.** Put the bread rounds in a well-buttered baking dish; place an apple on top of each round. In a large bowl, mix together butter and some soft brown sugar (*above*). Make more than enough stuffing to fill the raw apples; it will melt during cooking, leaving room to add the surplus.

5 **Stuffing the apples.** Pack the paste into the centres of the apples. If you like, add extra flavourings: here, pieces of dried orange peel are inserted into the stuffing and the apples are powdered with saffron and stuck with almonds. Sprinkle the apples with a little castor sugar and pour white wine into the dish to a depth of about 5 mm (¼ inch).

6 **Cooking and basting.** Put the dish in an oven preheated to 150°C (300°F or Mark 2) and bake the apples for 1 to 1½ hours, depending on their size, basting them occasionally with the cooking juices. Use a bulb baster (*above*) to take up liquid for basting without disturbing the apples. As the stuffing melts, use any surplus mixture to top up the cavities.

7 **Serving the apples.** Remove the dish from the oven. The cooking liquid will have caramelized and reduced to a buttery, golden syrup. Serve the apples just as they are, or with a bowl of pouring custard or, as here, whipped cream with chopped pistachio nuts. □

A Rich, Moist Purée of Chestnuts

In culinary terms, chestnuts defy classification. Although their hard shells would seem to categorize them as nuts, dessert cooks, guided by the chestnuts' tenderness and sweet flavour, prefer to treat them as fruit—poached and served whole in syrup, for example (*recipe, page 100*), or puréed and used either as a flavouring for other desserts or—as here—as a dessert in their own right (*recipe, page 96*).

Chestnuts destined for a purée must be cooked in two stages. First, they should be slit and parboiled to loosen their shells, which can then be peeled off relatively easily, provided that the slits are long enough. Parboiling also helps to loosen the tight brown membrane, or skin, covering the chestnut's flesh; this too must be removed so that no shreds of skin will mar the smoothness of the finished purée. An alternative way to shell the chestnuts is to score them and then roast them in a 180°C (350°F or mark 4) oven for about 20 minutes, then to remove the shells while the nuts are still warm. In either case nuts are then simmered in sweetened, vanilla-flavoured milk until they are tender enough to pass through a food mill.

You can serve the purée in a simple mound, but for a more inventive presentation, use a ricer—a kind of food press—to shape the purée. When forced through the small holes in the ricer (*Step 4, right*), the purée emerges in long threads.

Only a firm mixture can be riced; if the purée seems too liquid after it has been through the food mill, dry it out in a saucepan set over low heat (*Step 3, right*). Adding a little sugar at this stage will also help to thicken the purée, but take care not to over-sweeten it.

Serve the purée either chilled, or at room temperature, topped with whipped cream. If you like, you can mould the riced chestnuts into a more formal shape as shown in the box on the opposite page.

1 **Shelling and peeling the chestnuts.** With a small, sharp knife cut a cross through the shell on one side of each chestnut. The longer the arms of the cross, the easier the chestnut will be to peel. Drop the chestnuts in boiling water and parboil them for 10 minutes. Take the pan off the heat. With a spoon, lift out the chestnuts a few at a time, leaving the rest to soak. Cut away the shell from each chestnut (*above, left*) and—if the skin does not pull away with the shell— peel it off (*above, right*).

4 **Ricing the purée.** Using a spoon or a wooden spatula, fill a ricer with the chestnut purée. Hold the ricer over the centre of a large serving plate. Press the handles together to force the purée through the holes in the bottom of the ricer; it will emerge in long threads. Repeat until all the purée has been riced.

2 **Puréeing the chestnuts.** Place the chestnuts in a pan and barely cover them with milk. Add a vanilla bean for flavour. Bring the milk to the boil, then cover and reduce the heat. Simmer until the milk has been absorbed—about 45 minutes. Remove the vanilla bean. Purée the chestnuts through a food mill set over a bowl (*above*).

3 **Drying out the purée.** The chestnut purée should be smooth but firm. If the purée is runny, put it into a saucepan over a low heat. Add castor sugar to taste, and stir with a wooden spatula until it firms. If the mixture becomes dry and crumbly, add a little milk.

A Snowy Peak for Chestnuts

For a more symmetrical presentation, you can fill a ring mould with unriced chestnut purée or, as here, rice the purée directly into the mould. For extra richness, blend egg yolks and butter into the purée off the heat, before you rice it. There is no need to brush a mould with oil before filling it with riced purée. The purée can be unmoulded immediately, without refrigeration, by giving the mould a sharp tap.

1 **Filling the mould.** Force the chestnut purée through a ricer set over a mould, distributing the threads as evenly as possible. Gently push with a spatula to arrange the threads more uniformly, but avoid crushing the threads.

5 **Decorating and serving.** Leave the mound of riced purée untouched—manipulating it would mash the fragile threads. Spoon whipped double cream over the threads (*above*), and serve.□

2 **Decorating and serving.** Unmould the chestnut purée on to a serving plate. Fill the centre cavity with whipped cream. Dip a metal spatula into hot water, to prevent the cream from sticking to it, and shape the cream into a peak.

Two Ways to Construct Bread Cases

Bread makes an ideal container for moulded fruit desserts. If cooked in the mould, the bread becomes a rigid casing; if left uncooked, the bread sops up fruit juices yet remains firm enough to make unmoulding the dessert possible.

In an apple charlotte (*right, recipe; page 98*) buttered pieces of bread are arranged in an overlapping pattern in a mould. The bread case is filled with an apple purée (*page 26*) that has been reduced until it is too stiff to pour, and thus is firm enough to prevent the dessert from collapsing when it is unmoulded. When the charlotte is baked, the buttered bread case turns crisp and golden-brown; once the dessert has cooled, it will slip easily from its mould.

In summer pudding (*opposite page, recipe; page 99*) a bread-lined mould is filled with soft summer fruit—such as raspberries, redcurrants and blackcurrants—which have been cooked just enough to draw out their juices. The assembled pudding is not cooked. Instead, it is compressed overnight with a weighted plate so that fruit, juices and bread merge together in a moist, unified whole.

Apple Cooked in a Bread-Lined Mould

1 **Forming the case.** Cut slices of slightly stale bread into narrow rectangles slightly longer than the mould is deep. Brush one side with clarified butter, then place the buttered sides round the mould, slightly overlapping. Line the base with overlapping bread triangles.

2 **Filling the case.** Make a stiff purée of cooked apples (*page 26*) flavoured with sugar and cinnamon or cloves. Pack the purée into the bread case. Cut slices of bread to make a lid for the mould. Brush the lid with some clarified butter (*above*) and set it in place.

3 **Unmoulding the charlotte.** Bake the charlotte in an oven preheated to 200°C (400°F or Mark 6) for about 35 minutes, until the bread case is golden-brown. To check the colour, pull back a section of the side with a knife (*above*). Let the charlotte cool for about 20 minutes, then unmould it and serve with a fruit purée (*page 26*)—here, apricot (*above*). □

1 **Lining the pudding basin.** Cut a circle from a thick slice of slightly stale white bread to line the base of a pudding basin or a mould. Cut wedges of bread to line the sides of the mould. Use scraps from the bread wedges to fill any gaps in the bread lining.

2 **Preparing the fruit.** Pick over the fruit—here, blackcurrants, redcurrants and raspberries—and throw away any damaged specimens. Put the blackcurrants in a heavy pan, sprinkle them with sugar and cook gently for about 5 minutes to draw out their juices. Add the raspberries and redcurrants, and cook for 5 minutes more.

3 **Filling the case.** With a small metal strainer or a slotted spoon, lift the fruit from the pan and fill the mould half way to the top. Place a layer of bread on the fruit (*above, left*), then spoon over the remaining fruit. Cover the fruit with a lid of bread and pour over the juice from the pan so that the entire bread case is saturated (*above, right*).

4 **Weighting the pudding.** Put a plate that will just fit inside the basin's rim on the pudding and weight it heavily (*above*). Use kitchen weights, as here, or improvise. Place the basin on a tray or large plate to catch any juices that might overflow. Refrigerate the dessert overnight.

5 **Turning out the pudding.** Remove the weights and the plate. Gently loosen the pudding from the basin with a knife. Unmould the pudding on to a serving plate; choose a plate with a rim that will catch any escaping juice. Serve the pudding with double cream.□

Poaching: Matching Time and Tenderness

Fruit poached in syrup (*page 8*) gains in sweetness and flavour; the syrup itself, reduced after cooking, provides a translucent sauce that makes the poached fruit into a complete dessert.

Ripe, fresh fruits should be poached only briefly, or they will break up: peaches become very soft after 10 minutes, and currants would disintegrate after more than 2 to 3 minutes of poaching. If the dessert consists of a mixture of fruits—as in the compote of redcurrants, gooseberries, pears, peaches, apricots and nectarines demonstrated here (*recipe, page 101*)—poach different types of fruit separately so that none is overcooked.

In place of syrup, you can use wine sweetened with sugar or honey to poach fresh or dried fruit (*box, below; recipe, page 102*). The acidity in wine helps to keep fruit firm, so the fruit can cook longer without disintegrating. Lengthy simmering allows the fruit and the wine to exchange flavours and eliminates the harsh taste of undercooked wine.

1 Poaching redcurrants. Make a medium syrup (*page 8*) and bring it to a simmer. If possible, use an unlined copper pan, as here: a harmless chemical reaction caused by the metal will intensify the colour of red fruits. Gently tip redcurrants into the syrup (*above, left*) and cook them for about 2 minutes. Remove them with a strainer (*above, right*). The syrup will absorb colour and flavour from the berries: use it as a poaching liquid for other fruit (*Steps 2 and 3, right*), or reserve it to dress a fruit salad (*page 22*).

The Benefits of a Wine-Based Syrup

1 Simmering the figs. Put whole dried figs in a pan with enough red wine to cover them. Add honey and, for extra flavour, sprigs of fresh or dried thyme, wrapped up in muslin to prevent the leaves from dispersing into the wine. Bring the wine to a simmer, cover the pan and cook the figs gently for 1 hour or until they are tender, turning them from time to time.

2 Reducing the wine. Use a slotted spoon to remove the figs from the pan to a serving dish and discard the thyme. To make a sauce for the figs, turn up the heat a little and boil the wine until it has reduced to a syrupy consistency (*above*).

3 Serving the figs. Pour the wine syrup over the figs (*above*). Serve the figs tepid, or else chill them in the refrigerator. Accompany them, if you like, with double cream and crisp, sweet biscuits.

2 **Poaching firmer fruit.** Peel, halve and stone the other fruits—here pears, peaches, apricots and nectarines; reserve the peels. To prevent their discolouring, keep the fruits in a bowl of water acidulated with a squeeze of lemon juice. Simmer the fruits together in syrup. Use a toothpick to gauge tenderness, and remove each fruit as soon as it is ready (*above*).

3 **Simmering fruit peels.** Top and tail gooseberries and simmer them in the syrup for 2 to 3 minutes. Transfer them to the serving dish with the other fruits. Add the fruit peels to the syrup (*above*). Boil the syrup rapidly to extract colour and flavour from the peels and to reduce the volume of the syrup by about one-third.

4 **Serving the poached fruit.** Allow the syrup to cool a little, then strain it over the poached fruit in the serving dish (*above*). Discard the fruit peels. Serve the compote either warm or chilled (*right*). □

2
Custards, Creams and Meringues
The Adaptable Egg

In his encomium to the egg, the 19th-century Scottish philosopher and gastronome Eneas Sweetland Dallas wrote: "Nothing in the way of food more simple than an egg, and nothing so quick and marvellous in its manifold uses and transformations". Three of these "quick and marvellous" transformations are custards, creams and meringues. Whether the whole eggs are used, as in some creams, or just the separated yolks or whites, as in pouring custards and meringues, the key to making these desserts successfully is slow, even cooking.

Pouring custard, or *crème anglaise*, is made by stirring egg yolks, flavourings, sugar and cream or milk over a low heat (*page 38*). The yolks thicken during cooking to produce a smooth, rich custard—the foundation of a range of delicious desserts and sauces. If *crème anglaise* is topped with sugar and glazed under a hot grill, it becomes *crème brûlée* (*opposite page; recipe, page 106*). Whisk the egg yolks and sugar together over hot water, add some wine and you have a light and foamy *sabayon* (*page 39*). Stiffen the *crème anglaise* with gelatine and fold in whipped cream and you will have a mixture firm enough to hold the shape of an elaborate moulded Bavarian cream—the most spectacular of the custards.

Cooked dessert creams, another of custard's manifold varieties, usually contain a small proportion of egg white to help set the custard and give it a lighter texture. Depending on the proportion of whites, you can make lightly set *pots de crème* (*page 40*) or a *crème caramel* that is firm enough to turn out of a mould (*page 42*). These creams are gently cooked in a water bath, either on top of the stove or in a moderate oven. The constant temperature of the water—about 85°C (185°F)—causes the egg whites in the custard to set firm. Because the water never reaches boiling point, the creams remain voluptuously smooth, without separating, and no small bubbles form to coarsen the texture of the desserts.

The texture of meringues, made of egg whites, flavouring and sugar, can be fluffy or crisp, depending on whether they are poached as in *oeufs à la neige* (*page 47*), or baked at a very low temperature (*page 46*). Both kinds of meringues lend themselves to simple presentations as well as elaborate assemblies containing fruits and ice cream (*page 86*).

A firm tap with the back of a spoon cracks the caramel glaze of a *crème brûlée*, revealing the smooth custard beneath. To prevent the custard from curdling under the heat needed to melt its sugar topping, the cooking dish was set in a container packed with ice cubes.

Pouring Custard: Both Sauce and Starting Point

Smooth, pouring custard—*crème anglaise*—is best known as a sauce for puddings and cooked fruit, but it is also a key element in many other desserts. Stiffened with gelatine, for example, it is the basis of Bavarian creams (*page 44*); frozen, it becomes a classic ice cream (*page 72*).

Whatever role *crème anglaise* is to play, its main ingredients remain the same: milk or cream, sugar and egg yolks. A related custard called *sabayon*—a dessert in its own right—can be made by substituting wine for the milk or cream (*box, opposite; recipe, page 166*). In both formulations, egg yolks are the custard's thickening agent: when the mixture is gently heated, the protein of the yolks partially coagulate and bind the custard into a creamy emulsion. Too much heat, however, will completely coagulate the yolks and curdle the custard.

In fact every step in making a *crème anglaise* includes a precaution against curdling. First, the yolks are carefully separated from the whites. Egg whites solidify at a lower temperature than yolks, and even a few drops—if heated with the custard—may produce lumps. Next, sugar is beaten thoroughly into the yolks. Yolks blended with sugar stay smooth at higher temperatures and make it possible to cook the custard safely over direct heat. After hot milk is poured over the eggs to start the cooking, the mixture is removed to a heavy pan that will heat the custard slowly and evenly until thick.

The consistency of the finished custard depends on the proportion of egg yolks to milk: the more yolks, the thicker and richer the custard. The *crème anglaise* demonstrated here (*recipe, page 166*) uses 6 yolks for each 60 cl (1 pint) of milk.

For *sabayon*, the method varies somewhat. The egg yolks and sugar are first beaten together then whisked over a very gentle heat. Whisking aerates the hot yolks so that they will fluff up to more than twice their original volume. Just before serving *sabayon*, you can add lemon or vanilla—although the better your wine, the less need for additional flavourings. Almost any white wine can be used, from champagne to sauternes, fortified wines, too, are among the possibilities; Italians use marsala to make *zabaglione*, the original version of the dessert.

1 Separating the eggs. Crack each egg shell in half and slip the contents on to the palm of one hand, allowing all the white of egg to trickle through your fingers into a dish. With your thumb and forefinger, gently remove from the yolk any clinging threads of albumen, then drop the yolk into a mixing bowl.

2 Combining the yolks with sugar. Add sugar to the yolks in the mixing bowl and beat the mixture so that the sugar is completely absorbed. After about 10 minutes of beating, the mixture will be creamy in texture and almost white.

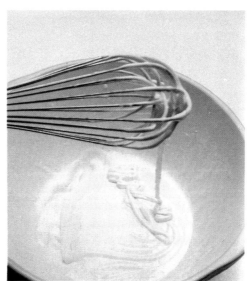

3 Testing consistency. Continue beating the mixture until it reaches the "ribbon" stage. To test, lift some of the mixture on the whisk and dribble it back into the bowl (*above*); it should form a trail, or "ribbon", that is visible on the surface.

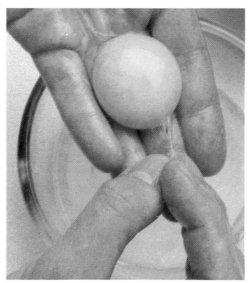

4 Adding scalded milk. Bring the milk to the boil over medium heat; when it nears boiling point, stir the milk to prevent a skin forming. Slowly pour the hot milk on to the yolk and sugar mixture, whisking constantly but gently. Do not whisk hard enough to form bubbles which would make a thick foam on the surface of the custard. Transfer to a heavy pan.

5 **Cooking the custard.** Put the saucepan over a low heat. Taking care to keep the custard below simmering point, stir it in a figure-of-eight motion (*inset*), so that you pass the spoon through the middle—the hottest part—twice in each complete motion. A square-edged spoon, as here, will reach into the corners of the pan and thus prevent patchy thickening. The consistency is correct when the custard coats the spoon. At this point, transfer the pan to a bowl of ice (*above*) to stop the mixture from thickening further.

6 **Straining the custard.** To ensure that the custard is smooth, strain it to remove any lumps from stray egg whites (*above*). Serve immediately. If you wish to keep the custard warm, transfer the pan to a hot water bath. To prevent a skin from forming, add a knob of butter or place a round of greaseproof paper on the surface of the custard. □

Sabayon: a Foam of Eggs and Wine

1 **Whisking eggs and sugar.** In a large bowl, or—as here—a *sabayon* pan, beat together the egg yolks and sugar until they are pale and creamy. Place the bowl over a large pan partly filled with water heated to just below boiling point, and continue to whisk.

2 **Adding the wine.** Pour in wine—here, champagne—and continue whisking for about 10 minutes, until the mixture froths up into a light mousse. Remove the pan from the hot water.

3 **Serving the sabayon.** As a dessert, *sabayon* is usually eaten hot. Pour it into individual glasses (*above*) and serve it immediately. As a sauce, *sabayon* may be used hot or cold. For a cold sauce, set the pan over ice to stop the cooking, and to chill the *sabayon* before use.

Lightly Set Confections, Rich in Flavour

By combining a little egg white with the yolks and milk that go to make a pouring custard (*page 38*), you can create lightly set dessert creams, such as the Peruvian creams demonstrated here (*recipe, page 108*). One whole egg to every five egg yolks produces a trembling, barely firm custard that is best cooked and served in individual ramekins—a custom that has earned these desserts their menu appellation *petits pots de crème*.

Since egg mixtures curdle readily, it is difficult to make a smooth custard cream by cooking it over direct heat. A water bath provides a more gentle cooking medium. The ramekins, filled with the custard mixture, are placed in a large, oven-proof pan that is partly filled with hot water, covered, and set over low heat or in a moderate oven. Inside the water bath, the hot water surrounds the ramekins and cooks the custards slowly and evenly.

Petit pots de crème may be flavoured in many ways: here, a rich blend of coffee, vanilla, chocolate and caramel is used. The purest coffee and vanilla flavours come from infusing the coffee beans and vanilla seeds separately in the hot milk used for the custard (*Steps 1 and 2, right.*) You can also use this method to perfume custards with orange or lemon peel.

Melted chocolate and caramel are added to the milk after the aromatic flavourings have been infused. In order to keep the mixture as smooth as possible, melt the chocolate very gently (*Step 3*); and make the caramel (*page 8*) fairly thin, so that it will blend easily with the milk.

1 Infusing the coffee. Heat whole, roasted coffee beans in a moderate oven for a few minutes, until they glisten with their aromatic oils. Bring milk to the boil in a pan over a moderate heat. Add the coffee beans (*above*), remove the pan from the heat; cover and keep warm. After about 30 minutes, strain the milk through a fine sieve into a bowl.

2 Adding vanilla. Return the milk to the pan and bring it back to the boil. Remove the pan from the heat. Break a whole vanilla bean in half and split one piece lengthwise. With the tip of a sharp knife scrape the seeds from one of the pod quarters into the milk. Leave the warm milk, covered, for about 15 minutes. Strain the milk back into the bowl.

3 Melting the chocolate. Break plain chocolate into chunks and put the chunks into the empty pan. Place the pan over a very low heat and add enough of the milk to barely cover the bottom of the pan (*above*). As it melts, stir the chocolate until it forms a smooth paste, then gradually stir in the remaining milk.

4 Adding caramel. In a small pan, make a little caramel (*page 8*). When it is a light golden colour, remove the pan from the heat and dip its base in cold water to arrest the cooking. Add a little hot water to the caramel, return it to a low heat and stir until it becomes a smooth syrup. Stir the caramel into the milk.

5 **Mixing the custard.** Place whole eggs and egg yolks—5 yolks to every whole egg—in a mixing bowl and whisk them until they are smooth. Gradually pour in the hot, flavoured milk, whisking it gently with the eggs (*above*).

6 **Skimming the custard.** To ensure that the custard is absolutely smooth, strain it by pouring the mixture through a fine sieve over a bowl. With a spoon, skim off any froth from the surface of the custard (*above*) so that bubbles will not spoil its appearance and texture when it cooks.

7 **Cooking in a water bath.** Fill the ramekins with the custard and place them in a wide, deep casserole. Pour in hot water to two-thirds of the depth of the ramekins; to prevent the water from splashing into the custards, pour it down a spatula held to one side of the bath (*left*). Bake, covered, at 150°C (300°F or Mark 2) for about 20 minutes. Chill, and serve with biscuits or wafers (*below*).□

A Moulded Sweet with a Caramel Glaze

Moulded custards that set firmly enough to be turned out can be made in essentially the same way as the *pots de crème* on page 40. However, to cause the desserts to set, you must include more egg white than is used in a basic *pots de crème* mixture. The proportion of egg white to yolk is critical. Too much white will produce a coarse, rubbery-textured custard; too little will produce a custard that will collapse when it is unmoulded. A ratio of 4 whole eggs and 4 egg yolks to every 60 cl (1 pint) of liquid provides the correct balance.

Such custards can be flavoured with finely grated orange or lemon peel, chocolate, coffee or vanilla, and baked in an oiled mould; but the classic version of the dessert is the *crème caramel* demonstrated here (*recipe, page 112*). *Crème caramel* is a vanilla custard which has been baked in a caramelized mould (*box, below*). As the custard cooks, the hard caramel lining melts in the heat, allowing the cooked custard to slide easily out of the mould. When the custard is turned out, it is capped with a layer of caramel and surrounded by a caramel sauce.

1 **Adding custard to a mould.** In a bowl, beat together the whole eggs, egg yolks, sugar, a few drops of vanilla extract and a pinch of salt. Stirring continuously, pour hot milk on to the mixture. Strain, then skim off any foam from the surface. Place a caramelized mould (*box, below*) in an ovenproof dish and ladle the mixture into the mould (*above*).

2 **Testing for doneness.** Pour warm water into the dish to immerse the mould to two-thirds of its depth. Bake the custard for 1 hour in a warm oven, preheated to 170°C (325°F or Mark 3). Test that the custard has set by inserting a knife into it. The knife should come out clean: if it does not (*above*), cook the custard for a further 10 minutes, then test again.

Caramelizing a Mould

1 **Making the caramel.** In a heavy pan over a low heat, dissolve sugar in a little water. Cook over moderate heat until the mixture is a light amber colour (*above*). Stop the cooking by dipping the pan momentarily in a bowl of ice-cubes and water.

2 **Coating the mould.** Immediately, pour the caramel into a warmed, dry mould. Using oven gloves, pick up the mould and rotate it so that the caramel runs round the inside of the mould, coating it completely. Allow the excess caramel to form a layer on the base.

3 **Oiling the mould.** To prevent the custard from sticking to the mould, use a pastry brush to put a little almond oil—or tasteless vegetable oil—on any areas of the mould that remain uncoated with caramel (*above*).

3 **Loosening the custard.** Remove the mould from the oven dish and leave it to cool. When the custard is tepid, insert a knife a little way down the side of the mould and run it round (*above*) to free the sides of the custard.

4 **Freeing the custard.** Hold the mould steady with one hand and use the fingertips of the other hand to ease the custard from the sides of the mould by pressing gently on the surface (*above*). Continue until the custard is not sticking to the mould at any point.

5 **Unmoulding the custard.** Choose a serving plate deep enough to hold the liquid caramel that will run down the sides of the custard as you unmould it. Invert the plate on to the custard and turn both over together. Lift the mould gently from the custard (*above*). Serve the *crème caramel* tepid, or chill it for a few hours in the refrigerator.☐

Sculptures of Cream and Gelatine

Bavarian creams, which rank among the world's most celebrated moulded desserts, depend on gelatine and whipped cream to make them firm enough to hold their intricate shapes. Included in this category are the classic *blanc-manger* (*right; recipe, page 114*), striped Bavarian cream (*below, right; recipe, page 118*), and a range of cold mousses and soufflés.

In each case, gelatine is added to a flavoured base; when the gelatine begins to set, whipped cream is folded in and the mixture is poured into a mould and chilled. Almond-flavoured milk is used for the *blanc-manger*; in the striped Bavarian cream, two flavoured bases—raspberry purée and vanilla pouring custard—provide the contrasting layers that give the dessert its name.

Choose a mould with a distinct pattern, and brush it with almond oil—or tasteless vegetable oil—before you start the cooking, so that the Bavarian cream will slip out effortlessly when it has set.

The skills essential to making these desserts are smoothly combining dissolved leaf or powdered gelatine (*page 16*) with the flavoured bases and adding whipped cream at just the right moment. A gelatine mixture sets—or takes—rapidly as it cools. The liquid gelatine must therefore be warm when you add it to a flavoured base—especially if the base is a cold one. Otherwise, the gelatine will take as soon as it makes contact with the base, and will form lumps, a mishap termed "roping" by professional cooks.

Once the gelatine has been added to the base, the mixture should be chilled to speed setting. Place it over a bowl of ice cubes and water while you whip the cream. Stir the mixture frequently, until it is just beginning to take. You should aim for a consistency close to that of the whipped cream. If the gelatine has not yet set sufficiently, it will be too liquid to blend easily with the cream; if it sets too much at this stage, its solidity will make it impossible for you to fold in the cream evenly. Premature setting can be remedied by warming the mixture: set the bowl over a pan of hot water for half a minute, stirring constantly.

An Almond-Flavoured Blanc-Manger

1 **Preparing the almond milk.** Pound blanched almonds (*page 12*) and mix them to a smooth paste with a little water. Put the paste in a pan, add milk and sugar, and heat the mixture to just below boiling point. Remove it from the heat and strain the liquid through a clean cloth. Gather up the corners of the cloth and twist (*above*) to wring out the last of the almond milk.

2 **Stiffening the almond milk.** Soften leaf gelatine (*page 16*), place it in a pan with just enough water to cover it and warm gently. When the gelatine begins to dissolve, combine it with the warm almond milk (*above*). Add more sugar to taste, and stir until the gelatine dissolves completely. Remove from the heat and pour the milk into a bowl over ice cubes. Stir the mixture as it cools.

Contrasting Layers of Bavarian Cream

1 **Preparing the fruit mixture.** Make a raspberry purée (*page 26*). In a separate pan, prepare an equal quantity of sugar syrup (*page 8*). When the syrup boils, remove it from the heat and add softened, powdered gelatine (*page 16*), stirring until it dissolves completely. Let the syrup cool; when it is lukewarm, blend it thoroughly with the fruit purée (*above*). Stir the mixture over ice or place it in a refrigerator to cool it further.

2 **Preparing the vanilla mixture.** Prepare a pouring custard (*page 38*) flavoured with vanilla. Stir the custard over a low heat and add powdered gelatine that has been dissolved in water (*above*). Continue stirring. Do not let the custard approach the boil or the custard will curdle. When the custard has thickened enough to coat the spoon, remove it from the heat and stir it over ice.

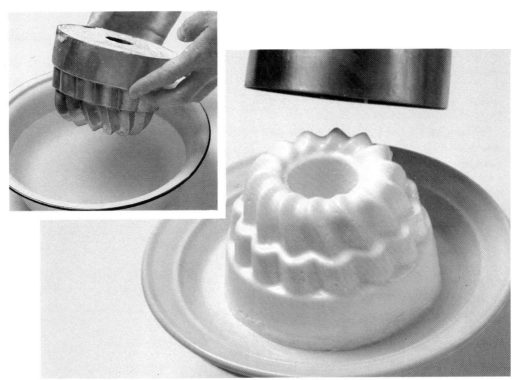

3 **Adding whipped cream.** While the almond milk cools, whip double cream until it forms soft peaks. Continue to stir the almond milk at intervals; as soon as the gelatinized liquid begins to take, stir in the cream (*above*) until it is thoroughly amalgamated with the milk. Pour the mixture into a lightly oiled mould. Cover and refrigerate for about 5 hours.

4 **Unmoulding and serving.** Remove the cover and test the dessert: when set, it should be firm to the touch. Loosen the edges of the *blanc-manger* with a knife and quickly dip the bottom of the mould into a basin of hot water (*above, inset*). Unmould the loosened *blanc-manger* using an inverted plate (*page 25*).□

3 **Adding whipped cream.** Whip sweetened double cream until it forms soft peaks. When the fruit and custard mixtures are equally cold and both are beginning to take, incorporate about half the cream into each (*above*). To keep the layers of the finished dessert from running into each other, the fruit purée and custard should have the same consistency: one mixture may need more cream than the other.

4 **Completing the dish.** Fill an oiled mould with alternate layers of the pink and white creams (*left*). Pour each cream gently so that the layers remain separate. Cover the mould and set it in a refrigerator for about 5 hours. Unmould as for *blanc-manger* (*Step 4, above*).□

Puffs of Egg White: Crisp or Soft

After you prepare a yolk-rich custard or cream such as one of those demonstrated on the previous pages, you can put the surplus egg whites to good use in the meringues demonstrated here.

A basic meringue mixture consists simply of egg whites and sugar—sometimes mixed with additional flavourings, such as coffee or chocolate. Depending on how it is cooked, the same mixture can make either of two quite different desserts. Baked meringues are brittle shells (*right; recipe, page 160*), often served sandwiched with whipped cream. Poached meringues are fluffy and yielding: they are usually served on custard—a presentation called *oeufs à la neige*, "snow eggs" (*opposite page; recipe, page 120*), which uses both yolks and whites.

The meringue mixture is simple to make but requires about 15 minutes' vigorous beating. First, the whites are whisked to a stiff foam, then sugar is beaten in. Too much sugar added at once will soften the whites: whisk it in a little at a time, beating after each addition.

For baked meringues, you can simply place spoonfuls of the mixture on a lined oven tray. But more decorative shapes can easily be made by squeezing the meringue from a flexible piping bag with a patterned nozzle, as here.

Slow, gentle cooking is necessary to produce baked meringues that are light and dry, without a trace of stickiness. Bake the meringues for about 3 hours at the oven's lowest setting: as a precaution against overheating, some cooks wedge the door ajar with a wooden spoon, or even bake the meringues overnight in the oven's plate-warming compartment.

For poaching, make the meringue shapes by gently sliding spoonfuls of the mixture on to barely simmering, sweetened milk. Poaching is much briefer than baking; 3 minutes of cooking will produce firm, fluffy meringues.

For the *oeufs à la neige* shown here, the poaching milk is used to make a pouring custard (*page 38*) on which the meringues are arranged for serving. Pile up the meringues, perhaps decorated with wisps of caramel (*Step 3, opposite page*), or float separate poached meringues on caramel-flavoured custard (*box, opposite page*).

Baked Meringues

1 Beating in sugar. Beat egg whites until they form stiff peaks (*page 14*). Add castor sugar, a little at a time (*above*), allowing about 60 g (2 oz) of sugar for each white. Beat well after each addition. Gently fold in the flavourings. For the assortment here, one third of the mixture is flavoured with cocoa powder, one third with strong coffee and the remainder is left plain.

2 Filling a piping bag. Insert a nozzle into a piping bag. Turn the upper one-third of the bag inside-out and spoon meringue into the lower two-thirds, then fold back the upper part of the bag to enclose the mixture. Twist the top of the bag to close it and provide a handle. Squeeze the top gently until the meringue mixture starts to appear at the nozzle end.

3 Forming the meringues. Lightly oil a baking tray and spread it with non-stick paper or oiled aluminium foil. Pipe the meringue mixture in spirals (*above*) using one hand to hold the top of the bag closed as you squeeze it, and the other to guide the nozzle.

4 Serving the meringues. Bake the meringues for about 3 hours in a very low oven. When they are dry enough to be detached easily from the baking sheet, remove them from the oven and leave to cool. Serve them sandwiched in pairs with whipped cream. If you like, flavour some of the cream with praline powder (*page 13*) and scatter more powder over the meringues. □

Poached Meringues

1 **Poaching meringues**. In a wide, shallow pan, heat sweetened milk to just below simmering point. Scoop up a tablespoon of the raw meringue mixture (*Step 1, left*) and slide it on to the milk with the tip of a spatula. Poach 3 or 4 meringues at a time: cook them for about 3 minutes, turning them over once with a spoon. Lift out the meringues and place them on a drum sieve or cloth to drain.

1 **Flavouring the milk.** Dilute some caramel (*page 8*) with a little warm water, so that it will blend easily with the milk. Poach the meringues (*Step 1, left*), drain them, and strain the milk. Stir the warm caramel into the still-hot milk (*above*).

2 **Making custard.** Continue poaching the meringues in small batches so that you can attend to them all and there is room for you to turn them. When all the meringues are cooked, strain the milk (*above*) to remove fragments of egg white. Stir the milk into beaten egg yolks and sugar and gently cook the mixture to make a pouring custard (*page 38*).

3 **Assembling the dessert.** Pour the custard into a glass bowl. Place meringues gently on its surface. When the surface is covered with meringues, pile the rest on top of the first layer. If you like, decorate the dish with threads of caramel (*page 8*), as shown here. Serve it either tepid or cold. □

2 **Arranging the meringues.** Make a custard by cooking the caramel-flavoured milk with beaten egg yolks (*page 166*). Pour the custard into a bowl; using a spatula or large spoon, arrange the cooked meringues in a pattern on the surface of the custard (*above*).

3
Soufflés and Puddings
From the Ethereal to the Weighty

Incorporating egg whites with a light touch
Melting and moulding chocolate
Gentle cooking in a water bath
Making the most of grains

Hot soufflés and hot or cold puddings run the gamut from airy flamboyant desserts to solid hearty ones. These two extremes seem to have little in common, yet between them lies a progression of overlapping cooking techniques that offer a dessert for any mood, season or appetite.

Hot, baked soufflés (*page 50*) are among the lightest of all desserts. Beaten egg whites are folded into a flavoured base; when the dessert is baked, air trapped in the egg whites expands and the soufflé rises to startling heights. Once cooked, the soufflé waits for no man; it must be rushed to the table before its fragile form collapses. In the lightest soufflés, egg whites alone are combined with a sweetened fruit purée; in most other soufflés, the basic mixture is enriched with egg yolks before it is mixed with the whites.

A chocolate mousse (*page 52*) is another dessert lightened with beaten egg whites—but for the mousse, the ingredients are not cooked. Instead, the dessert is chilled; as it cools, it becomes firmer and the bubbles of air remain trapped inside it. Although a mousse will never achieve the lightness of a soufflé, you can serve it without fear of its collapsing.

A little further from the miraculous lightness of the classic hot soufflé, comes the pudding-soufflé. A pudding-soufflé contains less egg white, and it cooks in the moist heat of a water bath. As a result, it does not expand as dramatically as a soufflé but neither does it fall so far as it cools. So a pudding-soufflé—such as a chocolate pudding (*opposite page and page 53*) or a semolina *flamri* (*cover and page 54*)—can be unmoulded and decorated at leisure before it is served.

Without the leavening of egg whites, semolina and other farinaceous ingredients make puddings that are even more substantial. Rice, for example (*page 56*), simmered in sweetened, flavoured milk makes a simple and nourishing dish; with the addition of cream and egg yolks, the rice becomes a rich and warming pudding.

Steamed puddings are cheering, filling winter food—perfectly appropriate at Christmas, which Englishmen would consider incomplete without the traditional spicy suet pudding filled with fruits and doused with brandy (*page 58*). A suet pudding may need as much as 12 hours steaming. Some types will keep—and mature in flavour—for 18 months or more.

Whipped cream is squeezed from a piping bag to adorn a chocolate pudding, which has been cooked by moist, gentle heat in a mould set in a water bath. To help the pudding slip easily from its heavily buttered mould, it was left to stand for 15 minutes so that it would become firm before being turned out.

The Art of Enfolding Air

The lightest of all desserts, a soufflé, is no more than beaten egg whites combined with a flavoured base. The soufflé's most important ingredient, air, does not appear in any recipe; but it is air, trapped in the beaten whites and expanding in the oven's heat, which causes the soufflé to rise. The cook's main task, therefore, is to incorporate as much air as possible into the egg whites (*page 14*).

The first step in making any soufflé is to heat the oven to the required temperature—usually about 180°C (350°F or Mark 4). While the oven is heating, you can prepare the dish and the flavoured base. To ensure that the soufflé will rise without hindrance, use a straight-sided container; coat it with softened butter and sugar to prevent the soufflé sticking.

When everything else is ready, beat the egg whites until they form stiff peaks. Always beat the egg whites at the last possible minute: if left to stand, they will soon lose their air and subside. Mix a portion of the beaten whites with the flavoured base; once the base has been lightened in this way, it can easily be folded into the remaining whites (*Step 4, right*). After the mixture has been folded together, pour it gently into the mould and cook the soufflé in the middle of the preheated oven for about 30 minutes.

The most frequently used base ingredients for soufflés are flour, milk, egg yolks, butter and sugar—combined in various proportions and mixed with any number of flavourings; in the vanilla soufflé demonstrated on the right, the flavourings are vanilla and crystallized fruit (*recipe, page 124*). But one kind of soufflé (*box, opposite page; recipe, page 123*) uses only a lightly sweetened fruit purée as its foundation. Such a soufflé is an excellent way to present soft fruits such as raspberries or, as here, wild strawberries. The fruit's flavour is not masked by other ingredients and the egg whites, unbound by yolks or flour, expand rapidly.

Since a fruit soufflé is very fragile it should be cooked as quickly as possible so that the whites set before air can escape from them. Preheat the oven to 190°C (375°F or Mark 5) and use a metal dish that conducts heat well. The whites rise high as well as fast: wrap a paper collar around the dish to prevent spillage.

1 Preparing the soufflé dish. Coat a straight-sided soufflé dish with softened butter and sprinkle it with a little castor sugar. Roll the dish around so that the sugar clings evenly to the buttered surfaces. Loosen any surplus sugar by gently tapping the sides of the dish, then shake out the loose sugar.

2 Making the base. Put flour into a cup or a small bowl and stir in enough cold milk to make a thin paste. Bring milk and sugar, flavoured with a vanilla pod, to the boil and stir in the flour and milk paste. Whisk over a low heat until the mixture thickens. Remove the pan from the heat and take out the vanilla pod.

3 Adding the yolks. After the thickened milk has cooled for a few minutes, add the egg yolks (*above*) and the butter. Whisk until the yolks are well blended into the base mixture, and then stir in the chopped, crystallized fruit.

4 Folding in the egg whites. Beat the egg whites until they form stiff peaks. Add about a quarter of the whites to the base mixture to lighten its texture. Pour this mixture over the remaining whites. Using a spatula or your hands, fold the whites from the bottom of the bowl over the top of the mixture. Continue folding until the soufflé is nearly homogeneous.

5 **Filling the soufflé dish.** Put the mixture immediately into the prepared soufflé dish (*above*) and place in a preheated oven. After about 30 minutes, check that the soufflé is cooked by inserting a thin knife blade into it. The blade will come out faintly moist if the soufflé is slightly underdone, but clean if well done. Serve the soufflé as soon as it is cooked to your taste (*right*). If it is allowed to cool, it will collapse—especially if it is slightly underdone. □

The Simplest Soufflé: Fruit and Whites

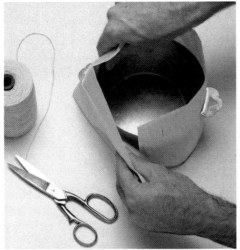

1 **Making a collar.** Wrap a double layer of kitchen or greaseproof paper around a charlotte mould or similar metal dish. If necessary, cut slits in the paper where it passes over the handles. Keep the paper in place by tying string around it. Brush the mould and the paper collar with softened butter and sprinkle them with sugar.

2 **Filling the mould.** Combine the stiffly beaten egg whites with a sweetened pureé of wild strawberries or other soft fruit (*as in Step 4, left*) to make an evenly coloured, foamy mixture. Spoon the mixture into the prepared dish; the soufflé should just reach the top of the charlotte mould, below the paper collar.

3 **Cooking and serving the soufflé.** Cook the soufflé in an oven preheated to 190°C (375°F or Mark 5) for about 25 minutes. The top will be lightly brown but the centre will still be a little moist. Remove the soufflé from the oven and serve it immediately, or it may collapse.

Chocolate Chilled and Chocolate Cooked

Blended with egg yolks and butter, then aerated with beaten egg whites, chocolate becomes a smooth, light mousse (*right; recipe, page 126*). And by reducing the proportion of whites, adding flour and baking the mixture, you can produce a substantial chocolate pudding (*box, opposite page; recipe, page 125*).

Make the foundation with plain dessert chocolate or, if you like, with bitter chocolate, which contains less sugar. Begin by melting the chocolate with a little water in a heavy pan over low heat. The water will keep the chocolate from burning; the low heat will prevent the curdling that would give chocolate a grainy texture: to rescue curdled chocolate, remove it from the heat, add a few drops of boiling water and whisk it vigorously.

After you have combined the chocolate with butter and egg yolks to give it smoothness—but before you lighten it with egg whites—you can stir in sugar, if it is needed, and a variety of flavourings. Rum or brandy is the classic choice whether you are making a mousse or a pudding; coffee or orange juice (or liqueurs flavoured with coffee or orange) also marry well with chocolate. Whipped cream is a traditional accompaniment.

1 Melting the chocolate. Break the chocolate into squares and put them into a pan with just enough water to cover the pan bottom. Place the pan on a very low heat and stir continuously with a wooden spatula (*above*) until the chocolate melts and blends with the water to form a smooth paste.

2 Blending in butter and eggs. Remove the pan from the heat. Add small pieces of butter, a few at a time, stirring until they have blended with the chocolate (*above, left*). Separate the eggs, keeping the whites aside in a mixing bowl, and add the yolks to the pan one by one (*above, right*), stirring continuously. Stir the mixture until it is smooth and glossy, then add sugar to taste and about 1 tablespoon of rum, brandy or other flavouring.

3 Introducing chocolate into egg whites. Whisk the egg whites until they form fairly stiff peaks (*page 14*). To combine the whites evenly with the chocolate, leaving no unflavoured pockets of egg white, dribble a little of the very dense chocolate mixture evenly over the surface of the beaten egg whites (*above*). Whisk gently until the mixture is evenly coloured.

4 Blending egg whites and chocolate. Pour the egg white mixture into the pan containing the bulk of the chocolate. Fold the chocolate into the egg white mixture, using a whisk to lift and slide the chocolate gently from the bottom of the pan on to the top of the mixture. Continue folding the mixture in this way until the mousse has a uniform colour and consistency.

5 **Serving the mousse.** Spoon the chocolate mousse into serving glasses (*left*) and chill for at least 2 hours to firm. Just before serving, decorate the mousse with whipped cream and, if you like, sugared orange peel (*page 11*). □

Baking a Moulded Loaf

1 **Sieving flour into the chocolate.** Melt the chocolate and add butter and egg yolks (*Steps 1 and 2, opposite page*). Stir sugar into the chocolate, then blend in sieved flour (*above*). Combine the chocolate mixture with beaten egg whites (*Steps 3 and 4, opposite page*).

2 **Moulding and cooking.** Pour the chocolate mixture into a heavily buttered mould (*above*) to within 2.5 cm (1 inch) of the top, leaving room for the pudding to rise. Place the mould in a water bath and add hot water to two-thirds the depth of the mould. Place in an oven preheated to 170°C (325°F or Mark 3).

3 **Serving the pudding.** After about 40 minutes, probe the pudding with a thin skewer. If the skewer comes out clean, the pudding is cooked. Let it rest for a few minutes to firm; then, using an inverted plate, unmould the pudding. Leave the pudding to cool, then decorate it with whipped cream and serve (*above*).

Two Classic Pudding-Soufflés

By blending a small quantity of beaten egg whites into a heavy base mixture, you can create a pudding-soufflé—a dish that combines some of the lightness of the classic soufflé (*page 50*) with the firmness of a more orthodox pudding (*pages 56 to 59*). In the *flamri* demonstrated here (*right; recipe, page 130*), boiled semolina—the granular product of partially milled wheat—provides the base; in the nut loaf (*bottom, right; recipe, page 126*), ground almonds and pistachios flavoured with fruit peels are the foundation. Since neither the *flamri*, nor the nut loaf is intended to be airy, both base mixtures are blended with just enough egg whites to lighten their textures.

Instead of being baked unprotected in the oven, pudding-soufflés are cooked in moulds in a water bath (*page 40*). Partially immersed in water kept just below boiling point—either in a moderate oven or on top of the stove—the pudding mixture will cook slowly and evenly. It will rise as it cooks, but not as dramatically as a classic soufflé. And although it will settle slightly when it is removed from the oven, there is no danger of its collapsing. In fact, a nut loaf can be kept for a day or two and will actually improve in flavour.

In most semolina pudding-soufflés, the grains are cooked in milk as a first stage. However, in the *flamri*, the semolina acquires more flavour by being simmered in white wine mixed with water. Adjust the amount of sugar added according to the sweetness of the wine and your own taste. Egg yolks are included to enrich the semolina before the beaten whites are folded in. The pudding is easier to unmould if it is cooked in a fairly shallow dish; you can build a taller, more formal dessert by using two or more moulds and turning them out one on top of the other, as here. *Flamri* is usually served with a tart sauce made from a purée of soft fruit, such as blackberries or raspberries.

The almond and pistachio loaf also includes white wine and egg yolks. Cooked orange and lemon peels added to the ground nuts help to balance the strong flavour of their aromatic oils.

Wine-Simmered Semolina

1 **Cooking the semolina.** Bring equal quantities of water and white wine to a rolling boil. Maintaining the same heat, sprinkle in semolina, stirring continuously with a whisk or wooden spoon. Cover the pan, reduce the heat and simmer for 20 minutes, until the semolina has cooked to a thick, smooth paste.

2 **Adding the eggs.** Remove the pan from the heat and let the semolina cool for a few minutes. Beat in sugar to taste, a pinch of salt and the whole eggs. Whisk egg whites until they form stiff peaks. Use a spatula (*above*) to fold them gently but thoroughly into the semolina mixture.

A Loaf of Pounded Nuts

1 **Making the nut paste.** Pound almonds and pistachios in a mortar until they are smooth. If you have an electric food processor, use it for this step. It will give good results and save much time. Simmer strips of orange and lemon peels in sugar syrup (*page 8*), then add the peels and syrup to the pounded nuts (*above, left*). Blend the peel and the nuts and stir small quantities of white wine and sugar alternately into the mixture (*above, centre*). Add the egg yolks and beat the mixture until it is stiff (*above, right*).

3 **Cooking the mixture.** Turn the mixture into two buttered moulds—one for the base, the other for a decorative top. Cover each mould with greaseproof paper and place it in a large pan (*above*). Pour in hot water to reach two-thirds of the way up the sides. Cover, and place the pan over a low heat for 25 to 40 minutes, until the *flamri* is firm.

4 **Unmoulding the pudding.** Let the moulds stand until the pudding-soufflé is lukewarm. Unmould the larger *flamri* first, using an inverted plate. Place a wide spatula over the smaller mould, then upend the mould and lower it gently on to the first pudding-soufflé (*above*). Carefully slide out the spatula before removing the mould.

5 **Decorating and serving.** Crown the *flamri* with whole blackberries, as here, or raspberries. Make a sauce by puréeing some of the fruit with sugar to taste. If fresh fruits are out of season, use frozen fruits, or, for the sauce, substitute a purée of dried apricots.□

2 **Folding in the egg whites.** Whisk the egg whites until they form stiff peaks. Blend a spoonful of the whites with the nut purée, then fold the purée gently into the remaining whites (*above*). Pour the mixture into a buttered mould. Set the mould in a water bath (*Step 3, top*) and place it in an oven preheated to 190°C (375°F or Mark 5) for about 25 minutes, or until the mixture has set firm.

3 **Serving the pudding.** Unmould the nut loaf using an inverted plate. Leave the loaf to stand for a few minutes to allow it to settle, then decorate it with whipped cream. If you like, include strips of sugared orange peel (*page 11*).□

Eggs and Cream to Transform a Staple

Cooked in milk until its grains are plump and tender, rice makes substantial and economical puddings that range from the basic to the luxurious. Because of its un-assertive taste, rice can accommodate many flavourings. In this demonstration, the rice is perfumed by a bouquet of orange and lemon peels (*recipe, page 133*). Cinnamon and vanilla are other popular flavourings: the Germans use cooking apples and sweet cider (*recipe, page 132*): the Indians favour almonds and rose water (*recipe, page 133*).

You can make puddings from long-grain rice, such as Patna, used here, or Carolina, or from short-grain rice—Piedmont rice or the pearl rice of Oriental cookery. The kernels of Patna or Carolina rice stay intact after cooking and produce a pudding with clearly separated grains. The kernels of short-grain rice absorb more liquid and merge together to produce a more homogeneous pudding.

Before cooking, wash the rice thoroughly in cold water to remove surface starch that would make the finished dish too glutinous. Parboil the rice (*Step 1, right*) for a few minutes, then give it another rinse with cold water to wash away any remaining starch and to stop the rice from cooking further at this point.

During the next stage of cooking , the rice will absorb about three times its own volume of sweetened, flavoured milk (wine or water in some recipes). You can serve the pudding when the milk has been absorbed, or go on to make more elaborate desserts. Here, egg yolks and cream are blended into the cooked rice, and then the pudding is baked at a fairly high heat to give it a brown crust. But you could combine the rice with egg whites, cook the mixture in a mould in a water bath, and serve it with stewed fruit (*recipe, page 131*). Or you can incorporate gelatine and crystallized fruits and chill the rice for *Riz à l'Impératrice* (*recipe, page 134*).

1 Parboiling the rice. Rinse the rice in cold water then plunge it into a heavy pan of boiling water. Boil the rice for about 5 minutes, stirring occasionally with a wooden spoon to keep the grains separate, then drain it in a colander. Rinse it under cold running water and leave it to drain again.

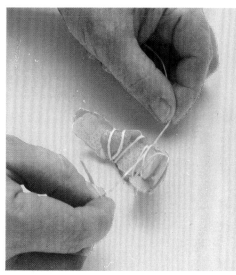

2 Preparing the flavouring. Set a pan of milk over a medium heat. While the milk heating, tie two strips of fresh lemon peel and three of fresh orange peel with string to make a bundle and set it aside.

3 Adding sugar. Add sugar to the milk, stirring to make sure that it dissolves thoroughly. Then add the bouquet of lemon and orange peels, some butter and a pinch of salt. For extra flavour, leave the milk to infuse for up to 1 hour.

4 Adding the rice. Bring the milk to the boil and stir in the drained, parboiled rice (*above*). Slowly bring the milk back to the boil, cover the pan and cook in a low oven or over a very low heat for about 30 minutes, until the rice is tender and the milk has been absorbed.

5 **Cooling the rice.** Remove the pan from the oven and take out the bouquet. Separate the grains of rice by stirring them gently with a fork. Serve the rice immediately, if you wish. If you plan to add cream and egg yolks, leave the rice to cool for 5 minutes, otherwise it will be so hot that it curdles the yolks.

6 **Adding the egg yolks.** Separate the egg yolks from the whites (*page 38*). Reserve the egg whites for use in other dishes, such as meringues (*page 46*). Add the egg yolks to the rice (*above*) and stir the mixture—taking care not to crush the grains—until the rice is thoroughly coated.

7 **Serving the pudding.** With a spoon, blend single cream into the mixture. Pour it into a buttered baking dish. Sprinkle 2 to 3 tablespoons of sugar over the pudding and bake it in a hot oven for about 25 minutes. If by this time the sugar has not formed a brown glaze, put the pudding under a grill for a minute or two. Serve directly from the baking dish.□

Steaming: an Age-Old Way to Make a Pudding

Steamed puddings, wrapped in cloth or packed into a basin and cooked in a large pan of boiling water, are a legacy from medieval times. As originally made, such puddings required a robust appetite on the part of the diner: they were dense, rich mixtures of savoury and sweet ingredients—meat or fish with fruits and spices.

Later, exclusively sweet puddings were developed as cold-weather desserts. These were usually made with flour, dried fruits and butter or suet—the fat that surrounds beef kidney. The English Christmas pudding demonstrated here (*recipe, page 136*) is an aristocratic example of the breed. In this dessert, suet is combined with breadcrumbs instead of flour, and the mixture is enlivened with generous quantities of dried and candied fruits, nuts and spices. The pudding is cooked in a basin, which is less messy than a cloth. Although the pudding would be edible after about 1½ hours, most cooks steam a Christmas pudding for up to 8 or 9 hours, to blend the flavours thoroughly and to allow the dried fruit to spread its dark colour throughout the pudding.

Good suet should be white, dry and crumbly to the touch. Buy it fresh from the butcher; pick it over to remove connective tissue and membrane before you grate it with a food processor or an ordinary kitchen grater.

Because of the exceptional keeping properties of cooked suet, and the preservative effect of sugar and alcohol, Christmas puddings can be made months, or even a year or two, in advance and stored; indeed, their flavours will often improve if they are left to mature in an airtight container (*box, opposite*).

Before you make a Christmas pudding, prepare the candied peel and dried fruit. Soak the peel in water for about 30 minutes; wash the dried fruits, spread them on a kitchen towel to dry, then pick them over and remove any woody stalks.

The time-honoured accompaniment for Christmas pudding is hard sauce, made by beating together equal volumes of butter and icing sugar, and flavoured with dark rum or brandy. Traditionally, a glass of warm brandy is poured over the pudding and set alight at table.

1 **Preparing the ingredients.** Chop blanched almonds (*page 12*), candied peel and cherries and place them in a large bowl with soft dark brown sugar and dried fruit—here, sultanas, currants and raisins. Grate the zest of an orange and a lemon over the mixture. Brush the zest off the grater with a pastry brush (*above*). Add minced or grated suet, breadcrumbs and spices such as grated nutmeg and ground ginger. Mix thoroughly with your hands.

2 **Binding the ingredients.** Beat eggs and pour them into the mixture. Add whisky, brandy or, as here, a glass of dark beer; stir with a wooden spoon to combine the ingredients. Traditionally, cooks add coins or charms to a Christmas pudding. If you do so, first sterilize them in boiling water and wrap individually in foil or greaseproof paper.

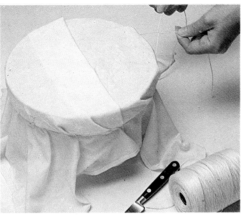

3 **Preparing the basin.** Brush a pudding basin with vegetable oil. Line the base with a circle of greaseproof paper, oiled on both sides so that the paper will not stick to the basin or the pudding. Fill the basin with the pudding mixture, packing it in tightly; level the mixture with a spoon. Cover with another circle of oiled greaseproof paper (*above*).

4 **Sealing the pudding.** Sprinkle a dampened cloth with flour and place it over the basin, floured side down. Pleat the cloth to allow the pudding to rise during cooking, and tie the cloth with string beneath the ridge of the basin. To help you lift the basin easily, make a handle by bringing the loose ends over the top of the basin; tie them together.

5 **Steaming the pudding.** Place a trivet in a large pan and lower the pudding basin on to it. Pour boiling water into the pan until the pudding basin is two-thirds immersed. Cover the pan and simmer the pudding for about 9 hours, adding more boiling water as necessary.

A Wax Seal for Storage

Brushing with wax. Remove the cloth and greaseproof paper top from the cooked, cooled pudding. Brush a large piece of greaseproof paper with vegetable oil and tie it tightly, oiled side down, over the basin with string. To make an airtight seal, melt some paraffin wax or a few candles in a metal bowl over boiling water and, using a pastry brush or a paint brush, coat the paper with the melted wax. Stored in a cool dry place, the pudding will keep for well over a year. To serve the pudding, remove the paper and scrape any wax off the basin. Steam for several hours and serve hot.

6 **Serving the pudding.** Remove the pudding basin from the pan, using the tied ends of the cloth as a handle. Uncover the pudding and unmould it from its basin. Decorate the pudding with holly. Just before serving, pour a glass of warmed brandy over the top; hold a lighted match near the pudding to ignite the brandy. □

4
Crêpes and Fritters
The Manifold Uses of Batter

A gleaming wine syrup drenches an array of crêpes rolled around poached figs (*page 34*). Crêpes make wrapping for almost any fruit and, once assembled, the fruit crêpes may be served with a complementary sauce, as here, or simply dotted with sugar and butter and glazed quickly under the grill.

An astonishing variety of desserts depend on one of the most basic of all cooking materials—batter, a dilute paste of flour and liquid. One type of batter yields wafer-thin crêpes that can be rolled around fruit (*opposite page*), filled with a soufflé mixture (*page 64*), or layered with custard and flavourings to make a cake (*page 65*). A similar batter baked with fruit makes a French *clafoutis*, a creamy, cake-like pudding (*page 66*). And pieces of fruit or flower blossoms coated with an especially light batter become sizzling, crisp fritters (*page 67*).

A batter's precise ingredients, and their proportions, vary according to its purpose. For crêpes (*page 62*), whole eggs are blended with the flour and enough milk added to produce a smooth, thin batter. Melted butter added to the mixture helps the cooked crêpes to slide easily from the pan. Flavourings can range from brandy and liqueurs to nothing more than a pinch of salt. It is the batter's consistency that is all-important. To make crêpes that are light and lacy, yet substantial enough to wrap around a filling, the batter should pour as easily as thin cream. A heavier batter made with a higher proportion of flour, would make leaden crêpes—but it is exactly right for the *clafoutis* pudding batter (*page 66*).

Fritter batter has still different requirements. In order to cook quickly into a crisp envelope, it must be very light. No egg yolks are included, therefore, and the flour is mixed with water or beer instead of the milk used in most other batters. To make the fritter batter even airier, beaten egg whites are folded into it just before cooking.

When flour is mixed with liquid, as in all batters, the flour's protein forms gluten, an insoluble, elastic substance. Beating increases the gluten's elasticity, with unwelcome results: if crêpe batter is too elastic, it will not flow evenly over the pan; elastic fritter batter will not cling to food. Leaving the prepared batter to stand, or "rest", at room temperature will reduce its elasticity. As a rule, it is wise to rest a fritter batter for about 1 hour, since deep fried food must be thoroughly coated. Crêpe batter should need no more than 30 minutes resting time; indeed, if you take care to blend the ingredients together gently, without beating too vigorously, you will be able to use the crêpe batter without delay.

How to Achieve the Perfect Crêpe

Served straight from the pan with a sprinkling of liqueur or of sugar and lemon juice, crêpes make a light, uncomplicated ending to a meal. For a more formal dessert, you can roll crêpes round a fruit or soufflé filling, or stack them to make a crêpe gateau (*pages 64-65*).

However crêpes are to be served, the basic batter mixture always includes eggs, flour, milk—and melted butter; brandy or liqueur can be added for flavouring (*box, opposite page; recipe, page 167*). Whisk the batter just enough to blend the ingredients: overbeating may make it so elastic that it will not coat the pan smoothly. Because crêpes must be cooked evenly, a fairly heavy iron or steel pan—reserved for crêpes—is essential. A new pan must be seasoned before use (*box, right*), otherwise the crêpes would stick, since the only cooking fat is a film of oil and the butter in the crêpe mixture.

Even with a seasoned pan, do not expect the first crêpe or two of any batch to be perfect. Consider them as test pieces to help you judge the quantity of batter needed and the precise degree of heat; discard these test crêpes if necessary.

Seasoning a Crêpe Pan

Seasoning a new crêpe pan. Wash and dry the pan, pour in 5 mm (¼ inch) of oil (*above, left*) and set the pan over a low heat until the oil starts to darken and smoke. Remove the pan from the stove, let it cool, pour out the hot oil and wipe the pan with a dry cloth (*above, right*). The pan is now ready for use. If a crêpe should stick during cooking, remove any batter residue by rubbing the pan with salt. Never wash the crêpe pan; if you do, you will have to re-season it. To prevent rusting, always wipe the crêpe pan with a well-oiled cloth before putting it away.

1 Forming the crêpe. Wipe the pan with an oiled cloth. Set the pan over medium heat. When a light haze forms above the pan, ladle in just enough batter to cover the bottom (*above, left*); the batter should sizzle as it touches the hot metal. At once, tilt the pan with a rolling motion to spread the batter as thinly as possible (*above, centre*). Pour any uncooked batter back into the mixing bowl (*above, right*).

A Well-Blended Batter

1 **Blending the ingredients.** Sieve the flour, together with a pinch of salt, into a mixing bowl. Form a well in the centre of the flour, break the eggs into the well and gradually whisk them into the flour, working from the centre of the bowl outwards. When the mixture is free of lumps, whisk in the milk (*above*).

2 **Flavouring the batter.** When the batter is smooth, add melted butter. If you like, pour in a dash of brandy or a liqueur (*above*) that will complement the filling you have chosen for the crêpe. Stir gently to blend the ingredients.

3 **Testing the consistency.** Crêpe batter should have the consistency of single cream and run freely from the spoon (*above*). If the batter is too thick, gradually whisk in a little more milk.

2 **Removing excess batter.** Use a palette knife or a spatula to cut off any trail left by pouring out excess batter from the side of the pan. Replace the pan over the heat for a few seconds. When the crêpe's upper surface looks dry and lacy, and the edges begin to curl—after about 10 seconds—it is time to turn the crêpe over.

3 **Turning the crêpe.** Free the edges of the crêpe with a palette knife or a spatula. Hold one side of the crêpe by its edge with your fingers and flip the crêpe over (*above*). The edge will be cool enough to handle. Alternatively, you can slide the palette knife or spatula underneath to turn the crêpe over.

4 **Stacking the crêpes.** The second side of the crêpe will cook even faster than the first. When it is cooked, slide the crêpe on to a warmed plate. If the pan's surface looks matt and dry, wipe it again with an oiled cloth. Stir the batter before making a fresh crêpe; the batter tends to separate while it stands. Stack the crêpes on top of each other (*above*). □

Rolling Crêpes Around Fruit

An apple filling. Halve, peel and core the apples, then slice them thinly. Soften the slices in a little butter over a low heat. Add sugar to taste. Put a little apple mixture on each crêpe, roll the crêpe around its filling (*left*) and place it, flap-side down, in a buttered baking dish. Dot the crêpes with butter and sprinkle with castor sugar. Set them in an oven preheated to 180°C (350°F or Mark 4) for about 20 minutes. To serve, slip a spoon under each crêpe, steady it with a fork and lift out (*below*).

Wrapping Up a Soufflé

Folding crêpes over a soufflé mixture. Prepare a *sabayon*-based soufflé mixture (*recipe, page 138*), flavouring it with Grand Marnier or other fruit liqueur. Put about a tablespoonful of the soufflé mixture on to each crêpe (*above*); the filling will expand during cooking, so do not add too much. Fold each crêpe over the filling and place the crêpe in a well-buttered, shallow dish. Sprinkle the crêpes with castor sugar and bake them in an oven preheated to 200°C (400°F or Mark 6) for about 8 minutes. Serve the crêpes at once (*right*), sauced with *sabayon* (*page 39*).

Moulding Crêpes into a Cake

Stacked in a deep dish and interlayered with an uncooked custard, plain crêpes become *crêpes à la crème* (*recipe, page 139*), a substantial, cake-like dessert. The assembly is baked in the oven to set the custard; then it is unmoulded and served, when cool, like a gateau.

You can vary the basic crêpe recipe by spreading each crêpe thickly with a purée of fruit or nuts. In this demonstration, puréed prunes and pistachios are used on alternate layers of the gateau before the custard is added.

To make a prune purée, cook the prunes in a little water until they are soft, strain them, remove their stones and pass them through a food mill (*page 26*). Add double cream, a pinch of salt, a dash of brandy, and sugar to taste. For the pistachio filling, simmer shelled pistachio nuts for a minute or so to loosen their skins. Peel the nuts, then blend them in a food processor or pound them in a mortar. Add sugar and sufficient cream to give the mixture the consistency of a rough paste.

1 **Layering the crêpes.** Prepare the crêpes (*page 62*). Butter a large mould and sprinkle the inside with fresh, white breadcrumbs; decorate the base with strips of angelica (*inset*) or crystallized fruit. Coat the crêpes alternately with the prune and pistachio fillings and stack them in the mould to within 5cm (2 inches) of the top.

2 **Pouring the custard.** With a knife, push the crêpes away from the mould's sides and pour uncooked custard around and over them to within 1 cm (½ inch) of the rim. Cover with buttered paper and cook for 30 to 40 minutes in an oven preheated to 150°C (300°F or Mark 2).

3 **Serving the gateau.** When the custard has set, remove the cake from the oven and let it cool. With a sharp knife, loosen the edges of the cake, then unmould it, using an inverted plate. Cut the cake into portions (*right*) and pour over a fruit purée—here, strawberries. □

Floating Fruit in a Batter Pudding

Crêpe batter that is thickened with extra flour forms the basis of the *clafoutis*—a pudding from the Limousin region of central France (*recipe, page 141*). *Clafoutis* is made by pouring the batter into a shallow ovenproof dish, studding the batter with fruit and baking it in a moderate oven until it has a firm, cake-like texture.

Traditionally, *clafoutis* is made with the wild black cherries of Limousin, but you can substitute almost any small, or peeled and cut-up, fruit, either fresh or dried. If you like, sprinkle fresh fruit with sugar and macerate it for an hour or so in a little brandy or a fruit liqueur. Dried fruits—prunes or raisins, for example—should be barely covered with wine or brandy, and left overnight to absorb the liquid: they will soak up most or all of it. Drain the fruits of any unabsorbed liquid before adding them to the *clafoutis*; reserve the liquid and sprinkle it over the dessert just before you bake it.

1 Ladling the batter. Lightly butter a shallow porcelain or earthenware baking dish; metal would conduct heat so quickly that the edges of the pudding would overcook. Ladle about half of the prepared batter mixture into the dish to form a base on which the fruit will rest.

2 Adding fruit. Arrange the fruits—here, pitted cherries—in a single, closely packed layer on the batter. Pour in the remaining batter so as to barely cover the fruit. If you like, sprinkle some brandy over. Bake the pudding for 25 minutes at 180°C (350°F or Mark 4).

3 Completing the cooking. Sprinkle a little sugar over the fruit, then return the *clafoutis* to the oven for another 10 to 20 minutes. Test for doneness by inserting a toothpick or, as here, a twig from a wooden whisk (*above*). If the toothpick comes out clean, the pudding is ready.

4 Serving the pudding. *Clafoutis* is best eaten warm, rather than hot or cold: let it cool for about 15 minutes after you remove it from the oven. If you like, dust icing sugar over the pudding before cutting it into slices, then serve with thick fresh cream (*right*). □

Golden Fruit Fritters

Deep-fried fruit fritters—pieces of fruit enclosed in bubbles of golden batter—are as delicious to eat as they are simple to cook. Bananas that have been steeped in green chartreuse are used here, but the same cooking method can be applied to most other fruits—and even to flowers *recipes, pages 140-144*).

Batter for dessert fritters must be very light so that it will cook quickly and produce a crisp coating, without a trace of sponginess. No egg yolks should be included in the batter, and water mixed with beer—which adds a refreshing bitter flavour—may be used instead of the milk called for in a crêpe batter. Let the fritter batter stand for about 1 hour so that it will lose some of its elasticity and cling evenly to the food. Finally, fold beaten egg whites into the batter just before using it, to guarantee its airy lightness.

Deep fry the fritters in a flavourless vegetable oil heated to about 190°C (375°F). Put only a few fritters in the oil at a time, otherwise the temperature of the oil will drop and the batter will not crisp.

1 **Preparing the batter.** Sift flour and a pinch of salt into a large mixing bowl. Add sugar to taste. Stir in melted butter, then pour in beer (*above, left*), water, and, if you like, a little brandy. Whisk the mixture just long enough to produce a smooth batter. Let the batter rest in a warm place for about 1 hour. Just before you use the batter, fold in beaten egg whites (*above, right*).

2 **Flavouring the fruit.** Peel and halve bananas and lay them on a plate. Pour brandy, rum or a liqueur—here, green chartreuse—over them, and add a sprinkling of sugar (*above*). Leave the fruit to absorb the flavour of the liqueur for an hour or so, turning over the banana halves several times.

3 **Coating the fruit.** Heat 5 cm (2 inches) of oil in a deep-frying pan to 190°C (375°F). Test the temperature by dropping a little batter into the oil: if the batter sizzles and colours immediately, the oil is hot enough. Dip each banana half into the bowl of batter, holding the half with the spread-out fingers (*above*) to allow excess batter to drop away.

4 **Cooking the fritters.** With a wire strainer, lower 2 or 3 fritters into the pan. Fry the fritters for 30 to 40 seconds on each side, or until they puff up into golden pouches. Lift the fritters out of the pan (*above*), and drain them on kitchen towels. Serve them immediately, dusted with icing sugar. □

5
Frozen Desserts
The Everyday Miracle of Ices and Ice Cream

Making water ices with minimum equipment

The uses of an ice cream churn

Freezing eggs and cream

The versatility of frozen custard

Moulding a bombe

Constructing a soufflé glacé

Ices and ice creams are among the great delights of summer. Once only a fortunate few, who were able to store unseasonal blocks of winter ice, could serve frozen delicacies on scorching midsummer days. But now, regardless of the season, anyone who has a freezer can enjoy the fresh flavours and inimitable textures of home-made ices.

The art in making such desserts is to freeze the ingredients without creating a rock-hard lump or a mass of coarse ice crystals, and the equipment you need will depend on the kind of ices you want to produce. The simplest water ices (*page 70*), for example, can be prepared in the ice tray of an ordinary domestic refrigerator or freezer; occasional stirring is enough to break up large ice crystals as they form, giving the finished dish a pleasant, granular texture. The richest ice creams, the parfaits (*page 72*), can be frozen in decorative moulds with no stirring at all, since they contain such a high proportion of egg yolks and cream that they do not crystallize as they freeze.

But to make smooth-textured water ices (*page 70*) or custard-based ices, you will need a hand-operated or electric-powered ice cream churn. The constant motion of the paddles within a churn prevents ice crystals from forming in the mixture.

In most churns, the paddles are fitted inside a metal mixing container, set in an outer bucket of crushed ice mixed with rock salt. The salt lowers the melting point of the ice, and the increased rate of melting has the effect of drawing heat rapidly from the contents of the churn. As a result, a good ice cream churn will freeze in minutes a mixture that would otherwise take hours to solidify in either a mould or an ice tray.

When you are making an ice cream mixture of any kind, bear in mind that the coldness of the finished dessert will mute its taste. The mixture therefore, should be more strongly flavoured than a similar, unfrozen dessert. Even so, you should never serve water ices or ice creams too cold. Allow them to stand for 30 minutes or so in the refrigerator, before taking them to the table. They will soften slightly and improve considerably in both flavour and texture.

Adorned with glazed cape gooseberries and the fragrant pulp of passion fruit, a mango parfait (*page 72*) is sliced for serving. Egg yolks and cream give the parfait its luxurious texture; mango purée, blended into the basic mixture, contributes a rich golden hue.

Water Ices: Capturing Clean, Clear Flavour

Water ices are the least complicated of frozen desserts—often no more than fruit juice or purée mixed with a light syrup and set to freeze in a metal refrigerator tray. Occasional stirring during the course of freezing breaks up the ice crystals and leaves the ices soft and semi-liquid, with a uniform grainy texture.

Water ices are often known as sherbets or *sorbets*; originally, these names referred to loosely frozen ice desserts—perhaps flavoured with wine or liqueur and often including beaten egg whites—that were served between the entrée and the meat course. Nowadays, these terms are used interchangeably by many cookery writers (*recipes, pages 145-147*).

All water ices owe their appeal to their clear, penetrating flavours—which can come only from the use of the best and freshest ingredients. In the melon and champagne ice demonstrated here, for example, (*recipe, page 146*) the melon must be fully ripe and the champagne of good quality. Begin by making a sugar syrup (*page 8*) so that it will have time to cool while you purée the melon flesh and mix it with the champagne. Cool syrup will blend smoothly with the fruit without cooking it; and the colder the mixture when it goes into the freezer, the less time it will need to solidify.

You can serve the ice in the empty melon shells, perhaps cutting them in a decorative pattern (*page 22*). Small melon halves will hold individual portions, as here; a large melon will make a serving dish for several guests.

An ice cream churn can be used to create water ices with a smooth texture (*box, opposite page*). The ingredients (*recipe, page 147*) are placed in the churn's central cylinder, surrounded by a freezing mixture of one part salt to three parts crushed ice. The churn's paddles, turning inside the cylinder, scrape the water ice from the sides as the water ice freezes and mix it constantly to keep it smooth. The water ice will be ready after about 20 to 30 minutes steady churning.

Most water ices made by either method may be prepared in advance and stored in sealed containers in the freezer, but they are best eaten within a few days: their fresh flavours fade rapidly.

1 **Producing the melon purée.** Make a syrup (*page 8*) and set it aside to cool. Halve ripe melons (*page 22*) and discard the seeds. Scoop out the flesh, and refrigerate the shells. Press the flesh through a sieve into a bowl (*above*). Stir in a little lemon juice to bring out the fruit's flavour. Add about half as much chilled champagne as you have purée.

2 **Adding sugar syrup.** Blend the cooled syrup into the melon and champagne mixture (*above*). Pour the mixture into a shallow ice tray and set it in a freezer or freezing compartment of a refrigerator.

3 **Stirring the mixture.** After about 30 minutes, remove the tray and use a fork to stir the frozen edges of the mixture into the centre (*above*), breaking up any large crystals as you do so. Replace the tray in the freezing compartment and repeat the procedure every hour.

4 **Whisking the ice.** After 3 to 4 hours of freezing, the mixture will be just firm enough to shape, with a granular texture. Remove the melon shells from the refrigerator and, if you like, rinse them with a little brandy. Scrape the mixture from its tray into a chilled bowl, and whisk it smooth, incorporating the brandy used to douse the melon shells.

Handling a Churn

1 Filling the cylinder. Place the freezing cylinder in the churn's outer bucket and fill the bucket three-quarters full with a mixture of rock salt and ice. Pour the water ice mixture into the freezing cylinder (*above*).

2 Packing the churn. Cover the freezing cylinder and add more rock salt and ice to fill the outer bucket. Turn the handle steadily until it is very difficult to move, indicating that the ice has frozen—allow about 20 to 30 minutes for this.

3 Serving the ice. Remove the cylinder from the ice bucket and wipe it clean of salty ice before you open it. Scoop out the water ice—blackberry flavoured, in this case—and serve it immediately (*above*) or store it in the freezer.

5 Serving the ice. Spoon the ice mixture into the melon shells (*right*), and serve immediately on cracked ice. If you have made the dessert a little in advance, you can keep the filled melon shells in the deep freeze. Do not leave this water ice for more than 1 to 2 hours, however, or the champagne will lose its sparkle, and the dessert much of its charm. □

Creating a Parfait from Eggs and Cream

The simplest ice cream is exactly what the name suggests—frozen cream. Double cream is beaten, flavoured and churned, or even set to freeze in a tray (*recipes, page 150*): because of its high fat content, there will be little crystallization, and the cream needs only occasional stirring.

Richer still is the parfait demonstrated here. Sugar syrup, beaten into warm egg yolks, creates a light egg mousse that is combined with its own volume of whipped cream and then frozen. Parfaits may be flavoured with liqueurs, coffee or puréed fruit: here, sieved, ripe mango provides a rich, golden colour and an exotic taste (*recipe, page 148*).

Since parfaits can be frozen undisturbed, they make excellent moulded desserts. Use a metal mould that will conduct heat freely away; to allow room for expansion as the ice freezes, never fill it quite full. To unmould the parfait—or any other moulded ice cream—loosen it by wrapping the mould in a towel soaked in warm water: a hot towel would melt the surface of the dessert and obscure any decorative pattern.

A third type of ice cream is based on a pouring custard, the *crème anglaise* demonstrated on page 38, but made with a higher proportion of egg yolks and often with single cream instead of milk. A custard-based ice usually contains fewer eggs and less cream than a parfait; as a result, it is best to make it in a churn (*box, right*) to prevent it from crystallizing. If you do not possess a churn, beat the mixture from time to time as it freezes.

Custard ices can be flavoured in innumerable ways. Vanilla (*recipe, page 166*), coffee and chocolate are all classic: use the techniques described on page 40 to flavour the cream or milk before you make the custard. Liqueurs or pounded nuts, used in the almond ice cream shown here (*recipe, page 151*), are also popular.

All ice creams can be made in advance and stored in airtight containers in a deep freeze. Indeed, a week or two's storage has a ripening effect that actually improves flavours, especially in the case of rich parfaits. But, if it is served directly from the freezer, stored ice cream will be too hard to cut—or eat. Let it soften in the refrigerator for 30 minutes or so before you bring it to the table.

1 Beating syrup into egg yolks. Make a 28° sugar syrup (*page 8*). In a pan placed in a water bath containing barely simmering water, beat the egg yolks with the syrup. Whisk steadily until the mixture is light and foamy—about 10 to 15 minutes.

2 Adding the flavouring. Take the pan off the heat and set it in a bowl of ice cubes to stop the cooking process. Continue whisking until the mixture has cooled. Gradually whisk in the flavouring— here, puréed ripe mango. Add a pinch of salt and a few drops of lemon juice to accentuate the flavour of the fruit.

Churning a Custard-Based Ice Cream

1 Flavouring the custard base. For an almond-flavoured ice cream, pound the nuts in a mortar (*page 12*), then add milk. Beat together egg yolks and sugar, pour on the milk and almonds. For a richer ice, you can add a little cream at this point. Stir the mixture over medium heat until it thickens, in the same way as *crème anglaise* (*page 38*).

2 Preparing for freezing. When the custard has a coating consistency, remove it from the heat and chill it, either in the refrigerator or by stirring over ice (*above*). Pour the cold mixture into a churn or ice trays for freezing.

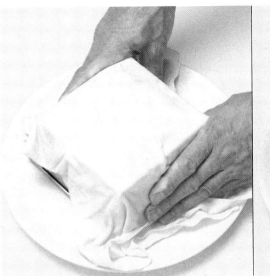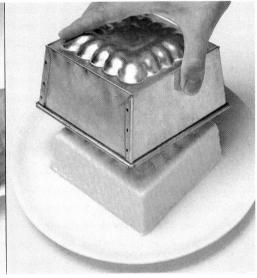

3 **Finishing the parfait.** Fold about an equal quantity of lightly whipped double cream into the mixture. Pour the mixture into a chilled metal mould to within 1 cm (½ inch) of the top (*above*). Cover the mould—with a lid, if it has one, or with aluminium foil—and set it in a freezer for at least 4 hours, or until it is solid.

4 **Unmoulding.** Soak a towel in warm water and wring it out. Remove the lid or foil from the mould, put a serving plate on top and invert mould and plate together. Wrap the warm towel round the mould (*above, left*). Remove the towel and lift the mould vertically to free the ice cream without spoiling its shape (*above, right*).

3 **Freezing and churning.** Churn for about half an hour (*page 71*) or freeze in ice trays for about 3 hours. If you use ice trays, at 30-minute intervals pour the mixture into a bowl and whisk it smooth. You can serve the finished ice cream as a dessert in its own right, or use it to make a composite dish, such as the *bombe* demonstrated on page 74.

5 **Serving.** If the surface of the parfait has melted slightly, smooth it over with the flat of a knife and return the parfait to the freezer for a few minutes. If you like, decorate the parfait with glazed fruit— here, cape gooseberries (*page 12*). Pour over a fruit sauce—in this case, passion fruit sweetened with a little light syrup.□

Packing Flavour Within Flavour

So called because of its shape, a *bombe* is a layered and moulded assembly of ice creams that excites the palate with contrasts of texture as well as of flavour. The New York Ice Cream demonstrated here (*recipe, page 151*) is a concoction of chestnut parfait and liqueur-flavoured fruit enclosed in an outer shell of almond-flavoured custard ice (*page 72*). Other *bombes* (*recipes, pages 152-153*) call for different ice creams or water ices; the only rule is that at least two textures—and flavours—should be included.

Bombes are a creative way to make use of any leftover ice creams or water ices you may have; or you can prepare the ingredients especially for this dessert.

Bombe moulds are traditionally copper—a good heat conductor that helps speed both freezing and unmoulding. If you cannot obtain such a mould, you can improvise with a deep, metallic mixing bowl or even a charlotte mould.

1 Lining the mould. Set a chilled *bombe* mould in a bowl of ice. Line it with a 1 cm ($\frac{1}{2}$ inch) layer of ice cream—here, almond-flavoured custard ice—that has been allowed to soften slightly. Smooth the ice cream with the back of a spoon; return the mould to the freezer while you prepare the other ingredients. Reserve some of the ice cream in the freezer.

2 Making a chestnut parfait. Sieve peeled, softened chestnuts (*page 30*) into a mixing bowl. Add egg yolks and sugar to the chestnut purée and place the bowl over a pan of water, heated to just below simmering point. Whisk the mixture steadily until it is smooth and glossy (*above*)—about 10 to 15 minutes.

5 Filling the bombe. Take the mould from the freezer and again set it in a bowl of ice. Use the raspberries, or other soft fruit, to fill the mould to about half its depth, then add the chestnut parfait to within 2 cm ($\frac{3}{4}$ inch) of the top of the mould (*above*). Cover the parfait with the remainder of the raspberries.

6 Finishing the bombe. Seal the mould with a final layer of the almond-flavoured custard ice reserved for this purpose (*Step 1*). Smooth the custard ice with the back of a spoon (*above*). Place a circle of greaseproof paper on top of the ice cream, then put the lid on the mould. Freeze the *bombe* for about 4 hours.

3 **Flavouring the parfait.** Take the mixing bowl from the heat and set it over a bowl of ice. Beat the mixture until it is cool. Remove the bowl from the ice and beat in a flavouring liqueur—such as the curaçao used here. Fold a roughly equal quantity of whipped double cream into the parfait mixture and set the bowl aside.

4 **Preparing the fruit filling.** Sprinkle kirsch (*above*) and sugar over soft fruit— in this case, raspberries. Toss the fruit gently to coat every piece. You can include the fruit whole in the *bombe* as here, or purée it first. If you use a fruit purée, freeze it until it is firm before you include it in the *bombe*.

7 **Unmoulding and serving.** Take the mould from the freezer. Remove the lid and the greaseproof paper, wrap a towel, soaked in warm water, around the mould (*above*) and invert it on to a chilled plate. Remove the mould and leave the *bombe* to soften in the refrigerator for about 30 minutes before serving (*right*). □

The Multiple Tiers of a Soufflé Glacé

A soufflé glacé is a magnificent illusion. Although it is served in a soufflé dish—over which it rises proudly, like a perfectly baked soufflé—it is made completely of ice cream. Because the soufflé glacé is based on a rich parfait mixture that needs no stirring as it freezes, you can build layer upon layer of different colours and flavours without fear of it collapsing.

For the rainbow effect in this demonstration (*recipe, page 154*), the various layers are flavoured with pistachio, raspberry, coffee, and hazelnuts and almonds. The sides of the dish are extended with a paper collar to raise the soufflé glacé to an impressive height—up to three times that of the soufflé dish, depending on how much room you have in your freezer.

The parfait base can be made by beating sugar syrup into egg yolks over heat, as shown on page 72; but if you have no syrup ready to hand, you can beat castor sugar directly into the yolks, as here.

1 Adding sugar to egg yolks. Place egg yolks in a bowl and set it over a pan of water kept at a low simmer. Slowly pour sugar on to the yolks. For extra flavour, include some vanilla sugar, made by burying a vanilla pod for at least a week in a closed container of sugar.

2 Whisking the mixture. Whisk the egg yolks and sugar steadily over low heat for about 10 minutes, until the sugar dissolves completely and no trace of graininess remains. At this point, the mixture will have tripled in volume, and will be pale, glossy and thick enough to form a ribbon (*above*). Remove the bowl and set it over ice to arrest the cooking.

3 Adding whipped cream. Continue to beat the mixture until it is so thick that it no longer clings to the surface of the bowl. Remove the mixture from the ice. In a separate bowl, whip double cream until it forms soft peaks, then fold the cream into the egg mixture.

4 Flavouring the mixture. Divide the mixture equally into as many bowls as you have flavouring. Here, the four flavourings are raspberry purée, ground pistachios, black coffee, and a mixture of crushed hazelnuts and almonds. Fold each flavouring into a bowl of the mixture and chill in the refrigerator.

5 **Building up the layers.** Wrap a collar of greaseproof paper, doubled over for increased rigidity, around a soufflé dish. Secure the collar with paper clips at top and bottom. Set the dish on a tray, to reduce the need for handling; add the first layer of flavoured mixture (*right*). Put the dish, on its tray, in the freezer for about 30 minutes, then add the next layer (*far right*). Continue, freezing each soufflé layer after you add it until you have completed the desired number of layers—here, two of each flavour.

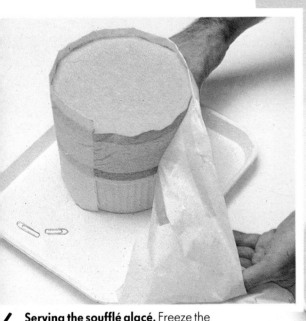

6 **Serving the soufflé glacé.** Freeze the soufflé glacé for 3 to 4 hours. Remove it from the freezer and gently peel off its paper collar. Set the soufflé glacé in the refrigerator to soften slightly and thus develop its full flavour. Decorate the dessert with chocolate scrolls (*page 11*) and pistachio nuts, as here, or any other garnish you prefer.□

6
Assemblies
From the Imposing to the Improvised

Desserts invite elaboration and artifice, and dessert cooks have always delighted in creating magnificent displays. Almost all of the desserts demonstrated on the following pages are striking dishes that will close a meal with panache, and many of them are classics. Charlotte russe, for example—a combination of Bavarian cream and sponge fingers set in a deep mould (*page 80*)—has featured on European menus since the early 19th century. And *paskha*—a dessert of sweetened, flavoured curd cheese formed in a tall mould and decorated with candied fruit (*page 82*)—is a traditional Russian Easter dish.

Most of these desserts owe their dramatic appearance to the assembly of two or more elements cooked by different techniques. Meringue, for example, is a valuable foundation. Cooked meringue can be fashioned into a commodious basket (*page 86*) and heaped high with fruit and ice cream—or, in the form of two large rounds, used to sandwich a similar filling (*recipe, page 161*). Uncooked meringue, piped over a block of ice cream so as to cover it completely, can be briefly baked until its surface has browned; the ice cream within remains unmelted, insulated from the heat by the airy meringue (*page 87*).

In a supporting role, fruit figures in most assemblies—as a filling, as a sauce or as decoration. But in the striking "supreme" on page 84, fruit occupies the centre stage. In that presentation, poached fruit, both fresh and dried, is combined with a moulded fruit purée to produce a spectacular arrangement of hues, ranging from pale tawny to crimson and black, united by a glistening sauce.

Not all assemblies are such formal dishes. In some, the ingredients and proportions are variable, offering plenty of scope for creativity—and for using up leftovers. Any scraps of cake and biscuit, for example, can be crumbled into melted-down leftover ice cream and baked to form a hot pudding (*page 90*). And trifle (*opposite page and page 88*), a lavish creation, heady with wine or brandy, can incorporate leftover cakes or biscuits, jam, jelly or over-ripe fruit. You can top it with custard, with cream, or with the rich yet refreshing old English treat known as syllabub: sweetened cream whipped with wine and lemon juice.

Whisked to a thick froth with an old-fashioned wig whisk, a syllabub is spread on top of a trifle. The layers of fruit purée, custard and cake have partially merged together, creating an attractive marbled effect.

79

A Rich Cream Enclosed by Biscuits

The first desserts to be called charlottes were simple fruit purées encased in bread and baked (*page 32*). But in the early 19th century, the celebrated French chef Antonin Carême invented charlotte russe (*right; recipe, page 155*), a version that required no baking. With its centre of Bavarian cream (*page 44*) and its casing of airy biscuit, charlotte russe retains the traditional contrast between soft interior and crisp exterior, but its ingredients are richer and its preparation more exacting—as befitted the tables of the great chef's illustrious clientele.

For the casing, use crisp sponge fingers—light, fat-free biscuits made with eggs, sugar and flour (*Steps 1 to 3, right; recipe, page 167*). The sponge fingers are cut to fit snugly together to line the base and sides of a deep, round mould. The scraps need not be wasted; reserve them for a trifle (*page 88*).

Carême flavoured his Bavarian cream filling with vanilla alone, but you can add chocolate, coffee, praline, fruit juice or puréed fruit; or you can mix nuts or fruit into the Bavarian cream.

Once you have spooned the Bavarian cream mixture into the biscuit-lined mould, the charlotte russe will need several hours in the refrigerator to set. When you have turned it out of the mould, decorate the charlotte russe with whipped cream and candied fruit; or serve it, as here, with a sweetened fruit purée. Tart fruits, such as blueberries or raspberries, provide a pleasingly sharp contrast with the creamy filling.

Many other desserts can be constructed in the same way as charlotte russe, but not all of them require a setting period in the refrigerator. Charlotte *à la chantilly*, for example, substitutes chilled, sweetened, vanilla-flavoured whipped cream for the Bavarian cream; the dessert is turned out as soon as the cream has been spooned into the mould. And for an ice cream charlotte, the biscuit-lined mould is filled with ice cream just before serving.

1 **Making the sponge mixture.** Beat egg whites until they form stiff peaks (*page 14*). In a saucepan, combine the egg yolks with castor sugar and set the pan in a water bath placed on a low heat. Beat the mixture until it is pale and frothy; then pour into a large bowl and gradually whisk in sieved flour (*above, left*). When the mixture becomes heavier and more difficult to work, stir with a spatula or a plastic disc (*above, right*). Continue until thoroughly blended.

4 **Making the base.** Cut a circle of greaseproof paper to fit the base of a charlotte mould. In the centre of the paper, place a small circle cut out from a sponge finger. To complete the base, trim the sides of other biscuits to make petal shapes that will fit closely together round the central sponge circle (*above*).

5 **Lining the mould.** Place the paper circle in the mould and arrange the cut biscuits on it, flat side up. Take some more sponge fingers and square off one end of each. Position the fingers, cut end down, with their curved surfaces against the sides of the mould. Line up the fingers on the sides with those on the bas

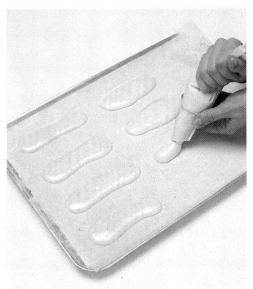

2 **Incorporating egg whites.** Blend a quarter of the beaten egg whites into the mixture (*above*); this will lighten the mixture and make it easier to fold in the remaining whites. Add the rest of the whites, folding them in gently with a whisk.

3 **Piping out the mixture.** Line an oven tray with non-stick baking paper or lightly oiled aluminium foil. Fill a piping bag (*page 46*) with the sponge mixture and pipe the mixture out to make fingers. Bake the fingers in the oven at 180°C (350°F or Mark 4) for about 20 minutes, until they are a golden colour.

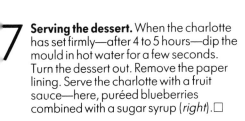

6 **Completing the assembly.** Prepare a Bavarian cream (*page 44*) and flavour it according to taste: here, puréed, dried apricots are used. Just before the cream sets, pour it into the mould. Cut the projecting finger ends flush with the filling (*above*). Refrigerate the charlotte.

7 **Serving the dessert.** When the charlotte has set firmly—after 4 to 5 hours—dip the mould in hot water for a few seconds. Turn the dessert out. Remove the paper lining. Serve the charlotte with a fruit sauce—here, puréed blueberries combined with a sugar syrup (*right*).□

A Monumental Cheese Dessert

Unsalted curd cheese such as *ricotta* can be turned into a soft, creamy dessert simply by mixing the cheese with sugar, a little cream and flavouring such as glacé fruits or brandy. Variations include adding eggs or melted butter, and shaping the dessert in a mould. One famous moulded cheese dessert is *paskha*, a Russian Easter dish (*recipes, page 122*). Like many other moulded cheese desserts, it is uncooked; its finished texture is similar to that of a baked cheesecake.

Curd cheese used to make a moulded dessert should be well drained and firm so that the dessert will hold its shape; if the cheese is very liquid, leave it for several hours in a sieve set over a bowl until most of the whey has drained from the curds. Then push the drained cheese through a sieve to eliminate lumps. The enrichments and flavouring ingredients for *paskha* include sugar, eggs, cream and butter; other ingredients, such as chopped nuts and candied fruits, may be added, as here. The mixture is beaten until it is as smooth and glossy as cream. Then it is poured into a muslin-lined mould—the muslin prevents the cheese mixture from escaping and simplifies unmoulding—covered with a weighted plate, and refrigerated overnight. The pressure forces out excess liquid and turns the *paskha* into a firm, compact mass that will hold its shape when unmoulded.

You can use any deep porous mould for the dessert, provided it has a hole in its base for drainage. Traditionally, *paskha* was prepared in a special perforated wooden box; an excellent substitute is a clay flowerpot, which allows excess liquid to drain through its porous clay sides as well as through the hole in its base. Scrub the pot clean before use and if the pot is a new one, soak it for 1 hour in cold water to rid it of any flavour of raw clay which could taint the dessert.

Paskha improves with keeping, and can be left in the refrigerator for two or three days before serving. Since it tastes best at room temperature, take it out of the refrigerator half an hour before serving. Slice the *paskha* horizontally; if you plan to serve it again, reserve the top slice to decorate the dessert when it reappears at the table.

1 Preparing the cheese. If the cheese is not sufficiently drained, pour it into a fine sieve set over a bowl and leave it to drain at room temperature until no more liquid drips from the sieve. Discard the liquid. Then, using a plastic disc, press the cheese through a drum sieve (*above*) to remove any lumps.

2 Assembling the ingredients. In a large bowl, beat the egg yolks with sugar until the mixture is very pale. Coarsely chop the almonds and the candied fruit, and add them to the egg mixture with the softened butter, the sieved curd cheese and a little grated lemon rind (*above*). Stir in the cream and a few drops of vanilla extract, and beat the mixture thoroughly until it is smooth.

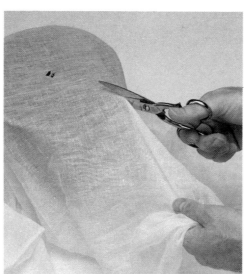

3 Lining the mould. Drape a large square of muslin over the mould—here, a clay flowerpot. Cut a slit in the muslin from the edge to the centre. Push the centre of the muslin down to the pot's base. Starting at one of the cut edges, smooth the muslin against the walls and base of the pot; the slit in the material allows you to overlap it without making a bulky fold, which could mark the dessert.

4 Filling the mould. Fill the mould with the cheese mixture, pressing it firmly into the pot. Fold the loose ends of the muslin lining over the top of the filling so that the mixture is completely covered.

5 **Draining the paskha.** Put a plate or saucer—slightly smaller than the mould—on top of the wrapped cheese mixture. Place weights on the plate— here, about 5 kg (11 lb) are used. Place the pot on a rack with a tray underneath to catch the liquid, and refrigerate the dessert overnight.

6 **Unmoulding the dessert.** Remove the weights and plate from the mould. Reverse the *paskha* and mould on to your hand and gently lift off the mould (*above, left*); then set the dessert upside down on the rack and peel away the muslin wrapping (*above, centre*). Place an inverted serving plate on the *paskha*, turn plate and *paskha* over together, and remove the muslin (*above, right*).

7 **Decorating and serving.** Cut candied fruit peel into thin strips and use your fingers or tweezers (*left*) to press the peel lightly on to the surface of the *paskha*, in the pattern of your choice. Here, the long vertical strips are composed of short pieces of angelica, cut to the width of each serving, for ease of slicing. Serve the dessert cut into horizontal slices (*below*).□

Concentric Rings of Cooked Fruit

The glowing colours of poached fruits (*page 34*) make them natural choices for a decorative assembly. By combining them with a ring of moulded apple pudding (*recipe, page 96*), as in this demonstration, you can create a glorious dessert that fully deserves the title "fruit supreme".

For the apple pudding, sieved apples are reduced to a stiff, dry consistency, blended with eggs and cooked in a ring mould placed in a water bath—the method used for a *crème caramel* (*page 42*).

The fruit you choose for poaching will of course, depend on what is available; here, fresh pears, peaches, apricots and nectarines are supplemented with currants and raisins. The dried fruits and any very firm fresh fruits require preliminary poaching—separately, so that each type of fruit receives just the right amount of cooking. The two poaching syrups are then combined and reduced by boiling before they are used to cook all of the fruit briefly together. Combined with almond milk and butter, the syrup makes a gleaming sauce for the fruit.

1 Mixing eggs and apples. Cook sliced apples with sugar and sieve the softened mixture (*page 26*). Stirring constantly, cook the sieved apple with more sugar and a little butter until it is too stiff to pour—about 15 minutes. Transfer the purée to a bowl; let it cool a little before beating in whole eggs: if the purée were very hot the eggs might curdle.

2 Filling the mould. Butter a ring mould; sprinkle it with breadcrumbs and shake out any that do not stick. Spoon in the purée and tap the mould to settle the mixture. Cook the pudding in a water bath at 180°C (350°F or Mark 4) for about 45 minutes, or until it is firm to the touch. Let it stand for 20 minutes, then unmould on to a large serving dish.

3 Pre-cooking the fruits. Poach dried currants and raisins in medium syrup (*page 8*) until they swell—10 to 20 minutes. Meanwhile, poach firm fresh fruits—here, pears and peaches—in medium syrup until tender. Pour the syrup into another pan. Add to the pears and peaches raw apricots and nectarines and the poached dried fruits.

4 Flavouring the syrup. To extract the flavour from the fruit peels, simmer them in one of the poaching syrups—here, the syrup used for poaching the firmest fruits. After 10 minutes' simmering, strain the syrup into the poaching syrup from the dried fruit (*above, left*) and discard the fruit peels. Boil the combined syrup to reduce it by about one-third. Add to the reduced syrup about one-third of its volume of almond milk (*page 13*). Continue boiling the syrup until it reduces to a quantity that will just cover the fruits.

5 **Simmering the fruits.** Pour the syrup over the fruits. Return to the heat and simmer gently for about 10 minutes, until the fruits are very soft but still intact. Leave the lid off the pan so that the syrup reduces a little more as the fruit cooks.

6 **Enriching the syrup with butter.** Take the pan off the heat. Add some thin slivers of unsalted butter and gently shake the pan to incorporate the butter into the warm syrup without breaking up the fruit. The butter will impart a sheen and a silky consistency to the syrup.

7 **Composing the supreme.** Arrange the poached fruits in a pattern on the serving dish. Here, nectarines and dried fruits surround the apple ring; the centre of the ring is filled with peaches, pears and apricots. Decorate the apple ring with strips of uncooked fruit—here, prune and peach strips—dipped in syrup (*above*). Pour the syrup over the assembly and add slivers of almond (*right*). Serve the dessert warm.□

A Meringue Basket Brimming with Fruit

By enclosing ice cream or fruit in meringue (*page 46*), you can make spectacular party desserts. In a baked Alaska (*box, opposite page*), soft meringue cocoons a block of ice cream; in the dessert on the right, rings of baked meringue form a rigid basket for ice cream and fruit. For a mixture stable enough to withstand the lengthy preparation, beat the meringue over simmering water (*recipe, page 161*); the heat will help to set it.

To make a 10 cm (4 inch) deep basket, you will need a circular base and six rings. If your oven lacks enough shelves to accommodate so many baking trays, make and cook the rings in batches. Or improvise with wire cake racks—on each tray, place a cake rack to support another tray.

When you assemble the baked base and rings, you will need some fresh meringue mixture to cement together the basket and to decorate it. To make the basket firm enough to handle, bake it in a cool oven for a further 1½ hours. You can then store it, empty, for up to a week in an airtight container.

1 Tracing the base of the basket. Line 7 baking trays with non-stick paper or aluminium foil. On each paper, invert a 20 to 22 cm (8 to 9 inch) plate and very lightly trace around its rim with a pencil (*above*). One circle will be needed for the base of the basket and one for each of the rings that will make up its sides.

2 Making the base. Prepare a meringue mixture. Fit a 1 cm (½ inch) nozzle on to a piping bag and fill the bag with the mixture. Take one of the lined trays and, starting from just outside the pencil mark and working inwards, pipe concentric circles of the meringue mixture to form a base for the basket. Smooth the base with a spatula.

3 Making meringue rings. Pipe a ring of meringue around the outside edge of the circles marked on the remaining sheets of baking paper (*above*). Put all of the trays into an oven preheated to its lowest possible setting and bake the meringue for 4 to 5 hours, or overnight. Remove the trays from the oven.

4 Removing the baking paper. Lift the papers, with the meringue still attached, from each tray and set them on wire racks to cool. To separate each meringue ring from its paper, place the paper on a board so that one side of the meringue projects over the board's edge. Then gently peel away the paper (*above*), turning the ring until it is free.

5 Assembling the basket. While the rings and base cool, make some fresh meringue mixture. Place the cooled base on a tray lined with fresh paper. Set the rings on the base, one on top of the other (*above*). Using a palette knife, spread a little fresh meringue mixture round the outside of the basket, filling in the gaps between the rings.

6 **Decorating the basket.** Fit a fluted nozzle on to the piping bag and fill the bag with meringue mixture. Working from the base upwards, pipe vertical lines of meringue around the basket (*above*) and scrolls or rosettes on the rim. Bake for 1½ hours in a very low oven. Cool, then remove the paper (*Step 4*).

7 **Filling the basket.** Sprinkle chunks of fresh pineapple with sugar and soak them for about 30 minutes in kirsch. Just before serving, spoon ice cream into the basket. Drain the pineapple chunks and put them on top of the ice cream.

A Hot Wrapping for Ice Cream

Served straight from the oven, the baked Alaska demonstrated below (*recipe, page 159*) yields an exciting surprise: an outer layer of hot meringue enclosing miraculously cold ice cream on a bed of sponge cake. In fact no magic is involved: the air trapped in the meringue insulates the ice cream and prevents it from melting during its brief spell in the oven. Make the ice cream in a paper-lined mould so that it can be turned out without dipping the mould in hot water. The ice cream must be frozen hard when it goes into the oven.

1 **Piping the meringue.** Unmould a block of ice cream—here, peach-flavoured—on to a sponge cake base, cut slightly larger than the ice and placed on a flat ovenproof dish. Pipe meringue over the ice cream (*above*), enclosing it completely.

8 **Serving the basket.** Purée soft fruits—here, raspberries—by pressing them through a nylon sieve. Sweeten the raspberry purée to taste, then pour it over the pineapple and ice cream in the meringue basket. Decorate the basket with a few whole raspberries (*above*). Serve immediately, cut into wedges. □

2 **Cooking and serving.** Cook the dessert in an oven preheated to 230°C (450°F or Mark 8) until the meringue is lightly browned—about 5 minutes. Remove the baked Alaska from the oven and serve immediately, cut into slices (*above*).

Trifle: a Basis for Improvisation

The word trifle may suggest something light and insubstantial, but the dessert known by that name is a glorious creation—layers of custard, jam, biscuit, fruit, nuts and cream built up on a foundation of wine-soaked sponge cake and displayed in a clear glass bowl (*demonstration, right; recipe, page 164*).

The precise ingredients of a trifle depend as much on the contents of your store cupboard as on any recipe. The only essentials are custard, a fruit flavouring, and some sort of cake to absorb the generous measure of fortified wine or brandy that invariably lends flavour and aroma to the dessert. Sponge fingers (*page 80*) can replace cake, for example, and any kind of sweet biscuit can be included in place of the almond-flavoured macaroons used here. You can add any sort of fruit, either cut up or puréed, or even omit it altogether and include extra jam or fruit jelly (*page 24*) in its place. The topping can be the classic syllabub (*box, opposite page*), or simply whipped cream.

1 **Building up the trifle.** Make a pouring custard (*page 38*) and set it aside. Cover the bottom of a deep glass bowl with pieces of sponge cake. Sprinkle the sponge with sherry or another fortified wine, such as Marsala or Madeira, and smear it thickly with jam. Add a layer of chopped nuts, one or two ladlefuls of the pouring custard and puréed fruit: here, both raspberries and blackberries are used. Top the fruit with more cake, or, as here, with macaroons that have been soaked in sherry.

2 **Topping with syllabub.** Add more jam, then more nuts: continue to build up the trifle, finishing with a layer of custard about 8 cm (3 inches) below the bowl's rim. Crown the dessert with a deep layer of syllabub (*box, opposite page*). Leave the trifle in the refrigerator for a few hours to firm. Just before serving, decorate it with candied fruit.□

Wine and Cream to Make a Syllabub

Syllabub is a dairy punch—a combination of cream or milk with a sweetened wine and, sometimes, brandy. In the past, syllabub was made by milking a cow straight into a bowl of wine: after a little while, the acidity of the wine separated the warm, unpasteurized milk into solid curds and clear whey. The less rustic syllabub demonstrated here (*recipe, page 119*) is called "everlasting" because it does not separate. Here, double cream is poured into flavoured wine: slow mixing and constant stirring ensure that the cream combines smoothly with the wine instead of curdling. Then the mixture is whisked to a light mass.

The usual proportions are two or three parts of cream to one part wine; you can vary the ratio quite widely as long as cream makes up at least half the volume. With less cream the mixture would not thicken. The syllabub should be whisked only until it forms soft peaks that barely hold their shape: further beating might curdle the cream. Use a hand whisk: if you used an electric beater, it would be difficult to stop at the right moment.

1 **Flavouring the wine.** Thinly peel the rind from 1 or 2 lemons. Put the rinds in a bowl and cover them with white wine and a little brandy. Halve the lemons, squeeze out their juice, and pour it into the bowl (*above*). Cover and leave to infuse overnight. The next day, strain the liquid through a nylon sieve (*inset*) and discard the rinds. Add sugar and stir until the sugar dissolves.

2 **Incorporating cream.** Pour double cream slowly into the liquid, stirring constantly. Grate in a little nutmeg. Beat the syllabub gently with a wire or twig whisk: to use a twig whisk, hold it upright between the palms of your hands, and twirl the whisk by rubbing your hands together. At first, no change will be evident, but after a few minutes the syllabub will thicken rapidly. Stop whisking as soon as it can hold its shape (*right*); its consistency should be that of lightly whipped cream.

3 **Serving the syllabub.** Chill the syllabub in the refrigerator. Use it as a topping for trifle (*opposite page*) or serve it as a refreshing dessert on its own, in glasses filled almost to overflowing. If you like, decorate the syllabub with a sprig of rosemary and a slice of lemon.

A Pudding from Leftover Ice Cream

An ingenious and economical dessert can be made from leftover cakes and biscuits and melted ice cream. The cake and biscuits are crumbled into the ice cream; the mixture is baked, uncovered, in a mould placed in a water bath until it is golden-brown (*recipe, page 161*).

Because most ice cream contains egg yolks, the dessert will set lightly in the same way as a custard (*page 40*), and can be spooned neatly from its dish. Add extra eggs before cooking the mixture if you prefer a firmer dessert, or if the ice cream was made with few or no eggs.

Whatever assortment of ingredients you have saved can be put to good use in the dessert. Use different ice creams if you have them: coffee, chocolate and praline combine well and most fruit flavours mix together successfully. Crisp almond macaroons, soft sponge cake and even bread can be included to vary the pudding's texture. A caramel lining for the baking dish (*page 42*) lends additional flavour: as the pudding cooks, the caramel melts to form a sauce.

1 Binding with egg. Stand leftover ice cream to melt in a large mixing bowl. Use whatever flavours you have, so long as they are complementary; here, vanilla-flavoured ice cream is used alone. If you wish, you can whisk one or two additional eggs into the mixture (*above*).

2 Adding cake and biscuits. Roughly crumble stale cake and biscuits into the mixture; allow about half as much cake and biscuits as you have ice cream. Use whatever is available; here, *petits fours*, macaroons, *langues de chat*, sponge cake and sponge fingers are included.

3 Filling the mould. Line the sides and bottom of a baking dish with caramel (*page 42*). Whisk the cake and ice cream mixture until the ingredients are well blended. When the caramel has set, spoon the mixture into the dish.

4 Baking the pudding. Place the baking dish in a large pan and add enough hot water to come two-thirds of the way up the sides of the dish. Place the water bath in a moderate oven, preheated to 180°C (350°F or Mark 4) for about 45 minutes, until the surface of the dessert has lightly browned (*above*).

5 Serving the pudding. Serve the dessert hot or leave it to cool—either overnight at room temperature or for 3 hours in the refrigerator. To serve, spoon the pudding and its caramel sauce straight from the baking dish (*above*).□

Anthology
of Recipes

Drawing upon the cooking literature and traditions of more than 20 countries, the Editors and consultants for this volume have selected 219 published dessert recipes for the Anthology that follows. The recipes may be as simple as a baked custard or as elaborate as a rainbow iced soufflé; as traditional as an English Christmas pudding or as exotic as a mango parfait; as informal as a bread and butter pudding or as impressive as an iced meringue *vacherin*. In each case, however, the emphasis is on authentic dishes meticulously prepared with fresh, natural ingredients.

The Anthology spans nearly 2,000 years, and includes recipes by more than 130 writers, from the Roman gastronome Apicius to such modern food authorities as Raymond Oliver, Jane Grigson and James Beard. But there are also recipes by little-known authors of now rare and out-of-print books held in private collections. A number of these recipes, including some from the cookery writers of pre-revolutionary and Stalin-era Russia, have never before been published in English.

Since many early recipe writers did not specify amounts of ingredients, these have been judiciously added; and where appropriate, introductory notes printed in italics have been supplied by the Editors. Modern terms have been substituted for archaic language, but to preserve the character of the original and to create a true anthology, the authors' texts have been changed as little as possible. Some cooking instructions have been expanded, but in cases where the directions may seem somewhat abrupt, the reader should refer to the appropriate demonstration in the front of the book to find the technique in question explained. Cooking terms and ingredients that may be unfamiliar are explained in the combined General Index and Glossary at the end of the book.

The Anthology is organized according to the chapters in the front of the book, with additional categories for jellies and cheese desserts. Recipes for standard preparations—batters, pouring custard, custard ice cream, basic jelly and sponge finger biscuits—appear at the end. The serving suggestions included in some recipes are, of course, optional.

All recipe ingredients are listed in order of use, with the main or title ingredients first. Metric and imperial measures for each ingredient are listed in separate columns. The two sets of figures are not exact equivalents, but are consistent for each recipe. Working from either metric or imperial weights and measures will produce equally good results, but the two systems should not be mixed for the same recipe. All spoon measures are level.

Fruit Desserts

Pineapple Surprise

Ananas en Surprise

To make a pineapple case, cut out the core of the pineapple first with a paring knife, then remove the flesh with a longer knife and a tablespoon. A melon surprise (page 22) can be prepared in the same way: scoop out the melon flesh, discard the seeds and cut the flesh into small cubes or balls. Suitable fruits to use for the filling include peaches, apricots and raspberries.

	To serve 6	
1	large, fresh, ripe pineapple	1
30 g	castor sugar	1 oz
2 tbsp each	kirsch and maraschino	2 tbsp each
125 g	mixture of fresh fruit, including strawberries, prepared according to kind	4 oz

Neatly cut off the top of the pineapple to form a lid, keeping the leaves intact. Reserve the lid. Cut out the flesh of the pineapple, using a circular movement: the sides of the case should be at least 1 cm ($\frac{1}{2}$ inch) thick.

Thinly slice the pineapple flesh, or cut it into small cubes, removing the hard centre. Flavour with the sugar, kirsch and maraschino and mix in the other fruits. Keep the fruits and the pineapple lid and case on ice, or refrigerated.

Just before serving, fill the pineapple case with the fruit and put on the pineapple lid. Arrange the pineapple on a napkin and surround, if possible, with ice and a few fresh flowers. To make this dessert more decorative, instead of simply placing the pineapple on a napkin, arrange it on a block of ice carved in any desired shape.

H. HEYRAUD
LA CUISINE À NICE

Dried Fruit Salad

Khoshaf

This is a great Middle Eastern favourite in which the fruit is not stewed but macerated for at least 48 hours. It is a superb dessert. Various dried fruits may be used, but purists feel that only apricots and raisins should go into this classic dish, together with the nuts.

A less common variation of the recipe given is to add 125 g (4 oz) each of dried figs and peaches, and a few fresh pomegranate seeds when these are available. The luminosity of the seeds brings out the rich orange, mauve and brown of the fruit, and the white and green of the nuts. Some people dissolve *amardine* (sheets of dried compressed apricot) in the water to thicken and enrich it.

	To serve 10	
500 g	dried apricots	1 lb
250 g	prunes	8 oz
125 g	raisins	4 oz
125 g	almonds, blanched and split	4 oz
60 g	pistachio nuts or pine-nuts	2 oz
125 to 250 g	sugar	4 to 8 oz
1 tbsp	rose water	1 tbsp
1 tbsp	orange flower water	1 tbsp

Wash the fruits if necessary and put them in a large bowl. Mix with the nuts and cover with water. Add sugar to taste and sprinkle with rose water and orange flower water. Let the fruits soak for at least 48 hours. The syrup becomes rich with the juices of the fruit and acquires a beautiful golden colour.

CLAUDIA RODEN
A BOOK OF MIDDLE EASTERN FOOD

Citrus Salad

Citrussalade

	To serve 4	
2 each	grapefruits, oranges and mandarins	2 each
3 to 4 tbsp	sugar	3 to 4 tbsp
2 tbsp	Grand Marnier	2 tbsp
	ground cinnamon	

Halve the grapefruits, remove the segments with a grapefruit knife, cutting away the white membrane, and chop the flesh coarsely. Scrape the inside of the empty grapefruit shells clean. Set them aside after cutting off a thin slice from the bottoms for better balance.

Grate the peel of one of the oranges, without removing any

of the pith, and reserve the grated peel. Peel the oranges, and divide them into segments; scrape the segments clean and chop them coarsely. Peel the mandarins, remove any pith from the segments and chop them coarsely.

Combine the chopped fruits loosely and fill the four grapefruit shells with the mixture. Sprinkle with sugar to taste, the grated orange peel and the Grand Marnier. Cover with plastic wrap and put the grapefruit halves in the refrigerator. Serve cold, sprinkled with a pinch of ground cinnamon.

HUGH JANS
VRIJ NEDERLAND

Chilled Melon Balls with Wine

Melon de Cavaillon à la Saint-Jacques

To serve 4

1	prime, ripe Charentais melon, halved, seeds removed, flesh scooped out with a ball cutter	1
About 2 tbsp	castor sugar	About 2 tbsp
About 10 cl	Muscatel, port or sweet dessert wine	About 4 fl oz

Put the melon balls in a bowl. Dust lightly with the sugar and pour over the wine of your choice. Place the bowl in the refrigerator or pack crushed ice around it and leave it to stand for about 1 hour before serving.

To serve, fill individual glass dishes with the fragrant melon balls and the chilled juices.

JEAN-NOËL ESCUDIER
LA VÉRITABLE CUISINE PROVENÇALE ET NIÇOISE

Strawberries with Wine

Fraises au Bordeaux

To serve 1

125 g	strawberries, hulled	4 oz
15 g	sugar	$\frac{1}{2}$ oz
1 tbsp	good claret or white wine	1 tbsp

Sprinkle the strawberries with sugar and add the wine. Cream should not be served with this.

X. MARCEL BOULESTIN
SIMPLE FRENCH COOKING FOR ENGLISH HOMES

Fresh Figs with Cream

Salade de Figues

To serve 4

500 g	fresh green figs, peeled and sliced	1 lb
15 to 20 cl	port, mixed with a few drops of curaçao and brandy	6 fl oz
15 cl	cream	$\frac{1}{4}$ pint

Put the sliced figs in a serving dish, standing on ice. Add the port, curaçao and brandy mixture. Pour the cream over all, stir and serve at once.

ELVIA AND MAURICE FIRUSKI (EDITORS)
THE BEST OF BOULESTIN

Caramel Orange Quarters

The author suggests that cherries, large strawberries, greengages, plums or grapes, first freed from their stalks, can also be prepared in this way. The technique of boiling sugar to the hard crack stage is explained on page 8.

To serve 6

3	large oranges, peel and pith carefully removed	3
500 g	sugar	1 lb
4 tbsp	water	4 tbsp

Pull the oranges apart into quarters, or rather into their natural segments, taking care not to tear the thin dividing skins. Place the orange segments on a wire tray to dry for an hour or so in the warmth of the kitchen, turning them once.

Boil the sugar and water to the crack stage and, spearing the orange segments on a delicately cut wooden twig about 15 cm (6 inches) long, dip them into the sugar without burning your fingers. Drain off all the excess sugar and rest the segments upon oiled wire trays. Set the trays aside in a cool place to allow the sugar to stiffen upon the fruit.

To serve, put your fingers under the wire in order to push up the orange segments without breaking or damaging their sugar coating. Arrange them either in a *compotier* upon green leaves or on a dessert dish.

CHARLES ELMÉ FRANCATELLI
THE ROYAL ENGLISH AND FOREIGN CONFECTIONER

Rum Persimmons

To serve 4

4	ripe persimmons, stems removed, halved lengthwise	4
6 tbsp	medium rum or dark Jamaica rum	6 tbsp
60 g	light brown sugar	2 oz
4 tbsp	soured cream	4 tbsp

Arrange the persimmons, cut-side up, on shallow dessert plates. Sprinkle each half generously with rum, sugar and soured cream. Spoon out of the shell to eat.

VICTOR J. BERGERON
TRADER VIC'S RUM COOKERY AND DRINKERY

Apricot Whip with Madeira

To serve 6

250 g	dried apricots, soaked in water overnight	8 oz
150 g	sugar	5 oz
15 cl	Madeira	$\frac{1}{4}$ pint
2	egg whites	2
$\frac{1}{4}$ litre	double cream, stiffly whipped	8 fl oz
30 g	almonds, blanched, sliced and toasted	1 oz

Place the apricots and their water in a saucepan. Add half the sugar and additional water, if necessary, to just about cover the fruit. Bring to the boil and simmer, uncovered, for about 25 minutes, or until the apricots are tender.

Drain the fruit, and reduce the remaining liquid until it is a syrupy glaze. Add this to the apricots, and set them aside to cool. Purée the fruit and syrup in a blender with 10 cl (4 fl oz) of the Madeira.

Beat the egg whites until they are stiff. Gradually beat in the remaining sugar, a little at a time. Continue to beat the egg whites until the sugar has dissolved. Fold the stiffly beaten egg whites and half of the whipped cream into the apricot purée. Pour the mixture into a serving dish, and sprinkle with the almonds. Chill well before serving. Beat the remaining Madeira into the remaining whipped cream, and serve with the apricot whip.

PAULA PECK
PAULA PECK'S ART OF GOOD COOKING

Strawberries with Orange Juice

Fraises à l'Orange

To serve 4 to 6

750 g	strawberries, hulled	1½ lb
125 g	castor sugar	4 oz
About 10 cl	orange juice	About 4 fl oz

Put aside about 500 g (1 lb) of the best strawberries. Pass the remaining strawberries through a sieve. Mix this purée with 40 g (1½ oz) of the sugar and dilute the mixture with the orange juice. Put the purée into a serving dish, arrange the reserved strawberries on top, sprinkle with the remaining castor sugar and serve the dessert very cold.

X. MARCEL BOULESTIN
RECIPES OF BOULESTIN

Pawpaw and Egg Yolk Pudding

Ovos Moles de Papaia

If desired, this dessert from Mozambique can be refrigerated for 2 hours or more and served chilled.

To serve 4

500 to 750 g	ripe pawpaw, peeled, seeded and coarsely chopped	1 to 1½ lb
4 tbsp	strained lime or lemon juice	4 tbsp
4 tbsp	water	4 tbsp
400 g	sugar	14 oz
7.5 cm	stick cinnamon	3 inch
4	cloves	4
5	egg yolks	5

Combine the pawpaw, the lime or lemon juice and the water in an electric blender, and blend at a high speed for about 30 seconds. Turn off the machine, scrape down the sides of the beaker with a rubber spatula, and blend again until the mixture is a smooth purée. With the back of a spoon, rub the purée through a fine nylon sieve into a 2 litre (3½ pint) enamelled or stainless steel saucepan.

Mix in the sugar, the cinnamon stick and the cloves and, stirring constantly, bring to the boil over a high heat. Stirring occasionally, cook briskly until the syrup reaches a temperature of 110°C (230°F), or until a few drops spooned into cold water immediately form coarse threads. Remove the pan from the heat and, with a slotted spoon, remove and discard the cinnamon and the cloves.

In a deep bowl, beat the egg yolks with a wire whisk or a rotary or electric beater for about 1 minute, or until the egg yolks thicken slightly. Beating constantly, pour the hot syrup into the yolks in a thin stream and continue to beat until the mixture is smooth and thick and is a deep yellow colour.

Divide the mixture among four small, heatproof dessert dishes and cool to room temperature. The dessert will become considerably thicker as it cools.

LAURENS VAN DER POST AND THE EDITORS OF TIME-LIFE
FOODS OF THE WORLD—AFRICAN COOKING

Gooseberry Huff

The technique of cooking sugar syrup to the small thread stage is shown on page 8. To make an Apple Huff, substitute 325 g (11 oz) puréed apple for the gooseberries in this recipe.

To serve 4 to 6

600 g	gooseberries, boiled until tender and puréed through a sieve	1¼ lb
250 g	castor sugar	8 oz
2 tbsp	water	2 tbsp
3	egg whites	3

Prepare a syrup with sugar and water, cooking it to the small thread stage. Let the syrup get almost cold. Beat the egg whites to a froth, combine them with the gooseberry purée, and beat until the mixture looks white. Add the syrup to the gooseberry mixture, and beat together until it is all froth. Pour into individual cups or glasses and serve.

J. STEVENS COX (EDITOR)
DORSET DISHES OF THE 17TH CENTURY

Gooseberry Cream

To serve 4

500 g	gooseberries, heads and tails removed	1 lb
15 g	butter	½ oz
60 g	sugar	2 oz
4	egg yolks	4

Take the gooseberries and boil them very quickly in enough water to cover them; stir in the butter; when the gooseberries become soft, pulp them through a sieve, sweeten the pulp with sugar to taste while it is hot, and then beat it up with the egg yolks. Serve in a dish, cups or glasses.

JOSEPHINE DAVID
EVERYDAY COOKERY FOR FAMILIES OF MODERATE INCOME

Strawberry, Raspberry or Bilberry Kisel

Kisel iz Klubniki, Maliny, Cherniki

This Russian recipe is taken from the best-selling cook book of the Stalin era.

To serve 4 to 6

250 g	strawberries, raspberries or bilberries, hulled and puréed through a sieve	8 oz
150 g	sugar	5 oz
90 cl	water	1½ pints
2 tbsp	potato flour	2 tbsp

Bring two-thirds of the water and all the sugar to the boil, stirring. Dissolve the potato flour in the remaining water and stir it into the syrup. Bring to the boil and boil for 2 minutes. Remove from the heat, add the fruit purée and stir well. Leave to cool a little before pouring into glasses. Serve hot or chilled, with cream if desired.

O. P. MOLCHANOVA
KNIGA O VKUSNOĬ ZDOROVOĬ PISHCHE

Rhubarb Cream

To serve 4

500 g	rhubarb, cut into 2.5 cm (1 inch) lengths	1 lb
8 cl	apple juice	3 fl oz
100 g	light brown sugar (or to taste)	3½ oz
¼ tsp	ground cinnamon	¼ tsp
2	eggs, yolks separated from whites	2
10 cl	double cream, whipped	4 fl oz

Place the rhubarb and apple juice in a saucepan. Bring to the boil, reduce the heat, cover and allow to simmer for about 10 minutes, or until the rhubarb is tender.

Pass the mixture through a food mill, or blend it until smooth in an electric blender. Return it to the saucepan.

Beat enough brown sugar into the rhubarb to sweeten it to taste. Add the cinnamon.

Beat the egg yolks with a spoonful of brown sugar and stir them into the fruit mixture. Heat briefly, stirring, until the mixture thickens slightly. Do not allow it to boil.

Cool and chill the mixture. Beat the egg whites until they are stiff but not dry and fold them into the chilled rhubarb mixture. Fold in the whipped cream.

JEAN HEWITT
THE NEW YORK TIMES WEEKEND COOKBOOK

Gooseberry Fool

Rhubarb fool is made in just the same way as gooseberry fool, but it needs an even larger proportion of sugar, preferably dark brown, and it is very necessary when the rhubarb is cooked to put it in a colander or sieve and let the excess juice drain off before the cream is added. The brown sugar gives rhubarb a specially rich flavour and colour.

To serve 6 to 8

1 kg	gooseberries	2 lb
250 g	castor sugar	8 oz
30 to 60 cl	double cream, whipped to soft peaks	$\frac{1}{2}$ to 1 pint

Wash the gooseberries. There is no need to top and tail them. Put them in the top half of a double saucepan with the sugar, cover, and steam them for about 30 minutes, or until they are quite soft. Strain off the surplus liquid (which would make the fool watery) and purée the gooseberries through a food mill. When the purée is quite cold, add the cream. More sugar may be necessary.

ELIZABETH DAVID
SYLLABUBS AND FRUIT FOOLS

Grape Cream

Grozdov Krem

In Bulgaria this dish is made with a product called petmez, *a thick syrup made from grape juice. The directions given here produce a result which is very similar, although it lacks the slightly caramelized flavour imparted by* petmez.

To serve 4 to 6

1 litre	unsweetened red or white grape juice	$1\frac{3}{4}$ pints
50 g	cornflour	2 oz
90 g	castor sugar	3 oz
About 100 g	shelled walnuts, two-thirds very finely chopped, the remainder very finely crushed	About $3\frac{1}{2}$ oz
1 tsp	ground cinnamon	1 tsp

In a saucepan, reduce the grape juice to $\frac{3}{4}$ litre ($1\frac{1}{4}$ pints) by boiling it gently, uncovered. Mix the cornflour with a little water and add it to the boiling juice. Stir until the mixture thickens, then add the sugar and the finely chopped walnuts. Continue to cook, stirring, until the sugar has dissolved. Leave to cool a little, then pour into individual dessert bowls or glasses. When the cream is quite cold, sprinkle with cinnamon and the finely crushed walnuts.

BULGARSKA NAZIONALNA KUCHNIYA

Chestnut Mont Blanc

Le Mont Blanc aux Marrons

To serve 6

1 kg	chestnuts, shells slit	2 to $2\frac{1}{2}$ lb
	salt	
About $\frac{1}{2}$ litre	milk	About 18 fl oz
75 g	sugar	$2\frac{1}{2}$ oz
1	vanilla pod	1
30 g	butter	1 oz
2	egg yolks	2
30 cl	double or whipping cream	$\frac{1}{2}$ pint
60 g	castor sugar	2 oz

Boil the chestnuts for 10 minutes in salted water. Cool them slightly. Peel them, removing both the outer shell and the inner skin. Put the chestnuts in a saucepan, cover with the milk, and add the sugar and vanilla pod. Simmer for about 1 hour, or until the chestnuts are tender. Remove the vanilla pod. Drain the chestnuts and purée them through a sieve using a pestle. Add a little of the hot milk to give the purée a good consistency. Stir in the butter and egg yolks. Form the purée into a mound and put to chill in the refrigerator.

Whip the cream with the castor sugar. Serve the dessert very cold, covered with the whipped cream.

ÉDOUARD DE POMIANE
LE CODE DE LA BONNE CHÈRE

Moulded Apple Pudding

Gâteau de Pommes

To serve 6

12	medium-sized apples, peeled, cored, and sliced, placed in a bowl of water with the juice of half a lemon to prevent them turning brown, and drained	12
About 500 g	sugar	About 1 lb
5 cm	stick cinnamon	2 inches
1	lemon, juice strained	1
1 tbsp	potato flour	1 tbsp
30 g	butter	1 oz
6	eggs	6
3 to 4 tbsp	dry breadcrumbs	3 to 4 tbsp

Put the apples in a saucepan with the sugar, cinnamon and lemon juice. Cover and cook over medium heat until the apples begin to soften; lower the heat and stir the apples until they are reduced to a purée. Strain through a sieve into a saucepan. Add the potato flour and the butter. Reduce the purée over a low heat, stirring all the while, until it is quite firm. Set the purée aside to cool.

Beat the eggs into the purée. Prepare a 1.5 litre (2½ pint) mould as follows: butter it and sprinkle with breadcrumbs, then turn the mould upside down and let any loose crumbs fall out. Pour the mixture into the mould to within 2.5 cm (1 inch) of the top. Bake in a water bath in a preheated 180°C (350°F or Mark 4) oven for about 45 minutes, or until the pudding is firm to the touch. Cool for about 15 minutes before unmoulding.

MICHEL BARBEROUSSE
CUISINE NORMANDE

Baked Bananas with Rum

Bananas Vieux Carré

This is a New Orleans speciality. The bananas can be prepared for baking before dinner, baked while you eat, then flamed at the table.

To serve 6		
6	large bananas, peeled and halved lengthwise	6
125 g	butter	4 oz
4 tsp	grated orange rind	4 tsp
10 cl	orange juice	4 fl oz
3 tbsp	lime juice	3 tbsp
½ tsp	ground cinnamon	½ tsp
4 tbsp	thin honey	4 tbsp
6 tbsp	white rum	6 tbsp
	double cream (optional)	

Melt half of the butter in an ovenproof dish that can be taken to the table. (An oval gratin dish is ideal.) Roll the banana halves in the melted butter to coat them well. Dot them with the remaining butter, sprinkle them with the grated orange rind, the orange juice and the lime juice, the cinnamon and the honey, and bake them for 15 minutes in an oven preheated to 190°C (375°F or Mark 5).

Flame the bananas with the rum by warming the rum in a small pan and igniting the liquid. Spoon the flaming rum over the bananas. Serve with double cream if desired.

JULIE DANNENBAUM
JULIE DANNENBAUM'S CREATIVE COOKING SCHOOL

Stuffed Peaches

Pesche Ripiene

To serve 6		
6	ripe peaches, halved, stones removed and cracked, kernels chopped	6
50 g	macaroons, crushed	2 oz
50 g	blanched almonds, chopped	2 oz
1 tbsp	cocoa	1 tbsp
100 g	sugar	3½ oz
1	egg	1
30 g	butter	1 oz
15 to 20 cl	moscato or other sweet white wine	6 fl oz

Using a teaspoon, scoop out some of the pulp from the peach halves. Put the peach pulp, macaroons, chopped almonds and peach kernels, cocoa, and 60 g (2 oz) of the sugar in a bowl, and mix well. Mix in the egg. Butter a shallow earthenware baking dish and put the peaches in it, hollowed side up. Fill the peaches with the stuffing mixture. Sprinkle with the rest of the sugar, dot with the butter and moisten with the wine. Bake in a preheated, 220°C (425°F or Mark 7), oven for 40 minutes. Serve either hot or cold.

LAURA GRAS PORTINARI
CUCINA E VINI DEL PIEMONTE E VALLE D'AOSTA

Pears, Baked and Stuffed

If desired, in place of the raisins, dates and chopped nuts, a stuffing of 125 g (4 oz) shredded coconut and 60 g (2 oz) tart jam or marmalade may be used.

To serve 6		
6	large pears, peeled and cored	6
40 g each	raisins, stoned dates and chopped mixed nuts	1½ oz each
	pouring custard (optional; *page 166*)	

Stuff the pears with a mixture made from the raisins, dates and chopped nuts. Place the pears close together in an ovenproof dish or pan, with just enough water to prevent them from burning. Bake them in a preheated oven, 180°C (350°F or Mark 4), for 40 minutes, or until they are tender. Remove the pears to a warmed glass dish, and allow them to cool. A plain cold custard may be poured over them before serving.

MAY BYRON
MAY BYRON'S PUDDINGS, PASTRIES AND SWEET DISHES

Apples Baked in Butter

Pommes au Beurre

The technique of peeling the apples and rubbing them with lemon juice, to prevent them from discolouring, is demonstrated on page 28.

	To serve 8	
8	large eating apples, all the same size, cored	8
8	slices stale bread, about 1 cm (½ inch) thick, cut into rounds of the same diameter as the apples	8
125 g	brown sugar	4 oz
250 g	butter	8 oz

Arrange the rounds of bread in a buttered ovenproof dish and stand an apple on each one. Work the sugar into the butter, and fill the centres of the apples with some of this mixture.

Bake in an oven preheated to 150°C (300°F or Mark 2) for about 1 hour, basting regularly, and placing lumps of the remaining sweetened butter on each apple from time to time to replenish the filling as it melts.

Serve very hot with whipped cream.

X. MARCEL BOULESTIN
THE FINER COOKING

Apple Charlotte

	To serve 8 to 10	
24 to 36	apples, peeled, cored and sliced	24 to 36
500 g	sugar	1 lb
60 g	butter	2 oz
1	bouquet of lemon peel and a cinnamon stick	1
30 cl	water	½ pint
1	2-day-old loaf finely grained white bread, crusts removed	1
About 125 g	clarified butter, melted	About 4 oz
About 30 g	icing sugar	About 1 oz
250 g	apricot jam, diluted with 2 to 3 tbsp boiling water	8 oz

First of all, some apple marmalade, or thick purée, must be prepared as follows: let the apples be placed in a stew-pan with the sugar, butter and some lemon peel and cinnamon tied together; moisten with the water, place the lid on the stew-pan, and then set the apples to boil on a brisk heat until they are softened. You then remove the lid and, with a wooden spoon, continue stirring the marmalade until it is reduced to a rather stiff consistency.

A plain round 2 litre (3½ pint) charlotte mould must now be lined at the bottom with small thin circular pieces of bread, dipped in the clarified butter, and placed so as to overlap each other until the bottom of the mould is well covered. Next, cut some thin, oblong squares of bread, dip them in clarified butter, and set these up the sides of the mould, overlapping each other—in order to hold firmly to the sides of the mould. Fill the cavity with the apple marmalade, cover in the top with a thin circular piece of bread dipped in clarified butter, place the charlotte on a baking sheet and bake in an oven preheated to 190°C (375°F or Mark 5) for 30 to 50 minutes, or until the bread is lightly coloured.

Remove the charlotte, let it cool for a few minutes, and carefully turn it out on to a heatproof serving dish. Sprinkle the top with sifted icing sugar and glaze under a hot grill for a few minutes. Pour the diluted apricot jam round the base of the charlotte and serve.

CHARLES ELMÉ FRANCATELLI
THE MODERN COOK

Plum or Apricot Croûtons

This is a delicious sweet for children, for the bread is crisp, the fruit soft and sticky, the sugar almost caramelized.

	To make 6	
9	plums or apricots, halved and stones discarded	9
6	slices day-old sandwich bread	6
About 40 g	butter	About 1½ oz
About 175 g	sugar	About 6 oz

Butter the slices of bread: place them buttered side up on a buttered baking sheet. On each slice, put 3 ripe plum or apricot halves, the spaces filled with sugar. Press the fruit well down on the bread. Bake near the top of a very moderate oven, preheated to 170°C (325°F or Mark 3), for about 40 minutes, and serve hot.

ELIZABETH DAVID
SUMMER COOKING

Summer Pudding

To serve 4 to 6

125 g each	raspberries, redcurrants and loganberries	4 oz each
250 g	blackcurrants	8 oz
175 g	castor sugar	6 oz
8	fairly thick slices white bread, crusts removed	8
	cream (optional)	

Remove the stalks from the fruit. Wash the fruit, if necessary, and put it with the sugar in a pan. Cover and cook gently for 5 to 10 minutes, or until the currants are tender. Drain off the juice, reserving 6 tablespoons. Line a 1 litre (2 pint) pudding basin with some of the bread slices, cutting them to fit the basin exactly. Spoon in the fruit, packing it in well. Pour in the reserved juice. Place the remaining bread on top of the fruit. Cover with a plate, small enough to rest on the pudding itself, and put the heaviest weight from your scales on the plate. Leave the pudding overnight in the refrigerator or other cold place. Turn out, and serve with cream if desired.

SUSAN KING
SUSAN KING'S COOK BOOK

Fruit and Pumpernickel Dessert

Götterspeise

To serve 4

500 g	fresh fruit such as wild or garden strawberries, redcurrants, raspberries, blackberries, morello cherries (stoned), one kind only or mixed	1 lb
2 to 3 slices	pumpernickel, lightly toasted and grated	2 to 3 slices
75 g	sugar	2½ oz
60 g	plain chocolate, grated	2 oz
1 tsp	vanilla sugar	1 tsp
¼ litre	double cream, whipped and sweetened with 1 tbsp sugar	8 fl oz

Sprinkle the fresh fruit with sugar. Put the fruit in a serving dish. Mix the pumpernickel with the chocolate and the vanilla sugar, and spread the mixture over the fruit. Heap the whipped cream on top. Chill the dessert in the refrigerator for 2 hours before serving.

HERMINE KIEHNLE AND MARIA HÄDECKE
DAS NEUE KIEHNLE-KOCHBUCH

Apple and Apricot Brown Betty

To serve 6 to 8

850 g	tart apples, peeled, cored and coarsely chopped	1¾ lb
125 g	dried apricots, soaked in water overnight, drained and coarsely chopped	4 oz
175 g	coarse fresh white breadcrumbs	6 oz
75 g	butter, melted	2½ oz
60 to 90 g	blanched almonds, coarsely chopped	2 to 3 oz
1	small orange, rind grated	1
125 to 175 g	brown sugar	4 to 6 oz
30 g	butter, cut into small pieces	1 oz

Toss the breadcrumbs in the melted butter until they have absorbed it evenly. Spread a thin layer of the crumbs in the bottom of a 1.5 litre (2½ pint) soufflé dish. Cover with a mixture of the apples, the apricots and the almonds. Sprinkle with a little orange rind and some of the sugar. Repeat the layers until the dish is full, finishing with a layer of crumbs. Dot with the butter pieces and sprinkle with any remaining sugar. Bake in a preheated 190°C (375°F or Mark 5) oven for about 30 to 40 minutes, or until golden and crisp. Serve very hot, with cream.

MARGARET COSTA
MARGARET COSTA'S FOUR SEASONS COOKERY BOOK

Green Apricot and Green Almond Compote

Compotes d'Abricots Verds et Amandes Verdes

Unripened apricots are very similar to unripened almonds: the hard outside flesh of the apricot later becomes the ripe flesh and that of the almond forms a dried-out husk round the shell.

To serve 4

500 g	green apricots or green almonds	1 lb
30 g	bicarbonate of soda	1 oz
About ¼ litre	medium sugar syrup (*page 8*)	About 8 fl oz

Put about ½ litre (1 pint) water and the bicarbonate of soda into a saucepan, bring to the boil, and leave to boil a moment or until the soda is dissolved. Toss in the apricots or almonds, and as soon as the water returns to a full boil, remove them with a skimmer. Rub them hard between your hands to remove the downy skin, tossing them into fresh water as soon as you have done this; boil 60 cl (1 pint) of fresh water in a saucepan, add the apricots or almonds, and cook gently for about 20 to 30 minutes or until, when pricking one with a pin, the point enters easily and the apricot or almond slips off the pin by itself. At this point remove the apricots and almonds and plunge them into fresh water. Bring the syrup to the boil, add the drained apricots or almonds and simmer gently over a low heat for 10 minutes or so, then serve.

MENON
LA CUISINIÈRE BOURGEOISE

Cherries in Red Wine

Ciliegie al Barolo

To serve 4

500 g	cherries, washed and stoned	1 lb
200 g	sugar	7 oz
10 cl	blackcurrant jelly	4 fl oz
1	orange, rind thinly peeled, cut into strips, and blanched for 5 minutes in boiling water	1
½	stick cinnamon	½
½ litre	Barolo, or other full-bodied red wine	18 fl oz
20 cl	double cream, whipped	7 fl oz

Put the cherries in a copper saucepan with the sugar, blackcurrant jelly, orange rind, and cinnamon stick; cover with the wine. Set the saucepan over a medium heat and when the wine comes to the boil, lower the heat and simmer the mixture very gently for 30 minutes.

Let the cherries cool in their sauce, remove the cinnamon stick and transfer the cherries and their sauce into individual serving dishes, garnishing with whipped cream. Refrigerate for 1 or 2 hours before serving.

LAURA GRAS PORTINARI
CUCINA E VINI DEL PIEMONTE E DELLA VALLE D'AOSTA

Chestnut Compote

The techniques of peeling chestnuts are shown on page 30.

To serve 6 to 8

1 kg	chestnuts, shells slit, roasted, peeled, and flattened a little with your hands	2 to 2½ lb
½ litre	medium sugar syrup (*page 8*), cooled	18 fl oz
1 tbsp	lemon juice	1 tbsp
2 tsp	fine *julienne* strips of lemon rind	2 tsp
30 g	icing sugar	1 oz

In a saucepan, put the chestnuts in the cold syrup and warm over a low heat, without bringing to the boil, so that the syrup may penetrate the chestnuts. Add the lemon juice and lemon rind, and put the chestnuts and syrup in *compotiers*. Sprinkle the chestnuts over with icing sugar, and glaze with a salamander, or beneath the grill.

G. A. JARRIN
THE ITALIAN CONFECTIONER

Pears in Red Wine

Poires Belle Angevine

This recipe is from Madame Prunier's restaurant in Paris.

To serve 4

4	firm, slightly under-ripe eating pears, peeled, halved and cored	4
About 60 cl	good red wine, preferably claret	About 1 pint
50 g	sugar	2 oz
1	small stick cinnamon	1
2 to 3 tsp	pear brandy	2 to 3 tsp

Wash the pear halves and put them in a heavy pan. Add the red wine, which should barely cover the pears, the sugar and the cinnamon stick.

Bring to the boil, then cover and simmer over a low heat for about 1 hour. Remove the pears with a slotted spoon, and place them in a *compotier*.

Over a brisk heat, reduce the cooking liquid until it has the consistency of a light syrup. Remove the cinnamon stick, add the pear brandy, and pour the syrup over the pears. Allow to cool thoroughly before serving.

ROBERT COURTINE
MES REPAS LES PLUS ÉTONNANTS

Fruit Compote

Compote de Fruits

The author suggests using sliced apples, pears, quinces, apricots and peaches for this dessert. Small fruits, such as strawberries, gooseberries, redcurrants, cherries and greengages may also be included, but they should be left whole.

To serve 6 to 8

1 kg	mixed fresh fruit, prepared according to type, and cut into slices or sections	2 to 2½ lb
60 cl	medium sugar syrup (*page 8*)	1 pint
	castor sugar	

Put the prepared fruit and the syrup into a saucepan, and simmer for about 15 minutes, or until the fruit is tender. Pour the fruit and syrup into a glass dish, sprinkle with sugar if necessary, and serve hot or cold.

ADRIEN-JEAN BOBINET
GASTRONOMIE

Peaches Aswim in Rose Petals

To serve 10

10	large, firm peaches, skinned, halved and stoned, 5 stones reserved	10
10	highly scented roses	10
1	rose-geranium leaf (optional)	1
300 g	sugar	10 oz
¾ litre	water	1¼ pints
2 to 3 tbsp	lemon juice	2 to 3 tbsp
½	vanilla pod or 1 tsp vanilla extract	½
10 cl	puréed raspberries, chilled and strained	4 fl oz
	pink rose petals, white part removed from base	

Remove the petals from the roses. Tie the rose petals and the rose-geranium leaf loosely in a muslin bag.

Make a syrup by combining the sugar, water and the petal bag. Bring to the boil and simmer for 5 minutes. Remove from the heat, add the lemon juice and the vanilla, and allow the syrup to steep for 10 minutes. With a spoon, press the petal bag to extract the maximum flavour, then remove the bag and, if using, the vanilla pod.

Crack the reserved peach stones and remove the almond-flavoured kernels. Add the peach halves and the kernels to the syrup and simmer until the peaches are tender. (Test for doneness with a fork.) Allow the peaches to cool in the syrup, then refrigerate until chilled.

With a slotted spoon, transfer the peaches to a pretty glass bowl. Spoon out the peach kernels and skin them. Mix the raspberry purée with the remaining syrup and pour this over the peaches. Chop the kernels and sprinkle them over the surface. Scatter the pink rose petals over the peaches.

JUDITH OLNEY
SUMMER FOOD

Compote of Dried Fruit

To serve 4

250 g	prunes or dried apricots, or 125 g (4 oz) of each, washed and soaked overnight in 90 cl (1½ pints) water	8 oz
90 g	demerara sugar	3 oz
1	strip lemon rind or 2.5 cm (1 inch) cinnamon stick	1
2 tsp	lemon juice	2 tsp
15 g	blanched, almonds, split and toasted	½ oz
6 to 8	glacé cherries	6 to 8

Strain the liquid from the fruit and put it into a saucepan with the sugar. Heat slowly until the sugar is dissolved. Add the lemon rind or cinnamon and the lemon juice. Boil over a brisk heat for 10 minutes without stirring, to thicken the syrup. Add the fruit and simmer gently over a low heat for about 20 to 30 minutes, or until the fruit is tender. Arrange the fruit neatly in a dish, strain the syrup over the fruit, and decorate with the almonds and the cherries. Serve hot or cold.

As an alternative method to cooking the fruit with the syrup in a saucepan, arrange the fruit in an ovenproof dish or casserole. Strain on the syrup. Put the lid on the dish and stew in an oven preheated to 150°C (300°F or Mark 2) for about 1 hour, or until the fruit is tender. When cooked, decorate with the almonds and the cherries.

CLAIRE MCINERNY AND DOROTHY ROCHE
SAVOUR: A NEW COOKERY BOOK

Figs with Thyme
Figues au Thym

To serve 4 to 6

500 g	dried figs	1 lb
2 or 3	small sprigs thyme, or ½ tsp crumbled dried thyme, tied in a bit of muslin	2 or 3
45 cl	red wine	16 fl oz
3 tbsp	honey	3 tbsp

Combine all the ingredients in a stainless steel or enamelled saucepan and simmer, covered, for about 1 hour, turning the figs over from time to time in their liquid if they are not completely covered. Remove the figs to a serving dish, discard the thyme, and reduce the cooking liquid over a high heat by about one third—or to the consistency of a light syrup—and pour it over the figs. This is good either tepid or chilled. Serve some kind of dry biscuit on the side.

RICHARD OLNEY
SIMPLE FRENCH FOOD

Dumplings Filled with Cherries
Vareniki s Vishnyami

Vareniki are a Ukrainian speciality and can also be filled with stoned plums or curd cheese. If only sweet cherries are available, use half the amount of sugar. An alternative method for cooking the dumplings is to poach them in the reserved cherry juice diluted with water, instead of using salted water. In this case serve the dumplings just with the soured cream.

To serve 6

600 g	sour cherries, stones removed	1¼ lb
250 g	sugar	8 oz
400 g	flour	14 oz
1 tsp	salt	1 tsp
2	eggs, beaten	2
7 tbsp	cold water	7 tbsp
30 cl	soured cream	½ pint

Place the cherries in a shallow bowl and sprinkle with the sugar. Leave in the sun or a warm place for 3 to 4 hours. Pour off the juice, which the cherries have released, into a saucepan and reserve for later. Sift the flour and salt together into a bowl, make a well in the centre, add the eggs and water, gradually work in the flour to achieve a firm dough. Knead for 5 to 10 minutes until smooth. Chill in the refrigerator for 15 minutes. On a floured surface, roll out the dough to a 3 mm (⅛ inch) thickness. Using a 7.5 cm (3 inch) cutter, make rounds of

dough and put a teaspoon of the cherry filling on each. Fold the dough over to form a half-moon shape, moisten the edges with a little water and pinch together firmly. Left over scraps of dough can be rolled out again to make more dumplings.

Bring a large saucepan of salted water to the boil, and add the dumplings up to 8 at a time. Cook for 10 minutes or until they float to the top. Remove the dumplings carefully with a slotted spoon and place them on a serving dish.

Reduce the reserved cherry juice by simmering for 10 minutes, then leave to cool. Serve the dumplings with the cherry syrup and the soured cream.

ELENA MOLOKHOVETS
PODAROK MOLODÝM KHOZYAÍKAM

Pumpkin and Dried Fruit Compote
Vahrena Tikva Sus Soosheni Plodove

If the pumpkin is watery and becomes too soft before the liquid has evaporated, to finish cooking uncover the saucepan and raise the heat a little. The dried fruits might include prunes, apricots, apples, pears, figs and sultanas.

To serve 4

500 g	pumpkin, peeled, seeded and cut into cubes like pieces of Turkish Delight	1 lb
300 g	mixed dried fruits, large pieces cut in half	10 oz
About 2 tbsp	water	About 2 tbsp
50 g	sugar or honey	2 oz

In a saucepan with a tight-fitting lid, place alternate layers of pumpkin and dried fruit. Add the water. Cover and simmer over a very low heat for 30 minutes, or until the fruit is cooked and the liquid has evaporated. A few minutes before the end of cooking, add the sugar or honey.

BULGARSKA NAZIONALNA KUCHNIYA

Jellies

Striped Jelly
Gelée Rubanée

These jellies may be made using a larger selection of flavours and colours; but take care to arrange them in the mould in such a way that they contrast well with each other.

	To serve 6 to 8	
15 g	leaf gelatine, softened in a little water	½ oz
400 g	sugar	14 oz
40 cl	cold water	¾ pint
6 tbsp	puréed redcurrants or mixture of redcurrant, raspberry and strawberry purée	6 tbsp
6 tbsp	kirsch, rum or anisette	6 tbsp

Put the gelatine, sugar and water into an untinned copper saucepan; stir, then whisk over a gentle heat until the sugar and gelatine have dissolved. Remove the mixture from the heat as soon as it begins to boil.

Add the red fruit purée to half of this liquid; add the white liqueur or rum to the remainder. Pour half of the red mixture into a 1 litre (1¾ pint) jelly mould. Leave to set in a cool place or in the refrigerator. When set, pour half of the white mixture on top. Leave this to set. Add the rest of the red mixture and when this is set, the remainder of the white mixture. Leave to set firmly in the refrigerator. When ready to serve, dip the mould in hot water so that the jelly will slip out easily.

ÉMILE DUMONT
LA BONNE CUISINE

Oranges Filled with Jelly

Any other variety of jelly, or different blancmanges, may be used at choice to fill the rinds; the colours, however, should contrast as much as possible.

	To serve 6	
6	large oranges	6
30 g	leaf gelatine, soaked in a little water	1 oz
	edible red food colouring	

With the point of a small knife cut out from the top of each orange a round about the size of a shilling (5p coin); then with the small end of a teaspoon or egg spoon, empty the oranges entirely, reserving the pulp and juice, taking great care not to break the rinds. Throw the rinds into cold water; strain the juice and pulp through a fine muslin cloth to obtain a clear juice. Measure the juice and add water to make up to a total of ¾ litre (1¼ pints) liquid.

Place the juice and softened gelatine in a bowl over simmering water, until the gelatine is completely dissolved. Remove from the heat; divide the juice into equal amounts and colour one half a fine rose colour with the red food colouring added, drop by drop, and leave the other very pale. When the juice is nearly cold, drain and wipe the orange rinds, and fill them with alternate stripes of the two jellies, allowing each layer of jelly to set before the next is added.

When the oranges are perfectly cold, cut them into quarters, and dispose them tastefully in a dish with a few light branches of myrtle between them.

ELIZABETH RAY (EDITOR)
THE BEST OF ELIZA ACTON

Orange Jelly
Gelée à l'Orange

To prepare this jelly in one 1.25 litre (2 pint) jelly mould, increase the quantity of gelatine to 30 g (1 oz), and use 400 g (14 oz) sugar. Refrigerate for about 2 hours before and after adding the orange segments.

	To serve 12	
1 or 2	oranges, peeled and cut into segments, pith and membrane removed	1 or 2
15 g	gelatine leaf, softened in a little water	½ oz
300 g	castor sugar	10 oz
½ litre	cold water	18 fl oz
1	sugar lump, rubbed on orange rind	1
15 cl	freshly squeezed orange juice	¼ pint
2 to 3 tbsp	freshly squeezed lemon juice	2 to 3 tbsp

Put the gelatine, castor sugar and water into a copper saucepan; stir and beat over a gentle heat until the sugar and gelatine have dissolved.

Dissolve the sugar lump in the orange and lemon juice, strain the juice, and stir it into the hot gelatine mixture.

Half fill little glass bowls or wine glasses with the jelly and allow it to set in the refrigerator for at least 1 hour. Put an orange segment in each bowl or glass, fill with the remaining jelly and leave to set in the refrigerator for about 2 hours, or until the jelly is required.

ÉMILE DUMONT
LA BONNE CUISINE

Red Fruit in Jelly Italian-Style

Miscela di Frutti Rossi all'Italiana

To serve 6 to 8

100 g	strawberries	3½ oz
100 g	raspberries	3½ oz
12	maraschino cherries	12
4 tbsp	maraschino liqueur	4 tbsp
	Raspberry jelly	
350 g	ripe raspberries	12 oz
4 tbsp	lemon juice	4 tbsp
100 g	sugar	3½ oz
15 g	powdered gelatine, dissolved in 2 tbsp hot water	½ oz

In an earthenware bowl, marinate the strawberries, raspberries, and cherries in the maraschino.

To prepare the jelly, purée the ripe raspberries through a nylon sieve. Add the lemon juice, sugar to taste, and just enough water to make up the quantity to 60 cl (1 pint). Stir in the dissolved gelatine.

Place a bowl or mould in ice, and coat the inside with a little liquid from the marinated fruit. Pour in raspberry jelly to a depth of 2 fingers and allow to set. With a slotted spoon, drain some of the marinated fruit and spread it in a uniform layer over the jelly. Pour on another few spoonfuls of jelly. After a few minutes, add another 2 spoonfuls of fruit and more jelly, and repeat this process until the bowl is quite full. Cover it with a lid with a piece of ice on top, or refrigerate, and leave to set. Just before serving, dip the outside of the bowl into warm water, wipe it dry, and turn out the jelly on to a dish covered by a napkin.

GIUSEPPE SORBIATTI
LA GASTRONOMIA MODERNA

Fresh Fruit Salad in Jelly

La Macédoine de Fruits Frais à la Gelée

Suitable fruits for use in this recipe include strawberries, raspberries, pineapple, peaches, apricots and oranges.

To serve 10

125 g each	mixed fresh fruits of 4 or 5 kinds, prepared according to type	4 oz each
½ litre	brandy	18 fl oz
100 g	sugar	3½ oz
	Kirsch jelly	
150 g	sugar	5 oz
1 litre	water	1¾ pints
30 g	leaf gelatine, softened in a little water	1 oz
¼ litre	kirsch	8 fl oz

Soak the prepared mixed fruits in the brandy and sugar for 1 hour. Meanwhile, prepare the jelly. Make a syrup by bringing the sugar and water to the boil together. Add the softened gelatine, and stir over a low heat until dissolved. Allow the jelly to cool, then add the kirsch.

Put a 1.5 litre (2½ pint) charlotte mould on ice and pour in about 20 cl (7 fl oz) of the jelly. Leave the mould on ice or in the refrigerator for about 30 minutes, or until the jelly is nearly set. Drain the fruits and arrange a quarter of them on the jelly. Cover the fruits with more jelly and allow to set as before. Continue these layers until the mould is full. Leave the mould on ice or in the refrigerator for 2 hours to set. Turn out the jelly just before serving.

ARISTIDE QUILLET
LA CUISINE MODERNE

Wine Jelly

To serve 10 to 12

40 cl	hock	¾ pint
5 tbsp	port wine	5 tbsp
250 g	grapes	8 oz
275 g	sugar	9 oz
75 cl	water	1¼ pints
50 g	leaf gelatine, softened in 6 tbsp of water	1¾ oz
6	lemons, juice strained	6

Remove the grapes from the stalks, but leave one small bunch intact. If desired, peel and seed the individual grapes. Dissolve the sugar in the water over a medium heat. Add the softened gelatine, and stir until the sugar and gelatine dissolve completely. Do not let the mixture boil. Off the heat, add the lemon juice and hock. Leave this mixture standing for about 20 minutes and then filter it through a napkin. Add the port. Surround a glass dish with ice and pour half of the jelly into the dish. When this jelly has set, lay grapes round the border of the dish and place the small bunch in the centre. Pour in about 1 cm ($\frac{1}{2}$ inch) of jelly and let it set so that it holds the grapes in place. Pour in the rest of the jelly and leave it in the refrigerator to set.

J. M. ERICH WEBER
THEORY AND PRACTICE OF THE CONFECTIONER

Champagne Jelly with Raspberries

To serve 4

15 to 20 cl	champagne	6 fl oz
21 g	powdered gelatine	$\frac{3}{4}$ oz
40 cl	water	$\frac{3}{4}$ pint
150 g	sugar	5 oz
1	lemon, juice extracted and finely pared rind (without any pith) cut into wide strips	1
10 cl	dry white wine	4 fl oz
350 g	raspberries	12 oz

Soften the gelatine in 3 to 4 tablespoons of the water. Heat the remaining water in a saucepan, add the gelatine, and stir until dissolved. Add the sugar, the lemon juice and the rind. Heat just to the point where the liquid is about to break into a boil. Remove the pan from the heat, cover, and steep for 20 minutes. Strain the liquid through a muslin-lined sieve, and discard the lemon rind.

Leave the jelly to cool. Watch, and as soon as it turns cold and just before it sets, stir in the dry white wine and the champagne. Pour into four shallow champagne glasses or balloon wine glasses. Leave to set until thoroughly cold. Serve with raspberries, sprinkled with castor sugar if desired.

JUDITH OLNEY
SUMMER FOOD

A Simple Lemon Jelly

To serve 6 to 8

6	lemons, rinds finely peeled, juice strained	6
60 g	leaf gelatine, soaked in a little water	2oz
500 g	sugar	1lb
60 cl	water	1 pint

In a saucepan, dissolve the sugar and soaked gelatine in the water, over medium heat, then add the lemon juice and rinds. Boil together for 1 minute, then strain through a muslin cloth into a mould, previously rinsed with cold water. When completely set, turn out the jelly and serve.

MRS. C. F. LEYEL
PUDDINGS

Black Coffee Jelly

To serve 4 to 6

60 cl	freshly made strong black coffee	1 pint
125 g	sugar	4 oz
5 tbsp	water	5 tbsp
15 g	leaf gelatine, soaked in 2 to 3 tbsp water	$\frac{1}{2}$ oz
	double cream, whipped	

Make a syrup by boiling the sugar and water together for 1 or 2 minutes. Add the freshly made coffee to the syrup, and stir in the gelatine, making sure it is completely dissolved. Pour the mixture into a 90 cl (1$\frac{1}{2}$ pint) mould, and allow it to get cold. Leave to set in the refrigerator. Serve with whipped cream.

RUTH LOWINSKY
MORE LOVELY FOOD

Custards and Creams

Burnt Cream

Crème Brûlée

This recipe was taken from *The Ocklye Cookery Book* (1909) by Eleanor L. Jenkinson.

	To serve 4 to 6	
60 cl	double cream or 30 cl (½ pint) each double and single cream	1 pint
4	large egg yolks, well beaten	4
60 to 90 g	castor sugar	2 to 3 oz

Bring the cream to the boil, and boil it for about 30 seconds. Pour it immediately on to the egg yolks and whisk them together. (At this point, although the recipe does not say so, I return the mixture to the pan, and cook it without allowing it to boil, until it thickens and coats the spoon.) Pour the cream mixture into a shallow heatproof gratin dish. Leave it to chill in the refrigerator overnight.

Two hours before the meal, sprinkle the chilled cream with the sugar in an even layer, and place it under a grill preheated to the maximum temperature. The sugar will caramelize to a sheet of brown smoothness: it may be necessary to turn the dish while under the grill to achieve an even effect.

JANE GRIGSON
ENGLISH FOOD

Tea Cream

	To serve 3 to 4	
7 g	black tea leaves	¼ oz
30 cl	double cream	½ pint
30 cl	milk	½ pint
2 tsp	rennet	2 tsp
60 g	sugar	2 oz

Boil the tea with the milk; strain off the leaves and add to the milk the cream, rennet, and sugar to taste. Set it over a very low heat in the dish it is to be served in, and cover it with a plate. When the dessert is thick it will be sufficiently done. Garnish with sweetmeats.

MARY JEWRY (EDITOR)
WARNE'S MODEL COOKERY AND HOUSEKEEPING BOOK

Almond Cream

Hsing Jen Lou

This dessert can be made in advance, reheated and served hot. It can also be served cold, if you prefer.

	To serve 6 to 8	
125 g	large blanched almonds	4 oz
1½ tbsp	long-grain or short-grain rice	1½ tbsp
1 litre	cold water	1¾ pints
About 6 tbsp	sugar	About 6 tbsp
1 tbsp	almond extract	1 tbsp

Rinse the almonds and rice together. Soak them in half of the cold water for at least 4 hours. Pour the almonds and rice with the water into an electric blender. Blend them for 5 minutes or until the liquid is no longer grainy.

Set a bowl underneath a 30 × 35 cm (12 × 14 inch) muslin bag and pour the liquid into the bag. Close the top of the bag by twisting it, then squeeze the bag to force the almond cream into the bowl. Put half of the remaining water in another bowl, mix the contents of the bag with it, pour the mixture into the bag and squeeze again to extract more cream. With the remaining water, repeat the process once more. You should have a total of 1 litre (1¾ pints) of almond cream. Pour the cream into a saucepan. Discard the residue in the bag and wash the bag for future use.

Heat the saucepan of almond cream. Add sugar to taste and the almond extract, and *slowly* bring to the boil over a medium to low heat, stirring constantly. This takes about 15 minutes. It is important that the cream is heated slowly, otherwise it will curdle. Remove from the heat and serve.

FLORENCE LIN
FLORENCE LIN'S CHINESE VEGETARIAN COOKBOOK

Butter'd Oranges

This is possibly my very favourite English recipe. Anne Blencowe's book, where I found it, was printed in 1694 (at least the copy that I have used), so it must have been on the go in the 17th century. I have yet to discover it in any other recipe book, so maybe it was a speciality of hers.

It is a simple job to crystallize your own rose petals. Pick a heavily scented rose. Pull each petal off and carefully paint with gum arabic. Dredge with castor sugar until every fragment of the surface is coated. Cover a cooling tray (wire cake rack) with a sheet of greaseproof paper; put each petal on to this, making sure they do not touch each other. Dry in an airing cupboard and store in an airtight jar.

	To serve 6	
8	large oranges	8
5	egg yolks	5
60 g	castor sugar	2 oz
1 tsp	rose water	1 tsp
125 g	unsalted butter, cut into 2.5 cm (1 inch) cubes	4 oz
15 cl	double cream	$\frac{1}{4}$ pint
1	large piece soft candied orange, shredded or cut into tiny pieces	1
	crystallized rose petals or 15 cl ($\frac{1}{4}$ pint) double cream, whipped	

First prepare 6 orange cases for filling with Butter'd Orange. Reverse each orange so that the "stalk" or "bud" is at the base. Holding a small pointed cook's knife at a diagonal angle, insert the tip into the orange 2.5 cm (1 inch) down from the apex, cut round and remove a "lid". Traditional zig-zag cutting can be used if you wish.

Take a teaspoon, if possible an old one which has a worn and rather sharp edge, and using the palm of the hand as a protective "wall", scoop and lever out all the orange flesh until the shell is quite clean. Do likewise with the lid. Take care not to pierce the skin at any point. You will be left with a "stalk" of pith sticking up from the bottom of the shell. Cut this out with a sharp knife or pair of scissors. Clean the edges of the base and lid of any bits of unsightly pith.

At this stage fix any decoration of your choice to the lid with a cocktail stick. Never use wire where it is likely to come into contact with food; but it is quite safe to wire any rosebuds or miniature flowers to the cocktail stick before pushing it through the orange peel lid.

The juice and flesh from the emptied oranges can be used as juice for breakfast or for adding to sauces.

Grate the rind from the remaining two oranges—which should give you 1 level tablespoon when pressed down. Squeeze the juice from the oranges.

Select a round-bottomed basin that will fit nicely and firmly into the top of a pan of boiling water. Mix together in the basin the orange juice and grated rind, egg yolks and sugar. Arrange the basin over the water, making sure that the water is in contact with the bottom of the basin.

Stir the mixture gently, but continuously, with a balloon whisk, until it is as thick as a good custard. Take care to scrape the sides of the basin during this operation, but do not whisk too briskly or you will create a foam which will prevent your seeing when the liquid has thickened. When the orange mixture starts to "ribbon", remove the basin from the top of

the pan and stand it in a large bowl of cold water to cool slightly. Continue stirring and add the rose water.

Remove the basin from the cold water. Whisk the pieces of butter into the mixture, making sure that each one is incorporated before adding the next. Lightly whip the cream and fold it into the mixture. As the Butter'd Orange starts to set, fold the candied orange pieces into it so that they stay suspended and do not all sink to the bottom.

Fill the orange "shells" and chill until set. Decorate the top of the Butter'd Oranges, with crystallized rose petals pouring from under the "lid" of the orange.

A simpler decoration is to use a "rose" piping tube and pipe a band of whipped cream round the rim of the orange base, letting it be somewhat thicker on one side than the other so that the "lid" stands at an attractive angle.

These oranges look most attractive when nestling in a folded organza napkin, or mounted into a pyramid.

MICHAEL SMITH
FINE ENGLISH COOKERY

Crème Carême

This dessert takes its name from Carême, the great early 19th-century chef who created it.

	To serve 8	
8	egg yolks	8
150 g	sugar	5 oz
1 tbsp	rice flour or 2 tsp cornflour	1 tbsp
$\frac{3}{4}$ litre	hot milk	$1\frac{1}{4}$ pints
6 tbsp	best maraschino	6 tbsp
35 cl	whipped cream	12 fl oz

In a bowl, whisk the egg yolks with the sugar and rice flour or cornflour until the mixture is pale yellow. Add the hot milk very slowly. Put the mixture in a saucepan over a very low heat, stirring with a wooden spoon until the spoon is thickly coated. Remove the custard from the heat, stirring occasionally until it is cold. Put it in the refrigerator. (Carême says put it on ice, surrounded by ice.) Remove it from the refrigerator from time to time to stir it. Just before serving, stir in the maraschino and whipped cream. You will then have, in Carême's words, a light velvety mellow cream.

ALICE B. TOKLAS
THE ALICE B. TOKLAS COOK BOOK

Chocolate Custard Cream

Pots de Crème Panisse

To serve 6

175 g	plain chocolate, broken into pieces	6 oz
¼ litre	water	8 fl oz
1	vanilla pod	1
6	egg yolks, well beaten	6
30 cl	double cream, whipped	½ pint

In a saucepan over a low heat, melt the chocolate with the water and the vanilla pod. When the chocolate is glossy and smooth, add the egg yolks. Continue to cook, stirring constantly, until the chocolate cream thickens and is perfectly smooth. Remove from the heat, take out the vanilla pod, and leave the mixture to cool a little, stirring the while. Pour it through a fine sieve into 6 ramekins or *petits pots*, filling to three-quarters full. Top each with a dome of whipped cream.

ÉDOUARD NIGNON
LES PLAISIRS DE LA TABLE

Red Wine Froth

To serve 4

20 cl	red wine (Burgundy or claret)	7 fl oz
4	egg yolks	4
125 g	sugar	4 oz
½	finely grated lemon rind	½ tsp
1 tbsp	raspberry or redcurrant jelly	1 tbsp

Whisk all the ingredients over a low to medium heat until the mixture thickens, but *it must not boil*. Remove from the heat and keep on beating vigorously until the mixture is cold. Serve in a glass dish or in small individual dishes.

INGA NORBERG
GOOD FOOD FROM SWEDEN

Wine Cream

Crème Bachique

To serve 6

½ litre	good white wine	18 fl oz
125 g	sugar	4 oz
1	strip finely pared lemon rind, or ½ stick cinnamon	1
7 or 8	egg yolks	7 or 8

Pour the wine into a saucepan, add the sugar and lemon rind or cinnamon. Bring to the boil and leave, covered, to infuse until tepid. In a bowl, stir the egg yolks with a spoon to mix

them well. Add the wine slowly, stirring constantly. Pour the mixture through a fine strainer into individual ramekins, and cook in a bain-marie in an oven preheated to 170°C (325°F or Mark 3) for about 20 minutes, or until set.

L. E. AUDOT
LA CUISINIÈRE DE LA CAMPAGNE ET DE LA VILLE

Peruvian Cream

Crème Péruvienne

To serve 6

60 cl	milk	1 pint
60 g	freshly roasted coffee beans	2 oz
¼	vanilla pod	¼
90 g	castor sugar or lump sugar	3 oz
2 tbsp	cold water	2 tbsp
2 to 3 tbsp	hot water	2 to 3 tbsp
100 g	plain chocolate, broken into 4 or 5 pieces	3½ oz
5	egg yolks	5
1	whole egg	1

In a saucepan, heat the milk to boiling point. Meanwhile, spread the coffee beans on a baking tray and warm them in an oven preheated to 180°C (350°F or Mark 4) for a few minutes, or until the beans start to sweat. Remove the boiling milk from the heat, and add the coffee beans along with the vanilla pod. Cover, and leave to infuse for 30 minutes over the lowest possible heat, protecting the pan with a flameproof pad.

Meanwhile, in a small saucepan, dissolve the sugar in the cold water and cook over a medium heat until the sugar reaches the golden caramel stage and is very pale in colour. Immediately immerse the bottom of the pan in a bowl of cold water, which should be standing close by; this immersion will arrest the cooking process. Add 2 to 3 tablespoons of hot water to dilute the caramel. Return the saucepan to a very low heat, and stir the mixture with a spoon until it turns into a smooth syrup. Set it aside until you need it.

Place the chocolate in a saucepan and add a few spoonfuls of the infused milk—just enough to cover the pieces of chocolate. Cover the pan and place it over an extremely low heat. When the chocolate has softened—after a few minutes— work it with a wooden spoon until it becomes a smooth paste.

Remove the remaining infused milk from the heat and pass it through a fine strainer into a clean bowl. Discard the coffee beans. Add the chocolate, then add the caramel syrup.

Place the egg yolks and the whole egg in a bowl and mix thoroughly with a little whisk. A little at a time, add the milk, chocolate and caramel mixture, whisking constantly to make sure that the eggs and liquid blend thoroughly. Do not, however, whisk too vigorously: this is unnecessary, and will cause an excessive amount of froth to form. Pass the mixture through a fine strainer to remove any particles of egg.

Choose a pan that is sufficiently large for the little individual cream pots to stand next to each other, without being wedged. Fill the pots with the cream, and place them in the pan. Pour into the pan enough boiling water to come two-thirds of the way up the sides of the pots (you can use a funnel for this operation). Put the pan in a preheated 150°C (300°F or Mark 2) oven. Cover the pan at once with a close-fitting lid: it is vital to seal the pan with a lid, in order to protect the surface of the cream from too strong a heat. The oven should be at a high enough temperature for the water in the pan to be almost boiling: that is to say as hot as possible without actually boiling. As soon as you notice the slightest trembling of the water, a sign that it may begin to boil immediately, add a couple of spoonfuls of cold water.

The cooking time varies according to the size of the pots used. For pots with a capacity of 8 to 9 cl (3 to 3½ fl oz), allow 18 to 20 minutes. For pots holding 10 cl (4 fl oz), allow a little longer—23 to 25 minutes. Before removing the pan from the oven, test whether the cream is cooked by tipping one of the pots slightly: the cream should tremble but remain firm.

Remove the pan from the oven. Leave the pots in the water for a few minutes, then take them out and leave them to chill, uncovered, for about 2½ hours.

To serve, wipe the pots carefully and arrange them on a napkin-covered serving dish or platter; the napkin will ensure that the pots do not slide around while being served.

MADAME SAINT-ANGE
LA CUISINE DE MADAME SAINT-ANGE

Caramel Custard

Crème au Caramel

To serve 6

175 g	sugar	6 oz
3 tbsp	water	3 tbsp
1.25 litres	milk	2 pints
1	egg	1
2	egg yolks	2
1 tsp	vanilla extract	1 tsp

Boil 60 g (2 oz) of the sugar with the water in a heavy saucepan until it is amber brown. Set aside to cool. Scald the milk, allow it to cool slightly, and pour it into the saucepan with the caramelized sugar. Stir over a low heat until the caramel is completely dissolved in the milk. Beat the whole egg with the yolks, and add the remaining sugar and the vanilla. Pour into the caramelized milk gradually, stirring to blend.

Pour the custard into individual cups, or into one large mould. Place in a pan of hot water and bake in an oven, preheated to 170°C (325°F or Mark 3), for 30 to 40 minutes, or until set. This can be tested by inserting a silver knife into the custard. If the knife comes out clean, the custard is set. Serve the custard warm or chilled.

CHARLOTTE TURGEON
TANTE MARIE'S FRENCH KITCHEN

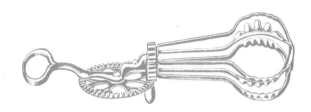

Tea Custards

Crème au Thé

To serve 12

¼ litre	black tea, as strong as possible	8 fl oz
1 litre	double cream	1¾ pints
125 g	sugar	4 oz
4	egg yolks	4
6	eggs	6

Orange flower sauce

60 g	sugar	2 oz
¼ litre	double cream	8 fl oz
1 tbsp	orange flower water	1 tbsp
2	egg yolks	2

In a saucepan, reduce the cream by half by boiling over a brisk heat. Beat in the sugar, tea, egg yolks and whole eggs, and pass the mixture through a fine strainer. Beat and strain again. Divide the mixture between 12 small pots, place the pots in a water bath, and cook in an oven preheated to 150°C (300°F or Mark 2) for 20 to 25 minutes, or until set. Cool the custards until tepid, then refrigerate until chilled. Invert the pots on to a serving platter to form small hillocks of the custard, arranged symmetrically.

To make the sauce, dissolve the sugar in the cream over a low heat. Whisk in the orange flower water and the egg yolks. Stir over a low heat without allowing the sauce to boil. Let it cool until tepid, and pour the sauce over the custards, which should be served cold.

JULES BRETEUIL
LE CUISINIER EUROPÉEN

Almond Pudding from Puerto Rico

Pudín de Almendras

To serve 6

150 g	finely ground almonds	5 oz
200 g	sugar	7 oz
2	eggs, beaten	2
¼ litre	milk	8 fl oz
¼ litre	double cream	8 fl oz
40 g	soft breadcrumbs	1½ oz
2 tsp	ground cinnamon	2 tsp
1 tsp	grated nutmeg	1 tsp
75 g	seedless raisins, soaked in 10 cl (4 fl oz) white wine for 15 minutes and drained	2½ oz
	whipped cream (optional)	

Add the sugar to the eggs, beating well. Add the milk and cream and mix well. Add the breadcrumbs, almonds, cinnamon, nutmeg and raisins and mix well. Preheat the oven to 180°C (350°F or Mark 4). Butter 6 individual custard pots or other individual ovenproof dishes. Pour the mixture into them. Place the dishes in a pan of water. Bake in the oven for 25 minutes, or until delicately browned on top and moderately firm. Serve hot or cold. Whipped cream may be placed on each portion, if you wish.

MYRA WALDO
THE COMPLETE ROUND-THE-WORLD COOKBOOK

Milk and Egg Sweet

Tyropatinam

This recipe is by Apicius, the 1st-century Roman gourmet.

To serve 4

60 cl	milk	1 pint
5	eggs	5
10 cl	honey	4 fl oz
	freshly ground pepper	

Mix the milk with the honey, then add the eggs. Work the eggs with the milk into a smooth mixture. Strain the mixture into a 90 cl (1½ pint) earthenware pot and cook in a water bath in an oven preheated to 170°C (325°F or Mark 3) for about 30 minutes, or until set. Grind over some pepper and serve.

BARBARA FLOWER AND ELISABETH ROSENBAUM
THE ROMAN COOKERY BOOK—A CRITICAL TRANSLATION OF
"THE ART OF COOKING BY APICIUS"

Caramel Water Custard

Oeufs à l'Eau au Caramel

To serve 4 to 6

125 g	sugar	4 oz
60 cl	water	1 pint
5 cm	cinnamon stick	2 inch
10 to 15	coriander seeds, lightly crushed	10 to 15
1	lemon, rind only	1
6	egg yolks, beaten	6

Put the sugar to boil in 10 cl (4 fl oz) of the water until it becomes caramel coloured; moisten promptly with the remaining water, adding the cinnamon, coriander and lemon rind, and boil gently for 30 minutes. Strain the mixture and, when half cooled, pour the mixture slowly over the beaten egg yolks in a mixing bowl, whisking at the same time.

Strain and pour into a 1 litre (1¾ pint) mould or into individual ramekins. Poach in a bain-marie until set—allow up to 40 minutes for a single mould, about 15 minutes for ramekins. Serve hot.

MENON
LES SOUPERS DE LA COUR

Little Pots of Pistachio Cream

Petits Pots aux Pistaches

The technique of blanching pistachio nuts is demonstrated on page 12. To obtain the spinach juice used as a colouring in this recipe, parboil a few leaves of spinach for 1 minute, drain and squeeze out any excess liquid. Pound or purée the leaves, and squeeze the juice through a cloth.

To serve 8

125 g	pistachio nuts, blanched and finely pounded	4 oz
60 cl	double cream	1 pint
125 g	sugar	4 oz
1	egg	1
4	egg yolks	4
1 tsp	spinach juice	1 tsp

Bring the cream to the boil in a saucepan. Add the sugar and stir until dissolved, then mix in the ground pistachio nuts, bring to the boil again, and leave to cool. Put the whole egg and egg yolks in another pan, mix, then stir in the cream mixture and add the spinach juice. Pass the mixture through a fine strainer. Pour into 8 small pots or ramekins, and cook in a bain-marie over a low heat for 20 minutes, or until set.

VIARD AND FOURET
LE CUISINIER ROYAL

Celeriac Cream

Crème au Céleri

To serve 14 to 16

1.5 litres	double cream or half cream and half milk	2½ pints
1	celeriac, peeled and quartered	1
8 to 10	egg yolks	8 to 10
250 g	sugar	8 oz

Boil the cream or cream and milk. Add the celeriac and simmer gently for approximately 20 minutes, or until the cream takes on the flavour of the celeriac: although boiling gently, neither the milk nor the cream will turn. While the mixture is infusing, beat the egg yolks until smooth; add the sugar to them. After removing the quarters of celeriac, gradually stir in the hot cream. Strain, pour the mixture into small porcelain pots and finish cooking in a bain-marie over a low heat, or in an oven preheated to 170°C (325°F or Mark 3), until set, approximately 15 to 20 minutes.

L. E. AUDOT
LA CUISINIÈRE DE LA CAMPAGNE ET DE LA VILLE

Sultan's Cream

Crème à la Sultane

To serve 4 to 6

15 cl	milk	¼ pint
30 cl	double cream	½ pint
5 cm	stick cinnamon	2 inch
6	coriander seeds	6
1	strip lemon rind	1
60 g	sugar	2 oz
6	egg yolks, lightly beaten	6
40 g each	chocolate sponge finger biscuits, and almond sponge finger biscuits, finely chopped	1½ oz each
15 g	crystallized orange flowers, or crystallized violets, crushed	½ oz
15 g	candied lemon peel, finely chopped	½ oz
¼ tsp	ground cinnamon	¼ tsp

Boil the milk and cream together with the cinnamon stick, coriander seeds, lemon rind and sugar. When it has come to the boil, allow the mixture to cool partially, then mix in the egg yolks and pour this custard through a fine strainer. Add the sponge finger biscuits, orange flowers or violets, the

candied lemon peel and the ground cinnamon to the cream mixture. Pour into a 90 cl (1½ pint) ovenproof dish and cook in a bain-marie in a preheated 170°C (325°F or Mark 3) oven for 30 to 45 minutes, or until set. Leave to get cold and serve.

LE CUISINIER GASCON

Marbled Eggs

Oeufs Marbrez

To prepare the green colouring for the eggs, parboil 250 g (8 oz) of chard or spinach, then purée it through a sieve. For the red colouring, purée through a sieve one sweet red pepper that has been grilled, peeled and seeded.

To serve 8 to 10

24	eggs	24
1	sweet red pepper, puréed	1
250 g	chard or spinach, puréed	8 oz
¼ tsp	powdered saffron, dissolved in 1 tsp boiling water	¼ tsp
	salt	
1 tsp	ground cinnamon	1 tsp
200 g	sugar	7 oz
30 g	butter	1 oz
	orange flower water	
	pomegranate seeds	

Break the eggs into four bowls, six eggs in each. Add the red pepper purée to one bowl, the chard purée to another, and the dissolved saffron to a third. Leave the eggs in the fourth bowl plain. Season the eggs in all four bowls to taste with a pinch of salt, the ground cinnamon and sugar, and beat the eggs in each bowl thoroughly.

Melt the butter over a low heat in an oven dish. When it is melted, pour in a layer of the red egg mixture. When it is barely firm, pour on a layer of the saffron-yellow mixture. Subsequent layers, with the exception of the top layer, may be barely set by passing the dish beneath a grill until just firm enough to pour on an additional layer. Continue making layers of the four colours in rotation until all the eggs are used. Put the dish into an oven preheated to 170°C (325°F or Mark 3) and bake for 30 minutes.

The dessert is served cut into slices, sprinkled with orange flower water, and decorated with pomegranate seeds.

PIERRE DE LUNE
LE NOUVEAU CUISINIER

Plum Custard

Oeufs à l'Anglaise

To serve 8 to 10

½ litre	plums preserved in syrup	7 oz
18	eggs	18
	salt	
1 tsp	ground cinnamon	1 tsp
200 g	sugar	7 oz
100 g	candied citrus peel, diced	3½ oz
100 g	raisins	3½ oz
125 g	macaroons, crumbled	4 oz
¼ litre	double cream	8 fl oz
1 tbsp	orange flower water	1 tbsp

Beat the eggs well, with the salt, cinnamon and sugar, and mix in the plums with their syrup, the candied peel, raisins, crumbled macaroons, and cream. Pour the mixture into a large buttered baking dish, place in a water bath, and bake in an oven preheated to 170°C (325°F or Mark 3) for 50 minutes or until the custard is just set. When the custard is done, sprinkle over the orange flower water and a spoonful of sugar and place under the grill to form a glaze.

PIERRE DE LUNE
LE NOUVEAU CUISINIER

Caramel Custard

Crème Caramel Renversée à la Vanille

The technique of caramelizing a mould is shown on page 42.

To serve 3

2	eggs	2
2	egg yolks	2
2 tsp	castor sugar	2 tsp
About ½ tsp	vanilla extract	About ½ tsp
	salt	
30 cl	milk	½ pint
	Caramel	
90 g	granulated sugar	3 oz
5 tbsp	cold water	5 tbsp
1 tsp	lemon juice	1 tsp

Put the ingredients for the caramel into a small tin-lined saucepan, and let them cook until they are a light coffee colour. Watch the caramel carefully, as it is apt to burn. When it is ready, pour it into a plain, dry, 60 cl (1 pint) soufflé mould which has straight sides and a flat bottom, and turn the mould round and round until the caramel coats it uniformly. It is a good plan to warm the mould first. Allow the caramel to become cold whilst making the custard.

Put the eggs and egg yolks into a basin with the castor sugar, vanilla extract to taste and a pinch of salt, and mix them to a cream with a wooden spoon. Heat the milk, and pour it slowly on to the egg mixture, stirring all the time. Strain the custard into the prepared mould and cover with greased paper. Steam *very* slowly for about an hour until the custard feels firm in the centre; or bake in an oven preheated to 180°C (350°F or Mark 4), with some warm water round the mould. Let the custard stand until tepid before turning it out. The pudding will have a glaze of caramel over the top, and some of the caramel will run round the sides as a sauce. Serve tepid, or chill and serve cold.

FLORENCE B. JACK
COOKERY FOR EVERY HOUSEHOLD

Alison's Orange Caramel Custard

Pudin de Naranjas

The technique of caramelizing sugar is shown on page 8.

To serve 6 to 8

250 g	sugar	8 oz
30 g	butter	1 oz
30 g	flour	1 oz
6	eggs, yolks separated from whites	6
30 cl	orange juice	½ pint

Caramelize 100 g (3½ oz) of the sugar in a heavy pan. Pour the caramel into a 90 cl (1½ pint), round, ovenproof glass dish, and tip the dish so that the bottom and sides are evenly coated with the caramel. Cream the butter with the remaining sugar. Add the flour and mix well. Beat the egg yolks very well, and add them to the butter mixture, then add the orange juice. Beat the egg whites until stiff and fold them into the mixture. Pour the mixture into the caramel-lined dish, set the dish in a pan of hot water and bake in an oven preheated to 180°C (350°F or Mark 4) for 1 hour. Turn the dessert out on to a serving dish so that the caramel glaze is on top. Serve the custard hot and, if you wish, flaming with brandy or rum.

HELEN BROWN
HELEN BROWN'S WEST COAST COOK BOOK

Macaroon Custard

Bonet

The technique of caramelizing a mould is shown on page 42.

To serve 3 or 4

50 g	macaroons, crumbled	2 oz
4	egg yolks	4
100 g	sugar	3½ oz
1 tbsp	cocoa	1 tbsp
1 tbsp	rum	1 tbsp
¼ litre	milk	8 fl oz
2 to 3 tbsp	water	2 to 3 tbsp

In a mixing bowl, beat the egg yolks with 4 tablespoons of the sugar. When the mixture is pale and creamy, add the crumbled macaroons, the cocoa, rum and milk, beating with a whisk until all the ingredients are well blended.

Dissolve the remaining sugar in the water, and cook over a moderate heat until the sugar caramelizes. Coat the base and sides of a 60 cl (1 pint) pudding mould with the caramel, then pour in the custard mixture. Put the mould into a pan filled with very hot, almost boiling water to come half way up the height of the mould. Cook in a preheated, 170°C (325°F or Mark 3) oven for 1 hour. Take care that the water does not boil.

When the custard is set, remove it from the oven, set it aside for 10 minutes, then unmould it on to a plate. The custard can be served hot or cold.

LAURA GRAS PORTINARI
CUCINA E VINI DEL PIEMONTE E DELLA VALLE D'AOSTA

Special Coconut Custard

To make the coconut milk called for in this recipe, grate the flesh of a coconut into a bowl and add about 60 cl (1 pint) of boiling water. Stir well, allow to stand for at least 30 minutes, then strain and squeeze through muslin. The technique of caramelizing a mould is shown on page 42.

To serve 6 to 8

½ litre	thick coconut milk	18 fl oz
150 g	brown sugar	5 oz
4 tbsp	water	4 tbsp
6	egg yolks	6
4	egg whites, lightly beaten	4
200 g	castor sugar	7 oz
1 tbsp	grated lime or lemon rind	1 tbsp

In a saucepan, dissolve the brown sugar in the water and cook the mixture over a moderate heat until it browns or caramelizes. Evenly line a 1 litre (1¾ pint) mould with three-quarters of the hot caramelized syrup, and set the mould aside. Stir the coconut milk into the remaining caramelized syrup. Place this over a low heat and stir continuously until all the caramel has dissolved. Set aside.

Mix the egg yolks and beaten whites and beat them lightly to mix them thoroughly. Add the castor sugar and grated lime or lemon rind. Then add the coconut milk mixture and mix well. Strain through cheesecloth or muslin and pour into the caramel-lined mould. Place the mould in a pan, filled with hot water to come half way up the sides of the mould, and cook slowly in an oven, preheated to 150°C (300°F or Mark 2), without allowing the water to boil. After about 1½ hours' cooking, place the mould under a very hot grill to brown the top. Cool and unmould before serving.

HELEN OROSA DEL ROSARIO (EDITOR)
MARIA Y. OROSA: HER LIFE AND WORK

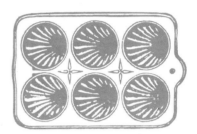

Old-Fashioned Cinnamon Custard

Lattaiolo

To serve 6

1.25 litres	milk	2 pints
	salt	
1	small piece lemon peel	1
1	small piece vanilla (pod or stick)	1
2	eggs	2
6	egg yolks	6
2 tbsp	flour	2 tbsp
	grated nutmeg	
½ tsp	ground cinnamon	½ tsp
100 g	icing sugar	3½ oz

Put the milk in a saucepan, along with a pinch of salt, the lemon peel, and vanilla, then set the saucepan on a medium heat. When the mixture reaches boiling point, reduce the heat and simmer very slowly for 30 minutes. Using a wooden spoon, keep removing the skin that forms on top. Remove the saucepan from the heat and let the milk cool completely.

Preheat the oven to 150°C (300°F or Mark 2). Place the eggs and egg yolks in a bowl, then add the flour and whisk very well. Add a pinch of nutmeg and the cinnamon. When the milk is cool, pour it into the bowl and mix thoroughly. Pass the contents of the bowl through a piece of cheesecloth into another bowl. Butter a 23 × 13 × 7 cm (9 × 5 × 2¾ inch) loaf tin and pour in the contents of the bowl. Bake in the preheated oven for 40 to 50 minutes, then remove from the oven and allow the custard to cool for 1 hour.

Cover the loaf tin with aluminium foil and place in the refrigerator for at least 4 hours, then unmould the custard on to a serving dish, sift the icing sugar over the top, and serve.

GIULIANO BUGIALLI
THE FINE ART OF ITALIAN COOKING

Chocolate Cream

Suave

To serve 8

250 g	butter	8 oz
250 g	bitter chocolate, grated	8 oz
250 g	castor sugar	8 oz
1 tbsp	flour	1 tbsp
5	eggs	5
	crème anglaise, flavoured with coffee (*page 166*)	

Melt the butter and grated chocolate over a low heat without letting them boil. When the chocolate is completely melted and very smooth, add the sugar.

Mix the flour with the eggs, add to the chocolate, and beat the mixture with a small whisk, as you would for an omelette. Line a 90 cl (1½ pint) mould with buttered paper. Pour in the chocolate mixture and cook for about 1¼ hours in a bain-marie on top of the stove or in an oven preheated to 190°C (375°F or Mark 5). Refrigerate the pudding overnight. Unmould and serve cold with the coffee-flavoured *crème anglaise*.

LE PETITS PLATS ET LES GRANDS

Quince Blancmange

For instructions on cooking sugar syrup to the thread stage, see page 8.

To serve 8

1 kg	ripe quinces, peeled and cored	2 to 2½ lb
1.75 to 2 litres	water	3 to 3½ pints
350 g	castor sugar	12 oz
40 g	leaf gelatine, soaked in about 4 tbsp cold water	1½ oz
30 cl	double cream	½ pint

Put the quinces into a saucepan with the water, and simmer them gently until they begin to disintegrate but are not reduced to a pulp. Strain the quince liquor through a jelly bag into another pan, discarding the quince pulp. Add the sugar

and stir the mixture over a brisk heat, boiling it until it reaches the thread stage. Skim it carefully. Add the gelatine and stir until dissolved. Pour the mixture into a basin, allow to cool until tepid, and stir in the cream. Continue stirring until the mixture is nearly cold, then rinse out a 2½ litre (4½ pint) jelly mould with cold water. Pour in the blancmange, and refrigerate until it is quite cold and set. To serve the blancmange, turn it out of the mould on to a fancy dish.

OSCAR TSCHIRKY
THE COOK BOOK BY "OSCAR" OF THE WALDORF

Almond Blancmange

Blanc-manger aux Amandes

The technique of peeling almonds is shown on page 12.

To serve 5

250 g	almonds, including 5 bitter ones, peeled	8 oz
10 cl	cold water	4 fl oz
10 cl	milk	4 fl oz
250 g	sugar	8 oz
21 g	leaf gelatine	¾ oz
½ litre	double cream	18 fl oz

In a mortar, pound the almonds as finely as possible, adding the water little by little. Then add the milk, and continue crushing the almonds by rotating the pestle. Put this almond milk into a saucepan, along with the sugar. Heat the mixture gently for 2 to 3 minutes over a low heat, taking care not to let it reach the boil.

Remove the pan from the heat. Place a cloth napkin over a large bowl and pour the mixture little by little into the napkin. Twist the napkin tightly in order to extract all of the almond milk. Melt the gelatine in a small pan over a low heat with 20 cl (7 fl oz) of water. Cook for a few minutes and skim off any froth or scum that forms. Combine the melted gelatine with the almond milk mixture.

Whip the cream until it stands in firm peaks. Allow the almond milk mixture to cool until it is tepid: at this point, and no sooner, blend in the whipped cream. Pour the mixture into an oiled 1.25 litre (2 pint) mould and leave in a cool place, or refrigerator, for about 5 hours.

To serve, unmould the blancmange (*page 45*).

J. B. REBOUL
LA CUISINIÈRE PROVENÇALE

French Flummery

This recipe is from a book published anonymously in 1747, but which is generally attributed to the English cookery writer of that period, Hannah Glasse.

To serve 6

90 cl	double cream	1½ pints
About 90 g	sugar	About 3 oz
21 g	leaf gelatine, softened in 3 to 4 tbsp water	¾ oz
1 tbsp each	rose water and orange flower water	1 tbsp each

Place the cream in a saucepan and boil gently over a low heat for 15 minutes, stirring all the time. Remove from the heat, sweeten to taste with sugar, add the gelatine and stir until dissolved. Add the rose water and orange flower water. Strain the mixture into a 1.25 litre (2 pint) mould. Put in the refrigerator for about 1½ hours or until set. Unmould the flummery on to a serving dish and arrange baked pears around it if desired. Serve with cream.

THE ART OF COOKERY, MADE PLAIN AND EASY

Fresh Apple Mousse

To serve 8

10	large cooking apples, peeled, cored and sliced approximately 1 cm (½ inch) thick	10
100 g	sugar	3½ oz
15 to 20 cl	water	6 fl oz
2 to 3 tbsp	lemon juice	2 to 3 tbsp
15 g	powdered gelatine, dissolved in 5 tbsp hot water	½ oz
2 tbsp	rum	2 tbsp
40 cl	double cream, whipped	¾ pint

Place the apples in a saucepan with the sugar, water and lemon juice. Cook for 10 to 12 minutes or until the apples reach the consistency of a thick apple sauce, stirring frequently to avoid burning. Remove the pan from the heat.

Add the dissolved gelatine to the cooked apple mixture and beat it well with a whisk or an electric mixer. Pour the mixture into a bowl and place it in the refrigerator or over cold water, stirring from time to time to accelerate cooling. When the mixture is cold and starts to set, fold in the rum and the whipped cream. Pour into 8 champagne glasses, chill for approximately 1 hour, or until set, and serve very cold.

DOMINIQUE D'ERMO
THE CHEF'S DESSERT COOKBOOK

Wine and Lemon Cream

Berliner Luft

To serve 4

15 cl	wine	6 fl oz
1	lemon, rind grated	1
15 g	leaf gelatine, dissolved in 10 cl (4 fl oz) hot water	½ oz
4	eggs	4
5 tbsp	lemon juice	5 tbsp
1 tbsp	cognac	1 tbsp
¼ litre	double cream, whipped	8 fl oz

Add the wine and the lemon rind to the dissolved gelatine. Whisk the eggs in a bain-marie over hot but not boiling water, until they begin to thicken slightly. Remove from the heat. Strain the gelatine mixture into the eggs, and add the lemon juice and the cognac. Beat the mixture until it is cold. Finally, fold in the whipped cream. Serve in glasses and garnish with macaroons or wafers.

GRETE WILLINSKY
KOCHBUCH DER BÜCHERGILDE

Strawberry Cream

To serve 4

250 g	strawberries, hulled	8 oz
60 g	sugar	2 oz
2 tbsp	lemon juice	2 tbsp
15 g	leaf gelatine, soaked in 4 tbsp cold water	½ oz
10 cl	milk	4 fl oz
30 cl	double cream, chilled	½ pint

Pass the strawberries through a nylon sieve into a bowl and add the sugar and lemon juice. In a saucepan, over a low heat, dissolve the gelatine in the milk, then strain it into the strawberry pulp. Whip the cream and blend it with the strawberry mixture. Mix together thoroughly, pour into a 1 litre (1¾ pint) mould. Leave the mould in ice, or in a refrigerator until wanted, then turn out and serve.

COL. A. F. KENNEY-HERBERT (WYVERN)
FIFTY DINNERS

Bavarian Cream Perfect Love

A chocolate cream is made by melting 90 g (3 oz) plain chocolate in the milk; a coffee cream by substituting freshly made strong coffee for the milk.

To serve 8 to 10

400 g	sugar	14 oz
8	egg yolks	8
45 cl	milk	16 fl oz
6	cloves	6
15 g	powdered gelatine, soaked in 4 tbsp cold water	½ oz
40 cl	double cream, whipped	¾ pint
2	lemons, rind grated	2

In a bowl, beat the sugar and egg yolks until the mixture is lemon-coloured. Heat the milk with the cloves. When the milk reaches the boil, remove the cloves and slowly add the milk to the egg yolks and sugar, stirring or whisking. Put this mixture in a saucepan over a very low heat. With a wooden spoon stir it continuously until the spoon remains thickly covered. Do not allow the mixture to boil. Remove it from the heat and pour it over the soaked gelatine. Stir in the same direction until the gelatine is completely dissolved, then strain and stir from time to time until it is cool. When the mixture begins to thicken, fold in the whipped cream with the grated lemon rind. Pour the mixture into a lightly oiled 1.75 litre (3 pint) mould and place in the refrigerator for 4 hours. Unmould on to a serving dish.

ALICE B. TOKLAS
THE ALICE B. TOKLAS COOK BOOK

Raspberry Cream

Crème Celesta

To serve 6 to 8

¼ litre	puréed raspberries, flavoured with 1 tbsp kirsch or maraschino	8 fl oz
20 cl	cold 22° Baumé sugar syrup (*page 9*)	7 fl oz
10	egg yolks	10
1	vanilla pod	1
30 cl	double cream	½ pint
60 g	castor sugar	2 oz

Pour the syrup into a medium-sized well-tinned copper saucepan placed inside a larger pan of simmering water. Add the egg yolks and beat well. Add the vanilla pod and cook, stirring constantly until the mixture is smooth and glossy. When the mixture has the consistency of a hollandaise sauce remove the vanilla pod. Transfer the mixture to an enamelled bowl and whisk until it cools.

Add the raspberry purée and pour the cream into individual cups or ramekins, filling to two-thirds full. Chill in the refrigerator for 1 hour. Whip the cream with the sugar. Fill the cups or ramekins to the top with the sweetened cream and chill again in the refrigerator until ready to serve.

ÉDOUARD NIGNON
LES PLAISIRS DE LA TABLE

Honeycomb Cream

The name of this dessert derives from its honeycomb texture.

When flavoured with lemon, honeycomb cream is delicious as a sweet in its own right. Alternatively it may be flavoured with a vanilla pod, to make a perfect accompaniment to any of the berry fruits, which can be piled high on a fruit stand as a foil to the cream. When served with a real egg custard into which a little whipped cream has been folded at the last minute, it becomes a really exotic dessert. It is best served on the same day it is made.

To flavour with vanilla, add a vanilla pod to the milk at least 30 minutes before you bring it to the boil. Remove the pod before pouring the milk on to the egg yolk mixture.

To serve 6 to 8

20 cl	single cream	7 fl oz
1	lemon, rind grated, juice strained	1
40 cl	milk	¾ pint
3	large eggs, yolks separated from whites	3
60 g	sugar	2 oz
20 g	leaf gelatine, soaked in 4 tbsp cold water	¾ oz

Add the grated lemon rind to the cream and milk. Bring these slowly to the boil over a low heat, thus allowing time for the lemon flavour to infuse into the liquid.

In a bowl, whisk together the egg yolks, sugar and lemon juice, and add the soaked gelatine. Whisking briskly, pour on the heated milk and cream.

Now stand the bowl in a sink of cold water, taking care that no water gets into the cream. Stir it from time to time as it cools, keeping the cream at the sides well-stirred into the rest, since the sides of the bowl is where the cream will set first.

While the cream is still cooling, whisk the egg whites until they just stand in peaks. Carefully, but fully, incorporate the egg whites into the now cold, but not set, cream.

Pour the mixture into a wetted 90 cl (1½ pint) mould or soufflé dish. Leave, until you need it, in a cool place like a pantry or cellar. Try not to put this pudding into a refrigerator unless the weather, or your kitchen, is very warm. All gelatine sweets are better if they are not refrigerated as they can turn rubbery if they are left too cold for more than a few hours.

MICHAEL SMITH
FINE ENGLISH COOKERY

Mocha Mousse with Tia Maria Sauce

The technique of making custard is shown on page 38.

Whenever a sauce should be clear, as in this recipe, arrowroot is preferable to cornflour. But cornflour may be used if arrowroot is not available. Kahlua, or any other coffee liqueur, may be used instead of Tia Maria.

To serve 8		
35 cl	strong coffee	12 fl oz
6	egg yolks	6
150 g	granulated sugar	5 oz
30 g	leaf gelatine	1 oz
10 cl	cold water	4 fl oz
90 cl	double cream	1½ pints

Tia Maria sauce		
4 tbsp	Tia Maria liqueur	4 tbsp
¾ litre	strong coffee	1¼ pints
300 g	sugar	10 oz
2 tbsp	arrowroot	2 tbsp
4 tbsp	cold water	4 tbsp

Make a soft custard with the egg yolks, sugar and coffee. Soften the gelatine in the cold water and add it to the custard. Stir and cool. Whip the cream and fold it into the custard. Pour into a 1.75 litre (3 pint) melon-shaped mould and chill.

To make the sauce, heat the coffee with the sugar. Stir the arrowroot into the cold water and add to the coffee mixture. Simmer and stir until thickened. Add the Tia Maria and chill.

Unmould the mousse and pour the Tia Maria sauce over the mousse just before serving.

JOSÉ WILSON (EDITOR)
HOUSE AND GARDEN NEW COOKBOOK

Cold Lemon Soufflé

If you like, you can decorate the top of the soufflé with swirls of piped whipped cream and press some chopped toasted nuts around the exposed sides.

To serve 4 or 5		
4	large lemons, rind finely grated, juice strained	4
4	eggs	4
15 g	powdered gelatine	½ oz
4 tbsp	cold water	4 tbsp
200 g	castor sugar	7 oz
30 cl	double cream	½ pint

Around a 14 cm (5¾ inch) soufflé dish (measured across the top), fit a standing collar of greaseproof paper to come at least 7.5 cm (3 inches) above the rim. Select two bowls, one larger than the other, and a saucepan over which the larger bowl will fit securely. Pour 5 to 7.5 cm (2 to 3 inches) water into the saucepan and put it on to a medium heat. Make quite sure that the smaller bowl is perfectly clean and dry.

Separate the eggs, dropping the yolks into the larger bowl and the whites into the smaller one. In a cup, sprinkle the gelatine over the cold water and leave to soften.

Add the sugar to the egg yolks. Fit the bowl over the pan of water, which should be barely simmering. Whisk the egg yolk mixture vigorously until it is thick and light, and leaves a trail on the surface when the whisk is lifted. Gradually whisk in the lemon juice and continue to whisk until the mixture thickens again. This time it will just manage to hold a trail on the surface. Take the pan off the heat and remove the bowl.

Stand the cup containing the softened gelatine in the pan of hot water; dissolve the gelatine, stirring occasionally. Meanwhile, continue to whisk the egg yolk mixture until just lukewarm. When the gelatine has completely dissolved, remove the cup from the water. Allow it to cool slightly. Whisk the gelatine into the egg yolk mixture. Fold in the lemon rind.

Whisk the cream until a trail just holds its shape on the surface, being careful not to let it get too stiff, or it will be difficult to fold in. The texture should be about the same as that of the egg mixture.

Make sure your whisk is perfectly clean and dry. Whisk the egg whites until they hold the shape of floppy peaks. With a large metal spoon or spatula, fold the cream into the egg yolk mixture, followed by the beaten egg whites, working as lightly and quickly as possible.

Stand the prepared soufflé dish on a plate. Pour in the soufflé mixture, taking care not to dislodge or crumple the paper collar. Leave it to firm slightly for 15 to 20 minutes before transferring the dish to the refrigerator. Chill the soufflé for 2 to 3 hours until firmly set. Just before serving, peel off the paper collar and decorate if desired.

ROBERT CARRIER
THE ROBERT CARRIER COOKERY COURSE

Striped Bavarian Cream

A striped Bavarian cream is made by alternating layers of vanilla cream with layers of cream of a contrasting flavour and colour. The strawberry cream used here can be replaced by a cream prepared in the same way using puréed raspberries, or any other red-coloured fruit, or dried apricots, soaked, cooked and puréed through a food mill. To make a coffee-flavoured cream, follow the instructions for vanilla cream, but infuse the milk with 30g (1 oz) freshly ground coffee, mixed with just enough boiling water to make a smooth paste and strained through several thicknesses of muslin.

To serve 12

Strawberry cream

350 g	strawberries, rubbed through a fine nylon sieve to yield about 30 cl ($\frac{1}{2}$ pint) purée	12 oz
250 g	castor sugar	8 oz
15 cl	water	$\frac{1}{4}$ pint
15 g	powdered gelatine, dissolved in 3 tbsp water	$\frac{1}{2}$ oz
$\frac{1}{2}$	lemon, juice strained	$\frac{1}{2}$
30 cl	double cream, whipped to soft peaks	$\frac{1}{2}$ pint

Vanilla cream

175 g	castor sugar	6 oz
6	egg yolks	6
	salt	
40 cl	milk, brought to the boil, and infused for 10 minutes with a vanilla pod, or mixed with 1 tsp vanilla extract	$\frac{3}{4}$ pint
21 g	powdered gelatine, dissolved in 3 tbsp water	$\frac{3}{4}$ oz
40 cl	double cream, whipped to soft peaks with 30 g (1 oz) castor sugar	$\frac{3}{4}$ pint

First prepare the strawberry cream. Make a heavy syrup by boiling the sugar in the water over a medium heat for 1 to 2 minutes. Off the heat, add the gelatine, stirring until it dissolves completely. Add the lemon juice to the strawberry purée. Pour in the warm syrup, stirring until thoroughly blended. Set the mixture aside to cool while you prepare the vanilla cream. As soon as the strawberry purée begins to set, fold in the whipped cream.

Using a wooden spoon, make the vanilla cream by blending together the sugar, egg yolks and a small pinch of salt in a heavy saucepan over a very low heat. When the mixture becomes quite smooth, gradually stir in the milk, then add the gelatine. Stirring all the time, keep the mixture on the heat until it coats the spoon, but do not allow it to boil. Transfer the vanilla cream to a bowl and cool by stirring over ice. As soon as the mixture begins to set, fold in the whipped cream.

Choose a 2 litre ($3\frac{1}{2}$ pint) mould, preferably a funnel mould, and brush the inside with sweet almond oil, or rinse the mould in iced water. Fill the mould with alternate layers of the two creams, taking care not to add a new layer until the preceding one has set properly. Cover the mould and place it in the refrigerator for about 5 hours.

To serve, dip the mould quickly into warm water, and wipe it dry. Unmould the dessert on to a serving dish, which may be covered with a folded napkin or a paper doily, if you like, or into a shallow glass dish.

PROSPER MONTAGNÉ
LAROUSSE GASTRONOMIQUE

Queen Mab's Pudding

Preserved ginger may be substituted for the glacé cherries, and blanched, chopped pistachio nuts for the candied orange peel. Currants may also take the place of the cherries, but must be steamed for 15 minutes before being used. Ginger syrup, or a sweetened purée of raspberries, strawberries or other fresh fruit may be served as a sauce.

To serve 6

6	bitter almonds, blanched and lightly crushed	6
1	lemon, rind very thinly peeled	1
90 cl	double cream, or 60 cl (1 pint) milk and 30 cl ($\frac{1}{2}$ pint) double cream	$1\frac{1}{2}$ pints
150 g	sugar	5 oz
6	egg yolks, well beaten	6
30 g	leaf gelatine, soaked in 3 to 4 tbsp water	1 oz
75 g	glacé cherries	$2\frac{1}{2}$ oz
60 g	candied orange peel, cut into shreds	2 oz

Put the bitter almonds and lemon rind into a stew-pan with 60 cl (1 pint) of cream or milk. Stir over a very low heat until the mixture is on the point of boiling, and the flavour of the lemon and almonds is well drawn out. Strain through a fine strainer or a muslin cloth into another stew-pan, and add the sugar and 30 cl ($\frac{1}{2}$ pint) of cream. Bring just to the boil. Turn the heat to low, then quickly stir in the beaten egg yolks.

Stirring constantly and carefully to prevent curdling, cook until the mixture becomes the thickness of a good custard. Add the soaked gelatine, stir until dissolved, and strain the mixture into a bowl. Continue stirring until nearly cold. Mix in the cherries and orange peel. Rub a drop of oil over a 1.25 litre (2 pint) mould, pour in the mixture, and leave to set in the refrigerator for about $1\frac{1}{2}$ hours. Unmould and serve.

MARY JEWRY (EDITOR)
WARNE'S MODEL COOKERY AND HOUSEKEEPING BOOK

Cream Mousse Moulds

Les Crémets d'Angers

	To serve 4	
¾ litre	double cream	1¼ pints
4	egg whites, stiffly beaten	4
30 g	castor sugar, vanilla-flavoured, if desired	1 oz

Whip ½ litre (18 fl oz) cream until stiff. Gently fold in the egg whites with the whisk, then pour the mixture into little perforated moulds lined with cheesecloth. Leave to drain in a cool place for 5 to 6 hours. Unmould carefully on to a serving dish, coat the cream mousses with the remaining unwhipped cream, sprinkle them with sugar and serve.

AUSTIN DE CROZE
LES PLATS RÉGIONAUX DE FRANCE

Devonshire Junket

The authentic Devonshire junket is topped with clotted cream. If unavailable, use lightly whipped double cream.

Junket is an English version of those curd and cream dishes that the French still make in such delicious variety (*crémets d'Angers, maingaux, coeurs à la crème*). Like their *fromage frais*, the junket is produced by curdling warm milk with rennet. Then it is left to set to a smooth jelly. The curd is not broken up and drained of whey as it would be in France, and as it once was in England (junket derives from old Norman French, *jonquet*, a little basket made from *jonques* or rushes and used for draining cheeses until recent times). When we had the idea of leaving the curd alone in its smoothness, I do not know. In *Food and Drink in Britain*, C. Anne Wilson quotes the earliest recipe she can find, from 1653, in which the junket was not drained, but eaten with cream and cinnamon, just as in this recipe. The junket will taste salty if your teaspoon of rennet was too generous.

	To serve 4 to 6	
60 cl	Channel Island milk	1 pint
2 tsp	sugar	2 tsp
2 tbsp	brandy	2 tbsp
1 tsp	rennet	1 tsp
125 g	clotted cream	4 oz
	ground cinnamon or grated nutmeg	

In a saucepan, bring the milk slowly to blood heat—if you are not used to judging this, use a thermometer; it is surprising how hot a liquid at 37°C (98.4°F) feels. Meanwhile, mix the sugar and the brandy in a 90 cl (1½ pint) china bowl in which you intend to serve the junket, and put it in a convenient place in the kitchen, where it can stay until required (junket sets best at room temperature). Pour the warmed milk into the bowl, then stir in the rennet gently. Do not disturb until the junket is firmly set—up to 2 hours. If the clotted cream is stiff, mix it with a little fresh cream, so that it can be spread over the surface without disturbing it. Sprinkle the cream with ground cinnamon or grated nutmeg.

JANE GRIGSON
ENGLISH FOOD

Everlasting Syllabub

In their heyday syllabubs were regarded as refreshments to be offered at card parties, ball suppers and at public entertainments, rather than just as a pudding for lunches and dinners. These syllabubs can be made at least 2 days in advance; they will keep well in a cool place.

	To serve 4 to 6	
1	lemon, rind finely peeled, juice strained	1
10 cl	white wine or sherry	4 fl oz
2 tbsp	brandy	2 tbsp
60 g	sugar	2 oz
30 cl	double cream	½ pint
	grated nutmeg	

The day before the syllabub is to be made, put the lemon rind and juice in a bowl with the wine and brandy and leave overnight. Next day, strain the wine and lemon mixture into a large and deep bowl. Add the sugar and stir until it has dissolved. Pour in the cream slowly, stirring all the time. Grate in a little nutmeg. Now whisk the mixture until it thickens and will hold a soft peak on the whisk. The process may take 5 minutes, it may take as long as 15. It depends on the cream, the temperature and the method of whisking. Unless dealing with a large quantity of cream, an electric mixer can be perilous. A couple of seconds too long and the cream is a ruined and grainy mess. For a small amount, a wire whisk is perfectly satisfactory and just as quick as an electric beater. The important point is to learn to recognise the moment at which the whisking process is complete.

When the cream is ready, spoon it into 10 syllabub or custard cups or sherry glasses which should be of very small capacity 5 to 7 cl (2 to 2½ fl oz) but filled to overflowing. Once in the glasses the cream will not spoil nor sink nor separate. A tiny sprig of rosemary or a little twist of lemon peel can be stuck into each little filled glass. Keep the syllabubs in a cool place—not in the refrigerator—until you serve them.

ELIZABETH DAVID
SYLLABUBS AND FRUIT FOOLS

A West Country Syllabub

The original instructions in this recipe, which dates from 1800, called for the bowl to be filled with warm milk straight from the cow. If desired, 60 cl (1 pint) white wine can be substituted for the mixture of port and sherry.

To serve 6 to 8

30 cl	port	½ pint
30 cl	medium sherry	½ pint
2 to 3 tbsp	castor sugar	2 to 3 tbsp
60 cl	milk	1 pint
15 cl	double cream, whipped	¼ pint

Pour the port and sherry into a 1.75 litre (3 pint) glass or pottery bowl: the bowl should be about one-third full. Stir in the sugar according to taste. Add the milk and stir a little. Leave to stand for about 20 minutes, or until the curd separates from the wine. Pour into individual glasses, spooning the curd on top, and put a spoonful of whipped cream on each.

ELISABETH AYRTON
THE COOKERY OF ENGLAND

Moulded Poached Meringue

Oeufs à la Neige Moulés

Moulded poached meringue is often served floating on a lake of chilled custard or crème anglaise *(recipe, page 166). To make the fruit purée called for in this recipe, use about 250 g (8 oz) raspberries, 150 g (5 oz) strawberries, and 100 g (3½ oz) redcurrants. Pass the fruit through a nylon sieve, and sweeten it to taste with about 100 g (3½ oz) sugar.*

To serve 4

4	egg whites	4
125 g	vanilla sugar, or sugar flavoured with orange or lemon rind	4 oz
½ litre	purée of redcurrants, raspberries and strawberries	18 fl oz

Beat the egg whites until stiff. Continuing to beat, gradually add the flavoured sugar in a fine stream. Liberally butter a 90 cl (1½ pint) plain or fluted funnel mould and sprinkle it with sugar. Fill the mould with the meringue mixture to within 2.5 cm (1 inch) of the brim. Bake in a water bath in an oven preheated to 190°C (350°F or Mark 4) for 15 minutes, or until firm to the touch and the meringue shrinks away from the side of the mould. Remove from the oven and let the meringue rest in a draught-free place for a few minutes. Unmould it on to a plate and leave to cool. Serve with the cold fruit purée.

JEAN DE GOUY
LA CUISINE ET LA PÂTISSERIE BOURGEOISES

Syllabub for Six

Recipes for syllabub vary in detail from place to place, and many include egg whites in the ingredients. This one does not and is said to be all the lighter for it.

To serve 6

15 cl	medium-dry white wine	¼ pint
2 tsp	very finely grated lemon rind	2 tsp
90 g	castor sugar	3 oz
2 tbsp	lemon juice	2 tbsp
30 cl	double cream	½ pint

Put all but the cream into a bowl and set aside for not less than 3 hours. Better still, leave overnight. Then add the cream and whip and beat and beat and whip until the mixture stands unaided in soft, seductive peaks. It will keep like this for several days, but never lasts that long! It looks its best when piled high into wine or sundae glasses.

JOYCE DOUGLAS
OLD PENDLE RECIPES

Snow Eggs

Oeufs à la Neige

For instructions on making a crème anglaise, *see page 38.*

To serve 6

8	eggs, yolks separated from whites	8
500 g	icing sugar, sifted	1 lb
1 litre	milk	1¾ pints
350 g	castor sugar	12 oz
1	vanilla pod, split lengthwise	1

Bring the milk to the boil with half of the castor sugar and the vanilla pod. Leave to infuse for about 10 minutes, then remove the vanilla pod.

Beat the egg whites until they stand stiffly in peaks, then gradually beat in the icing sugar. Scoop up the egg white mixture a spoonful at a time, rounding it into egg shapes with another spoon, and poach the snow eggs in the simmering milk, turning them so that they cook for about 1 minute on each side. The number of snow eggs, or poached meringues, you make will depend on the size of the spoons you use. When the poached meringues are firm, drain them and arrange them in a deep dish. Reserve the hot milk.

Make a *crème anglaise* with the egg yolks, the remaining castor sugar, and the reserved milk. Pour it into the serving dish, around, but not over, the meringues. The meringues should float on the sauce. Serve warm or cold.

RAYMOND OLIVER
LA CUISINE

Cheese Desserts

White Cheese Pudding

Pudding au Fromage Blanc

The pudding can be flavoured according to taste with grated orange or lemon rind, vanilla orange flower water, or a liqueur of one's choice.

To serve 4 to 6

250 g	curd cheese, sieved, or *ricotta*	8 oz
125 g	sugar	4 oz
10 cl	double cream	4 fl oz
	salt	
5	eggs, yolks separated from whites	5
2 tbsp	seedless raisins	2 tbsp
5 or 6	macaroons, finely crushed	5 or 6
About 40 cl	puréed raspberries or apricots, or a mixture of raspberries, red currants and strawberries	About ¾ pint

In a large bowl, combine the cheese, sugar, cream and a pinch of salt. Whisk together well, incorporating the egg yolks, one by one. Flavour according to taste. Beat until the mixture is light, then add the raisins and crushed macaroons.

In another bowl, beat the egg whites until stiff then fold them carefully into the cheese mixture. Pour into a well-buttered and floured 1 litre (1¾ pint) savarin mould and cook in an oven preheated to 170°C (325°F or Mark 3) for 45 minutes, or until the pudding puffs up and is firm to the touch at the centre. Turn the pudding out on to a heated dish and serve it immediately with a fruit purée passed separately.

JEAN DE GOUY
LA CUISINE ET LA PÂTISSERIE BOURGEOISES

Italian Cheesecake

Torta di Ricotta alla Casalinga

To serve 4 to 6

500 g	best *ricotta* cheese	1 lb
	salt	
4 tbsp	plain flour	4 tbsp
4 tbsp	castor sugar	4 tbsp
2	eggs, separated, whites stiffly beaten	2
1	orange, rind grated	1
60 g	raisins, soaked in warm water and thoroughly drained	2 oz
30 g	crystallized fruit, roughly chopped	1 oz
	icing sugar	

Using a wooden spoon, stir together in a bowl the *ricotta*, a pinch of salt, the flour, castor sugar, egg yolks and orange rind. Continue stirring until thoroughly blended, then add the raisins, the crystallized fruit and fold in the beaten egg whites. Butter and flour a 20 cm (8 inch) cake tin, pour the mixture into it and place in an oven preheated to 180°C (350°F or Mark 4) for about 1 hour. When the cheesecake is thoroughly cooled, turn it out and sprinkle with icing sugar.

MARIÚ SALVATORI DE ZULIANI
LA CUCINA DI VERSILIA E GARFAGNANA

Cottage Cheese Pudding

Ofenschlupfer mit Quark

To serve 6

300 g	cottage cheese, sieved	10 oz
	salt	
3 tbsp	soured cream	3 tbsp
75 g	castor sugar	2½ oz
40 g	sultanas, steeped in water and drained	1½ oz
4 or 5	soft bread rolls, crusts removed, thinly sliced	4 or 5
350 g	apples, peeled, cored and thinly sliced (optional)	12 oz
2	eggs	2
15 to 25 cl	milk	5 to 8 fl oz
1 to 2 tsp	grated lemon rind	1 to 2 tsp
30 g	butter, cut into small pieces	1 oz

Mix the cheese with a pinch of salt, the soured cream and 40 g (1½ oz) of the sugar, then mix in the sultanas. Line the bottom of a buttered oven dish with bread slices, then pour over the cheese mixture. A layer of thinly sliced apples may be added at this stage. Cover with the remaining slices of bread. Whisk the eggs with the milk, the grated lemon rind and half of the remaining sugar, and pour the mixture over the pudding. Sprinkle on the rest of the sugar, dot with the pieces of butter, and bake in an oven preheated to 180°C (350°F or Mark 4) for about 45 minutes.

HERMINE KIEHNLE AND MARIA HÄDECKE
DAS NEUE KIEHNLE KOCHBUCH

Paskha

A traditional *paskha* is shaped in a four-sided wooden Turks-head mould that has a small opening at the narrow end to drain off any moisture. Alternatively, a large clay flowerpot about 18cm (7 inches) tall with an upper diameter of 19cm (7½ inches) can be used. The flowerpot should be smoothly lined with two or three layers of fine cheesecloth or muslin, leaving a generous overhang to fold over the top.

To serve 15 to 20

1.5 kg	curd or cottage cheese	3 lb
125 g	blanched almonds	4 oz
125 g	glacé cherries	4 oz
175 g	raisins	6 oz
250 g	unsalted butter, softened	8 oz
1 tsp	rose water or vanilla extract	1 tsp
125 g	mixed candied citrus peel	4 oz
3	eggs	3
200 g	castor sugar	7 oz
10 cl	soured cream or double cream	4 fl oz

The curd or cottage cheese must be absolutely dry before it is used. Hang it in a muslin bag for 12 hours, or place it in a colander under a heavy weight. When dry, rub the cheese through a fine sieve into a basin. Set aside some of the almonds and glacé cherries for decoration, then chop the remainder and mix them with the cheese, together with the raisins, softened butter, rose water or vanilla extract, and the mixed peel. Beat the eggs and sugar together and add them to the cheese mixture. Beat thoroughly until no lumps remain. Then stir in the cream and, using a wooden spoon, beat the mixture until it is absolutely smooth.

Pour the mixture into a 3 litre (5 pint) mould lined with fine cheesecloth or muslin. Fold the ends of the cloth over the top of the *paskha*, cover with a small plate to distribute the weight and weigh the plate down with anything heavy. Stand the mould, small end downwards, in a deep plate and refrigerate the *paskha* for another 12 hours. When the *paskha* is removed

from the refrigerator, a lot of moisture will have drained out into the plate. Undo the cheesecloth or muslin, place a flat serving dish on top of the mould and turn them over, carefully removing the mould. Decorate the *paskha* with the reserved almonds and glacé cherries and serve it with *koulitch* (a not too sweet yeast bun).

SOFKA SKIPWITH
EAT RUSSIAN

Ordinary Paskha

Paskha Obiknovennaya

"Paskha" *means Easter in Russian and it is also the name given to a traditional Easter dessert. After being decorated with the Orthodox Cross and the letters XB—"Khristos Vosk-ryesye", "Christ is Risen", it is taken to the church to be blessed. Later it is taken back home and consumed on Easter Sunday.*

To serve 20

3 kg	curd cheese	6 to 7 lb
¼ litre	soured cream	8 fl oz
200 g	unsalted butter	7 oz
2 tsp	salt	2 tsp
About 125 g	sugar	About 4 oz

Place the curd cheese in a colander; cover with muslin or cheesecloth topped with a heavy weight, and leave at room temperature for 24 hours. Press the drained curd through a sieve into a large bowl. Add the soured cream, butter, salt and sugar and mix well so that not one lump remains. More sugar may be added, to taste, if desired. Transfer the mixture into a 3.5 litre (6 pint) mould, which should be lined with fine cheesecloth. Cover with a weight and chill in the refrigerator for 24 hours. Then carefully turn the *paskha* out on to a dish.

ELENA MOLOKHOVETS
PODAROK MOLODÝM KHOZYAĬKAM

Soufflés and Puddings

Strawberry Soufflé

This is a modern version of a recipe by Antonin Carême, inventor of the classic soufflé.

The mixture is so simple that the flavour of the soufflé depends enormously on the quality of the strawberries, which should be highly perfumed. If they are not, add a little kirsch or lemon juice to the purée.

	To serve 4	
250 g	strawberries, hulled	8 oz
125 to 175g	sugar	4 to 6 oz
	kirsch or lemon juice (optional)	
5	egg whites	5
1 to 2 tbsp	icing sugar	1 to 2 tbsp

Purée the strawberries in a blender or work them through a sieve. Add about 60 to 125 g (2 to 4 oz) of the sugar, depending on their sweetness. If desired, add kirsch or lemon juice to taste. Butter the inside of a 1.5 litre (2½ pint) soufflé dish and sprinkle it with sugar, discarding the excess. Preheat the oven to 180°C (350°F or Mark 4).

Up to an hour before serving, stiffly whip the egg whites. Add about 60 g (2 oz) of the sugar, and continue beating until this meringue mixture is glossy and forms a tall peak. Stir a little meringue into the strawberry purée, mixing it well, then add the purée to the remaining meringue, folding them together as lightly as possible. Spoon the soufflé mixture into the prepared dish (the mixture should reach the top of the mould) and bake it in the preheated oven for 25 to 30 minutes or until puffed and brown. The centre of the soufflé should still be slightly concave. Sprinkle the top with the icing sugar, and serve the soufflé at once.

A sauce of fresh strawberry purée makes an excellent accompaniment to this soufflé.

ANNE WILLAN
GREAT COOKS AND THEIR RECIPES

Frangipane Soufflé

Soufflé de Frangipane

If bitter almond macaroons are not available, use 5 sweet almond macaroons, and add a few drops of almond extract to provide the bitter almond flavour. The original recipe calls for 1 tablespoon of powdered caramelized orange flowers; orange flower water may be added to the egg mixture instead.

	To serve 8	
1	whole egg	1
8	egg yolks	8
6 tbsp	water	6 tbsp
½ litre	double cream	18 fl oz
2	bitter almond macaroons	2
3	sweet almond macaroons	3
1	dried sponge finger biscuit	1
60 g	castor sugar	2 oz
5	egg whites	5

Put the whole egg and 4 of the egg yolks in a saucepan, and mix them with the water. Stir in the cream. Place the mixture over a low heat, and stir constantly until it thickens. Remove from the heat and allow to cool.

Very finely crush the macaroons and sponge finger biscuit. Add them to the cooled egg mixture along with the castor sugar. Mix together well, then add the remaining 4 egg yolks. (More egg yolks may be added if your mixture is too thick to stir easily.) Beat the egg whites stiffly, and fold them in.

Pour the soufflé mixture into a buttered 1.25 litre (2 pint) charlotte mould or soufflé dish and cook in a preheated 180°C (350°F or Mark 4) oven for about 35 minutes, or until well risen and lightly browned.

VIARD AND FOURET
LE CUISINIER ROYAL

Prune Soufflé

	To serve 4 to 6	
250 g	prunes, soaked in water overnight and drained	8 oz
30 cl	water	½ pint
125 g	castor sugar	4 oz
5	egg whites	5
	double cream, whipped	

Cook the prunes in the water for about 10 minutes, or until they are tender. Drain them, remove the stones, then chop the prunes finely and mix them with the sugar. Beat the egg whites until stiff, and stir them into the prunes with a knife. Pour the mixture into a buttered soufflé or metal charlotte dish. Bake in an oven preheated to 190°C (375°F or Mark 5) for about 10 minutes. Serve at once with whipped cream.

INGA NORBERG
GOOD FOOD FROM SWEDEN

Chocolate Soufflé

To serve 3 to 4

90 g	plain or bitter chocolate, finely grated	3 oz
4	eggs	4
3 tsp	sugar	3 tsp
1 tsp	flour	1 tsp
	castor sugar	

Break the eggs, separating the whites from the yolks, and put them into different basins. Add to the yolks the sugar, flour and chocolate, and stir these ingredients for 5 minutes. Then whisk the egg whites until they are stiff, and fold them into the yolks until the mixture is smooth and light. Butter a 15 cm (6 inch) round cake tin, put in the mixture, and bake in a moderate oven, preheated to 180°C (350°F or Mark 4), for 15 to 20 minutes. Pin a white napkin around the tin, sift some castor sugar over the top of the soufflé, and send it immediately to the table. The proper appearance of this dish depends entirely on the expedition with which it is served. If it is allowed to stand after it is taken out of the oven, it will be entirely spoiled, as it falls almost immediately.

MRS. ISABELLA BEETON
THE BOOK OF HOUSEHOLD MANAGEMENT

Normandy Soufflé

Soufflé à la Normande

To serve 4

2	apples, peeled, cored, diced, and steeped for about 2 hours in about 2 tbsp calvados sweetened with a little sugar	2
10 cl	milk	4 fl oz
40 g	castor sugar	1½ oz
1 tbsp	flour, blended with a little cold milk	1 tbsp
15 g	butter	½ oz
2	egg yolks	2
2 tbsp	calvados	2 tbsp
3	egg whites	3
1 tbsp	icing sugar	1 tbsp

Butter a 1 litre (1¾ pint) soufflé dish and dust it with sugar. Put the milk and sugar into a saucepan and bring to the boil. Add the flour, and cook over a medium heat, stirring with a wooden spoon, for a few minutes or until the mixture thickens. Off the heat, stir in the butter, egg yolks and calvados. Whisk the egg whites until they stand in stiff peaks and fold them into the mixture.

Spoon a layer of the mixture into the soufflé dish. Sprinkle over about 2 tablespoons of diced apple. Add another layer of the soufflé mixture, and continue adding alternate layers of apple and soufflé mixture, finishing with a layer of soufflé mixture. Smooth the top of the soufflé, and cook in an oven preheated to 180°C (350°F or Mark 4) for 25 to 30 minutes. Two minutes before the end of the cooking time, sprinkle the soufflé with icing sugar and raise the oven temperature to 230°C (450°F or Mark 8) to form a glaze.

PROSPER MONTAGNÉ AND A. GOTTSCHALK
MON MENU

Vanilla Soufflé

Soufflé à la Vanille

The author suggests the following variations: flavouring the soufflé with a liqueur of your choice, such as chartreuse, Grand Marnier, kirsch or curaçao; with chocolate, by adding 50 g (2 oz) melted plain chocolate; or with praline, by adding 50 g (2 oz) praline almonds (see page 13).

To serve 4

10 cl	milk	4 fl oz
30 g	castor sugar	1 oz
1	vanilla pod	1
1 tbsp	flour, mixed with a little cold milk	1 tbsp
10 g	butter	⅓ oz
2	egg yolks	2
3	egg whites	3
15 g	icing sugar	½ oz

In a small saucepan, bring the milk to the boil, along with the castor sugar and the vanilla pod (or any other flavouring of your choice). As soon as the milk reaches the boil, add the flour and milk mixture. Cook for 2 minutes, whisking constantly (a wire whisk is a vital utensil for every household!). Take the pan off the heat, remove the vanilla pod, and add the butter and egg yolks. Mix thoroughly. Beat the egg whites until they form stiff peaks, and fold them into the mixture.

Butter a 60 cl (1 pint) soufflé dish and dust it with castor sugar. Pour in the soufflé mixture and smooth the surface. Cook in an oven preheated to 180°C (350°F or Mark 4) for about 25 minutes, or until the soufflé is well risen. Two minutes before removing the soufflé from the oven, sprinkle the icing sugar over the surface to glaze it.

PROSPER MONTAGNÉ AND A. GOTTSCHALK
MON MENU

Souffléed Oranges

Oranges Soufflées

A recipe created by Paul Bocuse for his restaurant at Lyons.

To serve 4

4	large oranges	4
4	eggs, yolks separated from whites	4
4 tbsp	castor sugar	4 tbsp
1 tbsp	cointreau	1 tbsp
	icing sugar	

Cut off and set aside the tops of the oranges, and scoop out the flesh; the hollowed-out oranges will later be filled with the soufflé mixture. Finely peel the rind from the tops of the oranges, cut the rind into thin strips, and blanch them in boiling water for 5 minutes. Drain and set them aside. Squeeze the juice from the orange flesh into a small saucepan, and reduce to about 1 tablespoon over a brisk heat. In a bowl, beat the egg yolks with the sugar until thick and creamy. Add the orange rind, the juice and the cointreau. Beat the egg whites until stiff and fold them into the yolk mixture.

Fill the orange shells with the soufflé mixture and cook in a preheated oven, 230°C (450°F or Mark 8), for 10 minutes. Sprinkle with icing sugar for the last few minutes of cooking.

LES PRINCES DE LA GASTRONOMIE

Banana Soufflé Pudding

Flamèri aux Bananes

To serve 6

4	bananas, peeled, sliced, soaked in 3 to 4 tbsp of kirsch, and the mixture puréed through a sieve	4
20 cl	milk	7 fl oz
100 g	butter	3½ oz
100 g	flour	3½ oz
8	egg yolks	8
6	egg whites stiffly beaten	6
	icing sugar	

In a saucepan, bring to the boil the milk and the butter. Gradually add the flour. Working the mixture with a wooden spatula, cook over a moderate heat until the paste detaches itself from the spatula.

Remove the saucepan from the heat and very gently incorporate the egg yolks, one at a time. Stir in the banana purée,

and then fold in the stiffly beaten egg whites.

Butter an earthenware soufflé dish of appropriate size, and pour in the mixture. Cook in an oven preheated to 170°C (325°F or Mark 3) for about 25 minutes. Remove the dish from the oven, and sprinkle the top of the soufflé with sifted icing sugar. Serve immediately.

PAUL BOUILLARD
LA CUISINE AU COIN DU FEU

Moulded Chocolate Loaf with Whipped Cream

Gâteau Moulé au Chocolat, Crème Chantilly

To serve 4

90 g	bitter chocolate, broken into small pieces	3 oz
4 tbsp	water	4 tbsp
90 g	unsalted butter, softened	3 oz
3	eggs, yolks separated from whites	3
200 g	sugar	7 oz
30 g	flour	1 oz
1 tsp	vanilla extract	1 tsp
	salt	
¼ litre	double cream	8 fl oz

Stir the water and chocolate pieces together in a round-bottomed metal mixing bowl, over a low heat, until the chocolate has melted. Remove the bowl from the heat, whip in the butter, then the egg yolks, and finally 150 g (5 oz) of the sugar, the flour and half of the vanilla. If, at this point, the mixture seems to curdle or disintegrate (it is only the action of the chocolate rehardening in contact with colder ingredients), place the bowl in another bowl filled with warm water, continue stirring, and the mixture will come back together.

Beat the egg whites with a pinch of salt until they stand stiffly in peaks, gently fold about one-third of the entire volume of egg whites into the chocolate mixture, then fold in the remainder. Pour into a buttered 1 litre (1¾ pint) mould (a savarin or a decorative jelly mould with a central tube). Place the mould in a bain-marie, filled with hot water to approximately the same level as the pudding's surface, and cook in an oven preheated to 180°C (350°F or Mark 4) for 40 minutes. Leave to cool slightly and unmould on to a serving plate, leaving the mould over the pudding until serving time. Chill in the refrigerator for about 1 hour.

Whip the cream with the remaining sugar and vanilla. Serve the chilled pudding either with the whipped cream separately, or with the central well filled with the whipped cream and a ribbon of cream piped around the base.

RICHARD OLNEY
THE FRENCH MENU COOKBOOK

Chocolate Mousse

Mousse au Chocolat

The author suggests two possible flavouring additions to this mousse: either 2 tablespoons finely chopped roasted almonds, or 1 tablespoon chopped candied orange peel.

	To serve 4 to 6	
250 g	plain chocolate, broken into pieces	8 oz
30 g	butter	1 oz
4 tbsp	water	4 tbsp
5	eggs, yolks separated from whites	5
1 tbsp	rum	1 tbsp

Put the chocolate in a saucepan with the butter and water. Cook over a very low heat until the mixture becomes a smooth paste. Off the heat, work in the egg yolks, one by one, using a wooden spoon. Then add the rum.

Beat the egg whites until they stand in stiff peaks, then fold them gently into the chocolate mixture. Pour the mousse into a deep 1.25 litre (2 pint) mould and leave to chill thoroughly overnight in the refrigerator.

LA MÈRE BRAZIER
LES SECRETS DE LA MÈRE BRAZIER

Milk and Macaroon Mould

Timballa 'e Latte

	To serve 4 to 6	
¾ litre	milk, brought to the boil with a small piece of vanilla pod	1¼ pints
200 g	macaroons, rubbed through a sieve	7 oz
3	eggs	3
200 g	castor sugar	7 oz
1 to 2 tbsp	lemon juice	1 to 2 tbsp

Beat the eggs and sugar together, then, still beating, gradually add the hot milk flavoured with vanilla. Set the mixture aside for 5 minutes, stirring it from time to time with a wooden spoon and discarding the foam on the surface. Add the macaroons and finally the lemon juice. Butter a 1.25 litre (2 pint) pudding mould and pour in the milk mixture. Bake in a bain-marie in a preheated, 180°C (350°F or Mark 4) oven. To test for doneness, stick a knife into the pudding after 20 minutes. The knife should come out dry and clean. Remove the pudding from the oven and wait for 5 minutes before unmoulding it on to a round serving plate. Serve at once.

LUIGI CARNACINA AND LUIGI VERONELLI
LA BUONA VERA CUCINA ITALIANA

Almond and Pistachio Loaf

Pain des Houris

The technique of peeling nuts is demonstrated on page 12.

Served directly from the oven, this is a soufflé. Tepid, much of the body is lost, but the savours may more easily be appreciated. Cold, it is moist and compact, heavy but delicious.

	To serve 4	
125 g	shelled almonds, parboiled for 2 minutes, rubbed between towels and peeled	4 oz
60 g	shelled pistachios, parboiled for 2 minutes, rubbed between towels and peeled	2 oz
1 tbsp each	slivered strips orange and lemon rind, parboiled for a few seconds and drained	1 tbsp each
140 g	sugar	4½ oz
6 tbsp	water	6 tbsp
4 tbsp	white wine	4 tbsp
3	eggs, yolks separated from whites	3
	salt	

In a saucepan, combine the strips of orange and lemon rind with 1 tablespoon of the sugar and the water. Bring to the boil, and simmer until the liquid is almost entirely reduced and the rind is coated with a thick syrup, but remove from the heat before the sugar begins to caramelize.

Pound the almonds and pistachios together in a large mortar until well crushed into a coarse purée. Add the rind and syrup and a little of the remaining sugar, and continue pounding, adding sugar from time to time, until the mixture becomes too stiff to work easily. Continue pounding, alternating additions of wine and sugar, until the wine is used up and only 1 tablespoon of the sugar remains. Add the egg yolks and work vigorously, pounding and stirring with the pestle.

Beat the egg whites with a small pinch of the salt until they stand firmly in peaks. Fold a healthy spoonful into the mixture in the mortar, then turn the contents of the mortar into the bowl containing the remaining egg whites, and fold the two gently together.

Pour into a buttered, loaf-shaped oven dish and half immerse the dish in a larger pan containing hot water. Place in a fairly hot oven, preheated to 190°C (375°F or Mark 5), and bake for about 25 minutes, or until the centre of the pudding is firm to the touch. Sprinkle the surface with the remaining sugar before serving.

The ingredients (except for the final incorporation of the beaten egg whites) may be added progressively to a food processor with extremely rapid and satisfactory results.

RICHARD OLNEY
SIMPLE FRENCH FOOD

Paradise Pudding

To serve 4 to 6

175 g	butter	6 oz
175 g	sugar	6 oz
3	eggs	3
175 g	flour	6 oz
2 tbsp	brandy	2 tbsp
30 cl	single cream	½ pint
	castor sugar	
	glacé cherries, halved, and angelica, cut in leaves	
	custard (*page 166*)	

Beat the butter and the sugar together to a cream; add the eggs, one at a time, and beat for 5 minutes after the addition of each egg. Lightly mix in the flour, then the brandy and the cream. Butter the inside of a 1 litre (1¾ pint) mould, dredge it with castor sugar, and decorate the bottom with the glacé cherries and the angelica. Pour in the pudding mixture, and tie a cloth over the top of the mould. Put it into a pan of boiling water, taking care that the water does not get into the pudding, and boil it for 1 hour. Unmould the pudding on to a plate and serve with custard sauce.

MAY BYRON
MAY BYRON'S PUDDINGS, PASTRIES AND SWEET DISHES

Algerian Date Pudding

Gâteau Algérien

This recipe is by Dr Pierre Uhry of Neuilly-sur-Seine.

To serve 6 to 8

250 g	dates, stoned and finely chopped— 210 g (7½ oz) when stoned	8 oz
210 g	sugar	7½ oz
110 g	almonds, blanched and chopped	3¾ oz
100 g	unsalted, roasted, hulled peanuts, finely chopped	3½ oz
4	egg whites, stiffly beaten	4

Mix together the dates, sugar, almonds and peanuts. Fold this mixture into the egg whites and place in a well buttered oven dish. Cook in a cool oven, preheated to 170°C (325°F or Mark 3), for 35 to 40 minutes. Serve hot, tepid or cold.

70 MÉDECINS DE FRANCE
LE TRÉSOR DE LA CUISINE DU BASSIN MÉDITERRANÉEN

Bread and Butter Pudding

To serve 4 to 6

60 g	currants, washed and picked over	2 oz
4	very thin slices of bread, buttered	4
3	eggs	3
1	egg yolk	1
125 g	sugar	4 oz
	grated nutmeg	
60 cl	milk	1 pint

Strew a few of the currants at the bottom of a 1¼ litre (2 pint) dish. Layer the buttered bread and remaining currants alternately on top. Put the eggs and egg yolk into a basin and beat them well. Add the sugar and pinch of nutmeg. Then add the milk and stir well together. About 10 minutes before putting the pudding in the oven pour the egg mixture over the bread and butter. Cook in a water bath in a preheated 180°C (350°F or Mark 4) oven. The pudding will take 45 minutes to bake.

MRS. RUNDELL
MODERN DOMESTIC COOKERY

Saxony Pudding

Pouding Saxon

To serve 4

125 g	butter	4 oz
60 g	castor sugar	2 oz
125 g	flour	4 oz
90 g	granulated sugar	3 oz
40 cl	milk	¾ pint
5	eggs, yolks separated from whites	5
	sabayon sauce (*page 166*)	

Put the butter and the castor sugar into a basin and cream them together. Beat in the flour. Melt the granulated sugar in a small saucepan and let it colour to a light brown. Add the milk to the pan, and bring the mixture to the boil. Stir it into the butter and flour mixture by degrees. Put this mixture into a saucepan, and stir vigorously over the heat until it thickens to a paste. Take the mixture off the heat and beat in the egg yolks, one at a time. Whisk the egg whites very stiffly, and fold them into the pudding lightly and quickly. Butter a 1.25 litre (2 pint) pudding mould and pour in the mixture. Steam the pudding for about 1 hour. When it is done, turn it out and serve it with *sabayon* sauce.

M. A. FAIRCLOUGH
THE IDEAL COOKERY BOOK

Baked Apple Pudding

Gebackene Apfelspeise

To serve 8 to 10

10	cooking apples, peeled, cored and diced	10
1	lemon, rind grated and juice strained	1
125 g	sugar	4 oz
	ground cinnamon	
150 g	butter, softened	5 oz
3	eggs, yolks separated from whites	3
100 g	currants	3½ oz
15 g	breadcrumbs	½ oz

Sprinkle the apples with the lemon juice, about 30 g (1 oz) of the sugar, and some cinnamon, and put them aside for 1 hour. Beat the butter until it is creamy. Gradually incorporate the remaining sugar, the egg yolks, lemon rind, currants and the apple. Beat the egg whites stiffly and add these to the mixture. Butter an ovenproof dish and sprinkle it with the breadcrumbs. Fill the dish with the apple mixture and bake for 1 hour in an oven preheated to 180°C (350°F or Mark 4).

DOROTHEE V. HELLERMANN
DAS KOCHBUCH AUS HAMBURG

Chestnut Pudding

Gâteau de Marrons

To serve 8

500 g	chestnuts	1 lb
60 cl	milk	1 pint
250 g	sugar	8 oz
1 tsp	vanilla extract	1 tsp
3	egg whites	3
	Caramel	
3 tbsp	sugar	3 tbsp
1 tbsp	water	1 tbsp

With a sharp, pointed knife make a cross on the flat side of each chestnut. Plunge the chestnuts into rapidly boiling water and boil them for 10 minutes. Remove them from the water and, while they are still hot, remove the shells. Scald the milk. Add the sugar and cook the chestnuts in the sweetened milk for 40 minutes. Force the chestnuts and milk through a food mill or strainer. Add the vanilla extract and allow the mixture to cool.

Put the 3 tablespoons of sugar into a 90 cl (1½ pint) plain or decorative mould. Melt the sugar and let it turn brown. Add

the water and move the mould around until the caramel has reached every part of the interior.

Beat the egg whites stiffly and fold them into the chestnut mixture. Pour the mixture into the mould. Place the mould in a pan of hot water and cook for 40 minutes in an oven preheated to 170°C (325°F or Mark 3). Unmould the pudding on to a dish, and serve plain or with sweetened whipped cream.

CHARLOTTE TURGEON
TANTE MARIE'S FRENCH KITCHEN

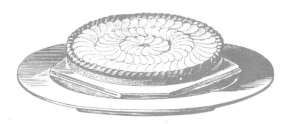

Steamed Chocolate Pudding

Mohr im Hemd

This is one of the most popular Viennese steamed puddings.

To serve 6

100 g	plain chocolate, broken into pieces	3½ oz
100 g	butter	3½ oz
4	large eggs, yolks separated from whites	4
100 g	castor sugar	3½ oz
60 g	flour, sifted	2 oz
75 g	ground almonds or hazelnuts	2½ oz
40 g	stale sponge cake, sponge fingers or bread, crumbled	1½ oz
15 cl	double cream, whipped	¼ pint
	Chocolate sauce	
60 g	plain chocolate, broken into pieces	2 oz
60 g	sugar	2 oz
15 cl	water	¼ pint

Butter a 1.25 litre (2 pint) pudding basin and dust it with either castor sugar or ground almonds.

Put the chocolate into a preheated oven, 140°C (275°F or Mark 1), to soften it. Cream the butter. Beat in the softened chocolate, the egg yolks and half the sugar. Continue beating with a wooden spoon until smooth. Whisk the egg whites as stiffly as you can, adding the remaining sugar towards the end. Fold the egg whites into the creamed butter mixture, simultaneously working in the flour, ground almonds or hazelnuts, and the cake crumbs.

Put the mixture into the prepared pudding basin at once, leaving a space of about 2.5 cm (1 inch) at the top for the pudding to rise. Steam it for 30 to 45 minutes in a covered water bath, or bake in a bain-marie in a 180°C (350°F or Mark 4) oven. To make the chocolate sauce, put the chocolate into a saucepan with the sugar and water, and boil gently for a few minutes, stirring continuously.

Test the pudding for doneness with a knitting needle or skewer. When this comes out clean, the pudding is ready. Invert a heated plate on to the pudding basin. With one gentle shake, unmould the pudding. Pour the chocolate sauce over and round it. Top with the whipped cream. Serve at once.

ROSL PHILPOT
VIENNESE COOKERY

Holyrood Pudding

This recipe comes from D. Williamson and Son, who were confectioners, caterers and teachers of cookery in Edinburgh in the mid-19th century.

To serve 4 to 6

60 cl	milk	1 pint
60 g	semolina	2 oz
90 g	castor sugar	3 oz
60 g	ratafia biscuits or macaroons, crushed	2 oz
30 g	butter	1 oz
3	eggs, yolks separated from whites	3
2 tsp	orange marmalade	2 tsp
	Almond sauce	
30 g	ground almonds	1 oz
1	egg	1
30 g	castor sugar	1 oz
15 cl	milk	¼ pint
1 tbsp	orange flower water	1 tbsp

Bring the milk to the boil and stir in the semolina with the sugar, ratafia biscuits or macaroons and butter. Let the mixture boil for about 5 minutes, stirring it all the time. Pour it into a basin and allow it to cool. Meanwhile, beat the egg whites to a stiff froth, and butter a 1.25 litre (2 pint) pudding mould. One at a time, beat the egg yolks into the semolina mixture. Add the orange marmalade, and lastly fold in the beaten egg whites. Mix gently and pour into the buttered mould. Place the mould in a water bath, and steam the pudding on top of the stove for 1¼ hours.

Meanwhile, make the almond sauce. Mix together in a small saucepan the egg, sugar, milk, ground almonds and orange flower water. Put the saucepan over a low heat and stir

the mixture with a whisk until it becomes like thick cream, but do not let it boil. Turn out the pudding and serve the almond sauce separately.

F. MARIAN McNEILL
THE SCOTS KITCHEN

Orange Semolina Pudding

Flamri à l'Orange

To serve 8 to 10

200 g	semolina	7 oz
60 cl	white wine	1 pint
40 cl	water	¾ pint
	salt	
1	bouquet orange and lemon rind, cut into strips	1
220 g	castor sugar	7½ oz
4	oranges, juice strained	4
30 g	orange sugar (prepared by lightly rubbing lumps of sugar on the skin of an orange)	1 oz
5	egg whites, stiffly beaten	5

In a saucepan combine the wine, water, a pinch of salt and the orange and lemon rind. Bring to the boil, then gradually pour in the semolina, stirring all the time, until a smooth mixture is obtained. Lower the heat, add the sugar and cook for 12 minutes, stirring often. Add the orange juice and orange sugar and bring back to the boil. Whisk in the beaten egg whites and when the mixture shows the first signs of boiling, quickly remove from the heat and pour into one large 1.75 litre (3 pint) or 2 small 90 cl (1½ pint) charlotte or jelly moulds, previously rinsed in cold water. Refrigerate for 4 to 5 hours. Unmould the puddng on to a serving dish and pour over a thick orange-flavoured syrup or alternatively serve with a purée of raspberries or strawberries.

URBAIN DUBOIS
CUISINE DE TOUS LES PAYS

Russian Semolina Pudding

Kasha Gureva Sladkaya Mannaya

To serve 6 to 8

200 g	semolina	7 oz
1.25 litres	single cream or rich milk	2 pints
1	vanilla pod	1
200 g	ground almonds	7 oz
200 g	castor sugar	7 oz
3 tbsp	water	3 tbsp
	toasted breadcrumbs	

Put the cream or milk and the vanilla pod in a saucepan and bring to the boil. Sprinkle in the semolina, stirring constantly, then simmer for about 10 minutes, or until the mixture thickens. Add the almonds, sugar and water, and return to the boil. Remove from the heat, discard the vanilla pod and pour the mixture into a buttered ovenproof dish. Sprinkle with breadcrumbs and bake in an oven, preheated to 190°C (375°F or Mark 5), for about 30 minutes.

ELENA MOLOKHOVETS
PODAROK MOLODÝM KHOZYAĬKAM

Semolina Pudding

Flamri

To serve 8

250 g	semolina	8 oz
½ litre	white wine	18 fl oz
½ litre	water	18 fl oz
300 g	sugar	10 oz
2	eggs	2
	salt	
6	egg whites, stiffly beaten	6
½ litre	puréed raspberries, strawberries, redcurrants, or other soft fruit, sweetened with sugar to taste	18 fl oz

Put the wine and water in a saucepan and bring to the boil. Gradually pour in the semolina, stirring constantly. Cover and simmer gently over a low heat, stirring occasionally, for 25 minutes or until the semolina is thick and smooth. Remove the pan from the heat and to this "porridge" add the sugar, the eggs and a pinch of salt. Fold in the stiffly beaten egg whites. Pour this mixture into a plain buttered mould. Place the mould in a pan of hot water, cover the mould and poach the pudding over a low heat or in a preheated, 170°C (325°F or Mark 3) oven for 25 to 40 minutes, or until it is firm to the

touch. Remove the mould from the pan and leave the pudding to cool. Turn out the pudding on to a serving dish, pour over the fruit purée and serve.

PROSPER MONTAGNÉ
LAROUSSE GASTRONOMIQUE

Macaroni Pudding with Pears

Mahal

To serve 6

125 g	macaroni, broken into very small pieces	4 oz
	salt	
60 cl	milk	1 pint
30 cl	single cream	½ pint
90 g	soft brown sugar	3 oz
60 g	butter	2 oz
1 tbsp	grated lemon rind	1 tbsp
60 g	ground almonds	2 oz
2	eggs, separated, and yolks thoroughly beaten with a whisk	2
6	dessert pears, peeled, halved and cored	6

Cook the macaroni in boiling salted water for 10 minutes. Drain the macaroni and put it into a saucepan with the milk and cream and simmer for 20 minutes. Remove the pan from the heat and let the mixture cool a little.

Add the sugar, and stir until dissolved. Add the butter, lemon rind, ground almonds and the beaten egg yolks. Whip the egg whites and fold in carefully.

Pour half the mixture into a buttered soufflé or oven dish, then arrange the pear halves on top, and finish with a layer of macaroni mixture. Cook in an oven, preheated to 180°C (350°F or Mark 4), for 30 minutes. Serve hot.

IRFAN ORGA
COOKING THE MIDDLE EAST WAY

Apricots with Rice Mould

Abricots Condé

The technique of preparing the syrup is shown on page 8.

When fresh ripe apricots are not available, use canned apricots in syrup and thicken the reduced syrup with a tablespoon of apricot jam.

	To serve 4 to 6	
10	large ripe apricots	10
150 g	sugar	5 oz
30 cl	water	½ pint
1	vanilla pod	1
4 tsp	kirsch	4 tsp
	Rice mould	
125 g	Carolina or Patna rice, well washed, blanched in boiling water for 2 minutes, drained, washed again and thoroughly drained	4 oz
½ litre	milk	18 fl oz
1	vanilla pod	1
1	small strip orange or lemon rind	1
¼ tsp	salt	¼ tsp
30 g	unsalted butter, melted	1 oz
About 60 g	sugar	About 2 oz
3	eggs, separated, yolks beaten lightly and thinned with 1 tbsp of single cream or boiled milk	3
About 1 tbsp	kirsch	About 1 tbsp
	angelica, candied fruits and peel, glacé cherries	

Prepare a light syrup with the sugar, the water and the vanilla pod. Plunge the apricots for a moment into boiling water, peel them immediately, then halve and stone them. Crack 4 of the stones, extract the kernels, cut them in half and add them to the syrup, along with the apricots. Bring the apricot halves slowly to the boil and poach, simmering, for 8 minutes, or until just tender, being careful that the apricots do not break or lose their shape. Keep the apricot halves warm in the syrup until time to use.

To prepare the rice mould, bring the milk to the boil with the vanilla pod, orange or lemon rind and the salt. Remove the vanilla pod and the rind. Put the rice into a saucepan and add 10 cl (4 fl oz) of the boiling milk, along with the melted butter. Cook, covered, over a low heat, stirring occasionally with a fork until the milk is absorbed by the rice. Continue to cook, adding about 10 cl (4 fl oz) of milk at a time until all of the milk is absorbed. Cool the rice slightly.

Sprinkle the sugar over the surface of the rice. Using a fork, and taking care not to break the grains of rice, mix in the egg yolks. Beat the egg whites, until they form soft peaks, fold them into the rice, and stir in the kirsch. Pour the mixture into a 1 litre (2 pint) buttered savarin mould. Cover with buttered greaseproof paper and cook in a bain-marie in an oven pre-heated to 180°C (350°F or Mark 4) for 45 minutes. To test for doneness, insert a trussing needle, which should come out clean. Let the rice stand for 10 minutes before unmoulding it on to a round plate.

Drain the apricot halves and boil the syrup, to reduce it to about 10 cl (4 fl oz); remove the kernels and vanilla pod. Place 16 of the apricot halves on the rice, overlapping them around the curved top of the ring. Decorate the apricots with angelica, candied fruits and peel and glacé cherries. Rub the remaining 4 apricot halves through a fine sieve and mix with the syrup. Flavour this sauce with the 4 teaspoons of kirsch. Coat the rice mould with the sauce and serve warm.

PAUL BOCUSE
THE NEW CUISINE

Alabaster Cream of Rice

This dessert can be served on its own, or as an accompaniment to a fresh or dried fruit compote or a chocolate mousse.

	To serve 4	
3 tbsp	Patna, or other long-grain rice	3 tbsp
60 cl	milk	1 pint
1	strip lemon rind	1
About 60 g	sugar	About 2 oz
15 cl	double cream	¼ pint

Put the rice and milk in a double saucepan with the lemon rind, and sugar to taste. Put on the lid and cook slowly, stirring occasionally, until the grains are quite cooked but still quite separate and white—about 25 minutes. Take the pan off the heat. Remove and discard the lemon rind, and pour the rice mixture into an enamel basin or mixing bowl. Add the cream and whisk both together until stiff. Care must be taken not to whip the mixture until the cream becomes butter.

Pour the mixture into a silver or glass bowl, and serve cold.

MRS. C. F. LEYEL
PUDDINGS

Apple Rice Pudding

Apfelreis

To serve 6

100 g	long-grain or short-grain rice	3½ oz
1 kg	cooking apples, peeled, cored and sliced	2 to 2½ lb
30 cl	milk	½ pint
½ tsp	grated lemon rind	½ tsp
100 g	sugar	3½ oz
½ tsp	salt	½ tsp
30 g	butter	1 oz
10 cl	sweet cider or apple juice	4 fl oz
2	egg whites	2
2 tbsp	icing sugar	2 tbsp

Cook the rice in the milk with the lemon rind, sugar and salt for about 25 minutes, or until the rice is soft. Place a layer of rice in a deep, 1.5 litre (2½ pint) baking dish, add half of the apples, dot with half of the butter, add the remaining rice and top with the rest of the apples. Dot with the remaining butter. Pour the cider or apple juice over the top. Bake for 45 minutes in an oven preheated to 180°C (350°F or Mark 4). Beat the egg whites until stiff, and blend in the icing sugar. Spread the meringue topping over the apples, and bake for about 20 minutes, or until the meringue is golden. Serve warm.

BETTY WASON
THE ART OF GERMAN COOKING

Rice Pudding with White Wine

Sutlach Sharapli

To serve 6

125 g	rice, washed and drained	4 oz
30 cl each	milk and single cream	½ pint each
30 g	butter	1 oz
90 g	seedless raisins	3 oz
3 tbsp	castor sugar	3 tbsp
	salt	
2	eggs, lightly beaten	2
60 g	ground almonds	2 oz
175 g	granulated sugar	6 oz
15 cl	dry white wine	¼ pint
30 cl	double cream, whipped	½ pint

Boil the rice in plenty of water until it is very soft. Strain off any surplus water and add the milk, single cream, butter, raisins, castor sugar and a pinch of salt. Cook over a medium heat until the mixture is quite thick, stirring frequently to prevent burning. Remove the pan from the heat and allow the mixture to cool.

Add the beaten eggs and ground almonds and stir thoroughly. Pour the whole into a well-buttered shallow baking dish and cook in a moderate oven, preheated to 180°C (350°F or Mark 4), for about 30 minutes, or until the top is golden-brown. Remove the pudding from the oven and let it rest for a few minutes. With a very sharp knife cut the pudding into triangular shapes in the baking dish and allow it to get cold.

Meanwhile, put the granulated sugar and the wine into a heavy saucepan and boil, uncovered, until a thickish syrup is obtained. This should take about 10 minutes, and be sure to stir until the sugar is dissolved. Pour this syrup over the rice shapes in the dish, and leave to be absorbed. Serve cold with the whipped cream.

IRFAN ORGA
COOKING THE MIDDLE EAST WAY

Rice and Wild Strawberry Pudding

Timbale de Fraises Germaine

To serve 8

100 g	rice, washed	3½ oz
250 g	wild strawberries, soaked for 1 hour in 2 tbsp each kirsch and maraschino liqueur	8 oz
½ litre	milk	18 fl oz
60 g	sugar	2 oz
½	vanilla pod	½
250 g	peeled, cored, fresh pineapple, diced and soaked in 2 tbsp of kirsch	8 oz
2 tbsp	double cream	2 tbsp
50 g each	raspberries and wild strawberries, puréed	2 oz each
2 tbsp	castor sugar	2 tbsp
10 cl	double cream, whipped	4 fl oz

Parboil the rice in water for about 5 minutes. Drain, and then put the rice into a saucepan or a heatproof oven dish. Stir in the milk, sugar and vanilla. Bring this mixture to the boil, then cover and cook for about 25 minutes in an oven preheated to 170°C (325°F or Mark 3). When the rice is cooked, empty it into a mixing bowl and place it to cool on ice. When it is cold, stir in the pineapple and the 2 tablespoons of double cream. Pour this mixture into a crystal bowl. Cover with the whole, macerated strawberries.

In a saucepan, combine the raspberry and strawberry purées with the castor sugar, cook for 3 minutes, remove from the heat, and allow to cool. As soon as the purée mixture is cool, fold in the whipped cream. Cover the strawberries with this cream mixture and serve.

PAUL BOUILLARD
LA CUISINE AU COIN DU FEU

Old Irish Rice Pudding

The original version of this recipe calls for an edging of puff pastry to be put round the pie dish.

To serve 8 to 12

125 g	long-grain rice, washed	4 oz
1.25 litres	water	2 pints
2.5 litres	milk	4 pints
15 g	bitter almonds, or a few drops of almond extract	$\frac{1}{2}$ oz
1	piece lemon rind	1
10 cm	stick cinnamon	4 inch
125 g	butter	4 oz
About 175 g	sugar	About 6 oz
12	egg yolks, beaten	12
6	egg whites, lightly beaten	6
15 cl	whisky or brandy	$\frac{1}{4}$ pint
	powdered saffron	

Heat the rice in the water. When it is hot, pour off the water. Add the milk to the rice, along with the bitter almonds or almond extract, the lemon rind and the cinnamon. Boil until the rice is quite soft, then remove the bitter almonds, if used, the cinnamon stick and the lemon rind. While the rice is still hot, mix in the butter and sweeten with sugar to taste. When the rice cools, add the egg yolks, the egg whites, the whisky or brandy and a pinch of saffron.

Butter a 2 litre ($3\frac{1}{2}$ pint) pie dish, and put the rice in. Bake in a preheated, 150°C (300°F or Mark 2) oven for $1\frac{1}{2}$ hours.

MAY BYRON
MAY BYRON'S PUDDINGS, PASTRIES AND SWEET DISHES

Rice Pudding

Riz au Lait

The author suggests the following variation: when the rice is cooked, stir in 3, 4, 5 or 6 beaten eggs and sweeten with sugar to taste. Pour the rice mixture into a buttered mould, and cook

in a bain-marie in a preheated, 180°C (350°F or Mark 4) oven for 20 minutes. Allow the pudding to stand for a few minutes before unmoulding. Serve hot or cold.

To serve 4 to 6

125 g	long-grain rice, thoroughly washed and drained	4 oz
	salt	
$\frac{3}{4}$ litre	milk	$1\frac{1}{4}$ pints
$\frac{1}{2}$	vanilla pod, or 1 tsp finely chopped orange or lemon rind	$\frac{1}{2}$
30 g	butter	1 oz
About 75 g	castor sugar	About $2\frac{1}{2}$ oz

Blanch the rice in lightly salted boiling water for 5 to 6 minutes. Drain the rice, rinse it in tepid water, and drain it thoroughly once again.

In a heavy casserole, bring the milk to the boil with the half vanilla pod or, if you prefer, the orange or lemon rind. Remove the vanilla pod if used, then add the butter and sugar to the milk and stir until the sugar is dissolved. Allow the milk to cool slightly, then pour in the rice. Bring to the boil, then cover and cook in an oven preheated to 170°C (325°F or Mark 3) for 30 minutes, without stirring. Transfer the rice to a *compotier* or serving bowl, and serve hot or cold.

ADRIEN-JEAN BOBINET
GASTRONOMIE

Creamed Rice

Kheer

This dessert can be served hot, but it is best well chilled and served in individual cups with a light scattering of slivered blanched almonds and pistachios. It is also customary to decorate the chilled *kheer* with edible silver or gold leaf.

To serve 4 to 6

90 g	short-grain rice, washed	3 oz
1.25 litres	milk	2 pints
175 g	sugar	6 oz
30 g	raisins	1 oz
4	cardamom pods, seeds extracted and crushed	4
2	cloves or 2 cm ($\frac{3}{4}$ inch) cinnamon stick	2
6 tbsp	slivered blanched almonds	6 tbsp
2 tsp	rose water	2 tsp

Bring the milk to the boil in a large saucepan. Add the rice, bring back to the boil, and stir and boil for 1 minute over a medium heat. Reduce the heat to low, and cook, stirring constantly, for 15 minutes. Continue cooking covered for $1\frac{1}{2}$ hours, stirring occasionally. Add the sugar, raisins, cardamom seeds and cloves or cinnamon, and cook, stirring slowly from time to time until the raisins plump out and the mixture thickens to a thick pouring consistency—about 10 to 15 minutes. Remove the cloves or cinnamon and add the almonds. Pour the mixture into a 1.5 litre ($2\frac{1}{2}$ pint) ovenproof dish and cook in an oven preheated to 180°C (350°F or Mark 4) for 25 minutes. Mix in the rose water just before serving.

DHARAMJIT SINGH
INDIAN COOKERY

Moulded Rice and Fruit Dessert

Riz à l'Impératrice

To serve 6

125 g	Carolina rice	4 oz
100 g	sugar	$3\frac{1}{2}$ oz
	salt	
30 g	butter	1 oz
1	vanilla pod, split	1
$\frac{3}{4}$ litre	milk	$1\frac{1}{4}$ pints
4 to 5 tbsp	apricot jam or preserved apricots	4 to 5 tbsp
60 g	mixed crystallized grapes, cherries, pineapple and angelica, diced and macerated in 4 tbsp kirsch, sweetened with 1 tbsp sugar	2 oz
$\frac{1}{2}$ litre	pouring custard (*page 166*), in which 30 g (1 oz) softened leaf gelatine has been dissolved	18 fl oz
3 tbsp	kirsch	3 tbsp

Blanch the rice in boiling water for 5 minutes; drain the rice, plunge it into cold water, and drain again. Put the sugar, a pinch of salt, the butter, vanilla pod and the milk into a heavy casserole and bring to the boil. Add the rice, cover the casserole tightly and place in a slow oven, preheated to 150°C (300°F or Mark 2), for 30 minutes or until the rice is tender and has absorbed the liquid but the grains still remain whole.

Remove the vanilla pod, place the rice in a bowl, and loosen its consistency with the apricot jam or preserved apricots. Stir in the diced fruits, the pouring custard and the kirsch. Pour the mixture into an oiled 1.5 litre ($2\frac{1}{2}$ pint) ring mould. Chill until set, for 2 to 3 hours if embedded in a bucket of crushed ice, or for 4 to 5 hours in the refrigerator. To serve, unmould the dessert on to a napkin-covered serving dish.

PHILÉAS GILBERT
LA CUISINE DE TOUS LES MOIS

Grandmother's Pudding

Pwdin Mamgu

This pudding is from the Gower peninsula, in South Wales.

To serve 6 to 8

250 g	stale breadcrumbs	8 oz
30 cl	milk	$\frac{1}{2}$ pint
60 g	shredded suet	2 oz
350 g	blackberries	12 oz
350 g	apples, peeled, cored and sliced	12 oz
90 g	sugar	3 oz

Soak the breadcrumbs in the milk, add the suet and mix well. Place a layer of the breadcrumb mixture on the bottom of a well-buttered 1.25 litre (2 pint) pie dish, and cover with a layer of blackberries, apple and sugar. Continue to fill the dish with alternate layers of the breadcrumb mixture and of fruit and sugar, finishing with a thick layer of the breadcrumb mixture. Bake in a moderately hot oven, preheated to 190°C (375°F or Mark 5), for approximately 1 hour, or until the pudding is golden-brown.

S. MINWEL TIBBOTT
WELSH FARE

Apple Dumpling

This is a fine old Scottish dish, much relished by children.

To serve 8

4	large cooking apples, peeled, cored and sliced	4
175 g	fresh butcher's suet	6 oz
500 g	flour	1 lb
	salt	
About $\frac{1}{4}$ litre	hot water	About 8 fl oz
1 or 2	cloves or $\frac{1}{2}$ tsp ground cinnamon	1 or 2
90 to 125 g	sugar	3 to 4 oz

Cut the suet into very small pieces, and soften it in hot water. When that is done, strain the suet and allow to cool, then press out any of the water that may remain. Work the suet in a basin with a wooden spoon until it is something like a batter. Sift the flour with a pinch of salt and add to the suet. Work the suet into the flour with your fingertips until it is all thoroughly absorbed, then gradually work in enough hot water to form a stiff paste. Mix the apples with the cloves or cinnamon and the sugar. Roll out the paste and place the apples in it. Gather the paste neatly over the lot, tie the bundle in a cloth and cook in a pan of boiling water for at least 2 hours. Alternatively, line a buttered 1.5 litre (2½ pint) basin with the paste, leaving an over-hanging flap, fill with the fruit mixture, and then turn up the paste over the top. Seal the paste, or pinch a lid of paste in place; tie the basin in a cloth, and boil for about 2¼ hours. Serve the dumpling with cream.

JENNY WREN
MODERN DOMESTIC COOKERY

Sussex Pond Pudding

The best of all English boiled suet puddings. In the middle, the butter and sugar melt to a rich sauce, which is sharpened with the juice from the lemon. The genius of the pudding is the lemon. Its citrus bitter flavour is a subtlety which raises the pudding to the highest class. When you serve it, make sure that everyone has a piece of the lemon, which will be much softened by the cooking, but still vigorous. Once when I had no lemons, I used a couple of small limes, which were equally successful. The name of the pudding refers to the sauce, which runs out of it, when it is turned on to a serving dish, and provides it with a moat of buttery brown liquid.

To serve 4 to 6

250 g	self-raising flour	8 oz
125 g	chopped fresh beef suet	4 oz
About 5 tbsp each	milk and water	About 5 tbsp each
125 g	slightly salted butter, cut into small pieces	4 oz
125 g	Demerara sugar	4 oz
1	large lemon or 2 limes	1

Mix the flour and suet together in a bowl. Make into a dough with the mixture of milk and water. The dough should be soft, but not too soft to roll out into a large circle. Cut a quarter out of this circle, to be used later as the lid of the pudding. Butter a 1.5 litre (2½ pint) pudding basin lavishly. Drop the three-quarter circle of pastry into it and press the cut sides together to make a perfect join. Put half the butter pieces into the pastry, with half the sugar. Prick the lemon (or limes) all over with a larding needle, so that the juices will be able to escape, then put it on to the butter and sugar. Add the remaining butter and sugar. Roll out the pastry which was set aside to make a lid. Lay it on top of the filling. Moisten the edges and press them together so that the pudding is completely sealed.

Put a piece of foil with a pleat in the middle over the basin. Tie the foil in place with string, and make a string handle over the top so that the pudding can be lifted easily. Put a large pan of water on to boil, and lower the pudding into it; the water must be boiling, and it should come half-way, or a little further, up the basin. Cover and leave to boil for 3 to 4 hours. If the water gets low, replenish it with boiling water.

To serve, remove the basin from the pan and take off the foil lid. Put a deep dish over the basin, and quickly turn the whole thing upside-down: it is a good idea to ease the pudding from the sides of the basin with a knife first. Put the pudding on the table immediately.

JANE GRIGSON
ENGLISH FOOD

Trinity College Pudding

To serve 6 or 7

250 g	fresh white breadcrumbs, sieved	8 oz
250 g	suet, shredded	8 oz
2 tbsp	crushed ratafia biscuits or macaroons	2 tbsp
125 g each	raisins and glacé cherries, chopped	4 oz each
125 g	castor sugar	4 oz
60 g	candied citron peel, chopped	2 oz
1 tbsp	flour	1 tbsp
1 tsp	mixed spice	1 tsp
	salt	
7	egg yolks, beaten, or 4 egg yolks beaten with 3 tbsp milk	7
5 tbsp	brandy	5 tbsp
2	egg whites	2
	custard sauce flavoured with rum (page 167)	

Mix the breadcrumbs, suet, ratafia or macaroon crumbs, raisins, cherries, sugar, citron peel, flour, spice and a pinch of salt in a basin. Gradually stir in the beaten egg yolks, or egg yolks and milk, then stir in the brandy. Beat the egg whites to a stiff froth. Fold them into the pudding mixture. Three-quarters fill a buttered 2 litre (3½ pint) pudding basin with the mixture. Cover the basin with buttered paper and tie down securely. Steam the pudding for 4 hours.

Unmould the pudding on to a heated platter. Serve with a custard sauce flavoured with rum.

ELIZABETH CRAIG
THE ART OF IRISH COOKING

Christmas Pudding

The quantities given here may be multiplied, and several puddings prepared at the same time. If they are well stored, the puddings will keep for up to 2 years. The techniques of creating an airtight seal for long-term storage, and of covering the pudding with a floured cloth for cooking, are shown on page 59.

To serve 8 to 10

150 g	fresh butcher's suet, or ready-shredded packet suet	5 oz
175 g each	currants, sultanas and raisins	6 oz each
150 g	white breadcrumbs, made from dryish bread	5 oz
150 g	soft brown sugar	5 oz
30 g	blanched almonds, roughly chopped	1 oz
30 g	mixed candied peel, chopped	1 oz
125 g	glacé cherries, halved	4 oz
1	lemon, rind finely grated	1
3	large eggs	3
2 tbsp	whisky	2 tbsp

If you are using fresh butcher's suet, remove the transparent tissue, then grate the suet on a fine or medium grater. Pick over the dried fruit; remove the woody stems from the sultanas if necessary. Then wash the currants, sultanas and raisins in cold water. Put them in a colander or a sieve and leave them to drain. Lay a clean tea towel on a cooling rack or tray. Spread the fruit over the tea towel and leave it in a warm place to dry. Roughly chop the raisins.

Thoroughly grease a 1.5 litre (2½ pint) pudding basin with vegetable oil. Cut rounds of greaseproof paper the same size as the top and the bottom of the basin. Brush the paper well with vegetable oil. It is very important to do all this, otherwise the pudding will stick.

Put all the dry ingredients in a large mixing bowl and mix them well together, then mix in the eggs and the whisky. Put a round of the oiled greaseproof paper in the bottom of the basin and spoon in the mixture. Place the other round of greaseproof paper on top of the mixture. Cover the basin with a piece of foil and put a foil sling round the pudding, or alternatively, cover with a floured cloth pleated and secured with string. Make a handle by tying together the corners of the cloth.

Put a small block of wood, or a trivet in the bottom of a large saucepan. This will ensure that the bottom of the pudding is not too near the heat. Lower the pudding into the pan. Fill the saucepan with water to about half way up the sides of the pudding basin. Cover the saucepan with a tightly fitting lid. Bring the water to the boil, then reduce the heat. Boil the pudding gently for 9 hours. Replenish the water in the saucepan at intervals with boiling water.

Remove the pudding from the saucepan. Wipe it well; and remove the foil or cloth and the top round of greaseproof paper. Brush a fresh round of greaseproof paper with vegetable oil and cover the pudding with it. Cover the basin with foil and tie around the top securely with string. Wrap the pudding in a clean tea towel and store it in a cool place until Christmas Day. Before serving, boil the pudding for a further 2 hours. Turn out of the basin, and serve with fresh whipped cream.

SUSAN KING
WOMAN'S REALM (MAGAZINE)

Fig Pudding with Lime Sauce

To serve 6 to 8

250 g	dried figs, cut into little pieces	8 oz
175 g	fresh breadcrumbs	6 oz
250 g	suet, very finely chopped	8 oz
5	eggs, well beaten	5
125 g	sugar	4 oz
2	limes, rind grated, juice strained	2
	grated nutmeg	
	salt	
15 to 20 cl	rum	6 fl oz
15 g	butter	½ oz
	Lime sauce	
2	limes, rind very thinly peeled, juice strained	2
3 tbsp	sugar	3 tbsp
20 cl	water	7 fl oz
2 to 3 tbsp	rum	2 to 3 tbsp
1 or 2 drops	red food colouring (optional)	1 or 2 drops

Take the breadcrumbs, suet and dried figs and mix them well together with the beaten eggs, the sugar, and the grated rind and juice of the limes; finally mix in a pinch each of grated nutmeg and salt, and the rum. Put the mixture into a well-buttered 1.25 litre (2 pint) mould, press it down tightly, cover with a buttered wax or greaseproof paper, tie it up in a cloth, and boil it for not less than 4 hours, topping up with water from time to time as necessary.

To make the lime sauce, put the sugar into a saucepan with the very finely peeled rind of the limes and the water; bring to the boil and simmer until a fine syrup is produced, then skim and add the juice of the limes and the rum. A drop or two of red food colouring will improve the colour of the sauce.

Unmould the pudding and serve it with the lime sauce. If liked, the pudding may be served "on fire" like a Christmas pudding, by pouring brandy over it and flaming it.

COL. A. F. KENNEY-HERBERT (WYVERN)
SWEET DISHES

Crêpes and Fritters

Pancakes with Curd Cheese Filling

Blinchiki s Tvorogom

This Russian pancake recipe is taken from the best-selling cookbook of Stalin's era.

To serve 6

1	egg	1
About 3 tbsp	sugar	About 3 tbsp
$\frac{1}{2}$ tsp	salt	$\frac{1}{2}$ tsp
$\frac{3}{4}$ litre	milk	$1\frac{1}{4}$ pints
250 g	flour, sifted	8 oz
60 g	butter	2 oz
20 cl	soured cream	7 fl oz

	Curd cheese filling	
500 g	curd cheese	1 lb
1	egg, separated, white lightly beaten	1
200 g	sugar	7 oz
$\frac{1}{2}$ tsp	salt	$\frac{1}{2}$ tsp
1	lemon or orange, rind finely peeled	1
15 g	butter, melted	$\frac{1}{2}$ oz
60 g	raisins, washed (optional)	2 oz

Prepare the pancakes; break the egg into a bowl and beat it with a wooden spoon. Add 1 tablespoon of the sugar, the salt and a third of the milk, and stir well. Add a little flour and some more milk, stirring continuously; add more flour and milk until all are incorporated into the batter. Melt a little butter in a 12 cm (5 inch) pancake or crêpe pan over a medium heat; pour in enough batter to cover the base of the pan thinly. As soon as the pancake is cooked on one side, remove to a side dish. Continue to make pancakes in this fashion until the batter is used up. If the pancakes become too thick, thin the batter with a little more milk.

To make the filling, first rub the curd cheese through a sieve into a bowl. Mix into it the egg yolk, sugar, salt, lemon or orange rind, melted butter and, if desired, the raisins. Place 1 tablespoon of filling on to the fried side of each pancake, and roll up the pancake, folding in the sides when it is partly rolled. To keep the filled pancake roll from coming apart while it is frying, smear the last edge with beaten egg white before folding it down.

Fry the pancakes in butter on both sides, starting with the flap side down and turning once, until the pancakes are nicely browned. Serve the pancakes hot, sprinkled with the remaining sugar, with a bowl of soured cream on the side.

O. P. MOLCHANOVA
KNIGA O VKUSNOĬ I ZDOROVOĬ PISHCHE

Crêpes with Tangerine Butter

Crêpes Suzette

Robert Courtine, in his introduction to this recipe, notes that it is not flames, as many people imagine, that differentiate crêpes Suzette from other crêpe preparations, but the presence of tangerine juice and curaçao.

To serve 6

	crêpe batter (*page 167*)	
1 tsp	tangerine juice	1 tsp
1 tsp	curaçao	1 tsp
40 g	clarified butter	$1\frac{1}{2}$ oz

	Tangerine butter	
2	tangerines, juice strained	2
2	lumps sugar	2
60 g	butter	2 oz
40 g	sugar	$1\frac{1}{2}$ oz
1 tsp	curaçao	1 tsp

To make the tangerine butter, rub the sugar lumps over the skin of the tangerines until the lumps have absorbed the colour and flavour of the zest. In a bowl, work the butter with a wooden spoon until soft; add the sugar and blend until creamy. Crush in the sugar lumps, add the tangerine juice and the curaçao; mix well.

Add a teaspoon of tangerine juice and a teaspoon of curaçao to the crêpe batter. Heat a small crêpe pan containing a little of the butter, pour in a small ladleful of the batter, and cook the crêpe on both sides. Remove it to a warmed plate, and keep the crêpe warm. Make 12 crêpes in this way.

Spread each crêpe with a spoonful of the tangerine butter, fold it in four and transfer to a very hot serving dish before spreading the next crêpe. Arrange the crêpes four by four with their points together so that they make a round. Serve immediately on to hot plates.

ODETTE KAHN (EDITOR)
CUISINE ET VINS DE FRANCE

Curd Cheese Pancakes

Túróspalacsinta

It is the pride and joy of every Hungarian housewife to know that her pancakes are thinner than anyone else's pancakes. To achieve this paper thinness and lightness this batter recipe is made with soda water.

To serve 6

125 g	flour	4 oz
1	egg, beaten	1
15 cl	milk	$\frac{1}{4}$ pint
	salt	
15 cl	soda water	$\frac{1}{4}$ pint
	oil for frying	
30 g	butter	1 oz
30 g	sugar	1 oz
	Curd cheese filling	
250 g	fresh curd or cottage cheese	8 oz
2	eggs, yolks separated from whites	2
175 g	vanilla sugar	6 oz
1	lemon, rind finely grated	1

Sift the flour into a bowl, add the egg, milk and a pinch of salt. Beat with a fork until the mixture is smooth. Add the soda water and, using a wooden spoon, beat until the batter is smooth. Put it aside and let it rest for 10 to 15 minutes. Put a little oil in a pancake pan and let it get hot. Pour in a very small amount of batter, just enough to cover the pan thinly, and fry on one side until the pancake is crisp. Turn the pancake over, add a little more oil and fry on the other side. If the batter gets too thick towards the end, squirt in a little more soda water. You should get a dozen paper-thin pancakes out of this amount of batter.

For the filling, rub the curd cheese through a sieve into a bowl and beat in the egg yolks, sugar and rind. Beat the egg whites until stiff and fold them into the curd cheese mixture. To fill the pancakes, either put a small portion of the filling on each pancake, roll up each pancake round the filling and place them, flapside down, in a heated baking dish. Alternatively, put layers of pancake sandwiched with layers of filling in a heated ovenproof dish, beginning and ending with a pancake. Dot the pancakes with butter, sprinkle with sugar and put in a preheated, 220°C (425°F or Mark 7) oven for 10 minutes.

KATO FRANK
COOKING THE HUNGARIAN WAY

Crêpes Soufflées with Champagne Sabayon

Crêpes Soufflées au Sabayon

The technique of preparing crêpes is demonstrated on page 62.

This recipe is from the restaurant, Le Taillevent, in Paris.

To serve 4

12	small crêpes (*batter, page 167*)	12
4	eggs, yolks separated from whites	4
75 g	castor sugar	2$\frac{1}{2}$ oz
30 g	flour	1 oz
$\frac{1}{4}$ litre	milk, heated to boiling point	8 fl oz
10 cl	Grand Marnier	4 fl oz
4 tbsp	icing sugar	4 tbsp
	Champagne sabayon	
4	egg yolks	4
50 g	castor sugar	2 oz
15 cl	champagne	$\frac{1}{4}$ pint

First prepare the crêpes. Set them aside until required.

To make the soufflé mixture, in an enamelled saucepan, whisk the egg yolks with the castor sugar for 1 minute. Add the flour, stirring, then gradually stir in the boiling milk. Stirring constantly, bring to the boil, reduce the heat to low, and cook for 2 minutes. Remove from the heat and add the Grand Marnier. Beat the egg whites until they stand in stiff peaks, then fold them into the mixture.

Butter a large ovenproof dish. Fill the prepared crêpes by placing a generous spoonful of the soufflé mixture on to one half of each crêpe, then folding the other half loosely over the top. As the crêpes are filled, arrange them side by side in the dish. Cook in an oven preheated to 220°C (425°F or Mark 7) for 7 minutes. Half way through the cooking, sprinkle the crêpes with the icing sugar, so that they become glazed.

Serve the crêpes accompanied by the champagne *sabayon*, prepared as follows: put the egg yolks, castor sugar and champagne into a copper saucepan. Place the saucepan in a water bath over a moderate heat, and whisk the mixture constantly until it has a creamy, frothy consistency.

LES PRINCES DE LA GASTRONOMIE

Crêpes with Wild Strawberries

Crêpes Richelieu

The technique of preparing crêpes is demonstrated on page 62.

To serve 4 to 6

About 12	crêpes (*batter, page 167*)	About 12
250 g	wild strawberries	8 oz
60 g	castor sugar, mixed with 4 tbsp kirsch	2 oz
	Pastry cream	
25 g	castor sugar	1 oz
1½ tbsp	flour	1½ tbsp
10 cl	milk	4 fl oz
	salt	
½ tsp	vanilla extract	½ tsp
1	egg yolk	1

Macerate the strawberries in the sugar and kirsch for 30 minutes. Meanwhile, cook the crêpes and keep them warm.

To make the pastry cream, mix together the sugar, flour and milk with a pinch of salt and the vanilla extract. Transfer the mixture to a saucepan, and bring to the boil, stirring constantly. Remove from the heat, and whisk in the egg yolk. Allow to cool completely, then gently incorporate the strawberries, taking care not to crush them. Place a little of the strawberry filling in each crêpe, roll up and serve.

PAUL BOUILLARD
LA CUISINE AU COIN DU FEU

Crêpes Soufflées

The technique of preparing crêpes is demonstrated on page 62.

To serve 4

10	crêpes (*batter, page 167*)	10
3 tbsp	castor sugar	3 tbsp
5	eggs, yolks separated from whites	5
	vanilla extract	

To prepare the soufflé mixture, first put the sugar, egg yolks and a drop or two of vanilla extract into a bowl. Mix with a wooden spoon, stirring until the mixture becomes thoroughly amalgamated. Beat the egg whites until stiff, and fold them into the yolk mixture.

Lightly butter a gratin dish. Stack the crêpes, one on top of the other, spreading a generous tablespoon of the soufflé mixture over each. Cover completely with the remaining soufflé mixture, then place in an oven preheated to 200°C (400°F or Mark 6) for 20 minutes. Serve immediately.

LES PETITS PLATS ET LES GRANDS

Cream Filled Crêpe Charlotte

Pain de Crêpes à la Crème

The technique of preparing crêpes is demonstrated on page 62.

To serve 6 to 8

250 g to 300 g	flour	8 to 10 oz
1 tbsp	sugar	1 tbsp
	salt	
4	eggs, yolks separated from whites, whites stiffly beaten	4
½ litre	milk	18 fl oz
50 g	butter, melted and cooled	2 oz
	oil	
	dry breadcrumbs	
	Cream filling	
4	egg yolks	4
About 90 g	sugar	About 3 oz
30 cl	double cream	½ pint
½ tsp	vanilla extract and/or 1 tsp finely grated lemon rind	½ tsp

Put the flour, sugar and salt in a bowl. Make a well in the centre, add the egg yolks, and whisk, adding the milk and butter, until the batter is smooth. Fold in the egg whites.

Heat a little oil in a crêpe pan. Pour in enough batter to cover the base of the pan. When the edges start to brown, turn the crêpe to cook the other side. Continue to make crêpes until all of the batter is used up.

To make the filling, beat the egg yolks with the sugar until pale and creamy, then add the double cream and beat well together. Add the vanilla extract or lemon rind or, better still, both. Butter a 1 litre (1¾ pint) charlotte mould and sprinkle it with dry breadcrumbs. Layer the crêpes in the mould, separating each layer with some cream filling. Top with a crêpe.

Cook in an oven preheated to 180°C (375°F or Mark 4) for about 20 minutes to set the cream. Unmould and sprinkle with sugar. Serve cold.

H. WITWICKA AND S. SOSKINE
LA CUISINE RUSSE CLASSIQUE

Slid Pancakes

Csúsztatott Palacsinta

To serve 8 to 12

60 g	butter, softened	2 oz
1 tbsp	granulated sugar	1 tbsp
4	eggs, separated, whites stiffly beaten	4
	salt	
10 cl	milk	4 fl oz
3 tbsp	flour	3 tbsp
4 tbsp	double cream	4 tbsp
	clarified butter	

Pancake filling

50 g	vanilla sugar	2 oz
125 g	plain chocolate, grated	4 oz
250 g	jam	8 oz

In a bowl, beat together the butter, sugar, egg yolks and a pinch of salt. Gradually incorporate the milk, then the flour, and beat until the batter is smooth. Finally, add the cream, and let the batter rest for 1 hour.

Preheat the oven to 180°C (350°F or Mark 4). Fold the beaten egg whites into the batter. Heat a 20 cm (8 inch) crêpe pan with a little butter. With a ladle, dip out about 10 cl (4 fl oz) of the batter and pour it on to the hot pan. With a circular motion, swirl the batter so that it covers the bottom of the pan. Adjust the amount of batter to conform to the size of your pan. Fry the pancakes slowly, but only on one side.

Slide the first pancake, cooked side down, into a fairly deep 20 cm (8 inch) ovenproof dish. Sprinkle the pancake with some of the vanilla sugar and grated chocolate and/or jam. The chocolate and jam can be used on alternate layers, or one or the other can be used throughout.

When the second pancake is cooked, slide it on top of the other. Sprinkle with more sugar and/or jam. Continue to cook and layer the pancakes in this fashion.

Cook the last pancake on both sides, and use it as a cover to the torte of stacked pancakes. Bake in the preheated oven for 10 to 15 minutes. To serve, cut the torte as you would a cake.

GEORGE LANG
THE CUISINE OF HUNGARY

Layered Crêpe Gateau with Cheese Filling

Gâteau Livonien

The technique of preparing crêpes is shown on page 62.

To serve 8

10 to 12	crêpes (*batter, page 167*)	10 to 12
1 kg	fresh white curd cheese	2 lb
175 g	butter, softened	6 oz
250 g	castor sugar	8 oz
	salt	
8	egg yolks	8
60 g each	raisins, dried currants, candied citron and angelica	2 oz each
4	egg whites, stiffly beaten	4
	double cream	

First prepare the crêpes. In a bowl, mix together thoroughly the cheese, butter, sugar, a pinch of salt and the egg yolks. Put the mixture through a sieve into a bowl, and add the raisins, currants, citron, angelica and stiffly beaten egg whites.

Generously butter a charlotte mould, and line the bottom and sides of the mould with crêpes. Pour in a quarter of the cheese mixture, cover with a crêpe, and continue layering, finishing with a crêpe. Place in an oven preheated to 190°C (375°F or Mark 5) for about 45 minutes, or until golden.

Turn out on to a napkin-covered serving platter, and serve a sauceboat of double cream at the same time.

A. PETIT
LA GASTRONOMIE EN RUSSIE

Prune Fritters

Pruneaux en Beignets

To serve 4 or 5

20	prunes, soaked for at least 3 hours in water, drained and stones removed	20
20	walnut halves	20
	fritter batter (*page 167*)	
40 g	cocoa, sifted	1½ oz
100 g	castor sugar	3½ oz
	oil for deep frying	

Stuff each prune with a walnut half. Close the prunes up well and dip them in the fritter batter. Fry them in hot oil until they are golden. Drain, and immediately roll the prune fritters in a mixture of the cocoa and sugar. Arrange the fritters in a pyramid and serve hot.

HUGUETTE COUFFIGNAL
J'AIME LES NOIX

Cherry Batter Pudding

Le Clafoutis

An alternative presentation is to ladle a layer of batter into the baking dish, cover it with a layer of cherries and add the remaining batter so that the cherries are barely submerged (see page 66). If the dessert is arranged in this way, serve it straight from the baking dish instead of unmoulding it.

The *clafoutis* (which some people mistakenly spell *clafouti*) is one of the two or three most popular dishes of Limousin. It is an excellent dessert made with juicy black cherries.

To serve 6 to 8

750 g	black cherries, stems removed, stoned	1½ lb
500 g	flour	1 lb
4	eggs	4
2 tbsp	castor sugar	2 tbsp
	salt	
½ litre	milk	18 fl oz
4 or 5 tbsp	cognac	4 or 5 tbsp
2 tbsp	icing sugar	2 tbsp

Sift the flour into a bowl. Add the eggs, sugar and a pinch of salt, and knead the mixture until you have a smooth dough, free of lumps. Add the milk, followed by the cherries which should be evenly distributed in the dough. Next, pour the cognac over the mixture.

Generously butter a 1.75 litre (3 pint) pie dish, to ensure that the *clafoutis* will come out easily once it is cooked. Put the pie dish into an oven, preheated to 180°C (350°F or Mark 4), and leave to cook for 30 to 45 minutes.

Unmould the *clafoutis* and sprinkle icing sugar over it.

GASTON DERYS
L'ART D'ÊTRE GOURMAND

Rhubarb Fritters

To serve 4 to 6

750 g	young rhubarb, cut into 2.5 cm (1 inch) lengths	1½ lb
125 g	castor sugar	4 oz
3 tbsp	brandy	3 tbsp
	batter (*page 167*)	
	oil for deep frying	

Boil the rhubarb pieces in water for 10 minutes; then drain them and place them in cold water. When quite cold, drain the rhubarb pieces. Lay them in a shallow dish, strew sugar over, moisten with the brandy and let them marinate for 2 hours.

Remove the rhubarb pieces, dip them in the batter and deep fry them in hot oil until they get a nice colour. Drain the fritters on kitchen paper to absorb the fat. Place them neatly on a dish that has been spread over with a folded napkin or a fancy paper, and serve.

OSCAR TSCHIRKY
THE COOK BOOK BY "OSCAR" OF THE WALDORF

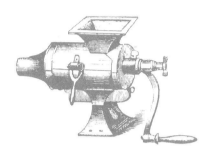

Indonesian Banana Batter Pudding

Kue Talam Pisang

To make the *santen*, or coconut milk, called for in this recipe, grate the flesh of a coconut into a bowl, and add about 35 cl (12 fl oz) of water. Leave for 20 minutes, then squeeze handfuls of the grated nut so that the water becomes white and takes up the juices from the flesh. Go on doing this until you are convinced you must have squeezed out every last drop; this is likely to take at least 1 minute or so. Strain the liquid through a fine sieve, then squeeze the grated flesh hard to make sure that all the liquid is out of it. Put the gratings back in the bowl, add a further 35 cl (12 fl oz) water, and repeat the process.

To serve 6

3	large bananas peeled and cut into thin rounds	3
250 g	rice flour	8 oz
60 g	cornflour	2 oz
	salt	
¾ litre	*santen*	1¼ pints
100 g	brown sugar	3½ oz

Sift the rice flour and cornflour into a mixing bowl, and add a pinch of salt. Heat the *santen* in a saucepan, taking care not to let it boil. Put about 10 cl (4 fl oz) into a small saucepan and use it to dissolve the sugar. Use the rest of the *santen*, with the flour, to make a smooth, fairly thick batter. Mix the dissolved sugar into this. Spoon the batter into small baking cups, or ramekins, leaving room to put several rounds of banana on top of each, then add the banana rounds. Stand the baking cups, or ramekins, in a bain-marie with water to reach half-way up the sides of the moulds. Steam until the batter is set and cooked, about 25 to 30 minutes. Serve warm or cold.

SRI OWEN
THE HOME BOOK OF INDONESIAN COOKERY

Curd Cheese Croquettes
Cyrniki ou Croquettes de Fromage Blanc

To serve 4

500 g	fresh white curd cheese	1 lb
3 or 4	eggs	3 or 4
3 tbsp	sugar	3 tbsp
	salt	
150 g	flour	5 oz
20 to 30 cl	double cream	7 to 10 fl oz
100 g	butter	3½ oz
	vanilla extract (optional)	
30 g	castor sugar	1 oz

Press the cheese through a fine strainer; add the eggs, the sugar, a pinch of salt, the flour and 1 to 2 tablespoons of the cream. When mixed together thoroughly, form the mixture into oval or round croquettes a finger-width thick. Cook the croquettes in hot butter until golden on all sides. Drain and serve with the remaining cream (which may be flavoured with vanilla if you wish) and the castor sugar.

H. WITWICKA AND S. SOSKINE
LA CUISINE RUSSE CLASSIQUE

Custard Fritters
Crema Fritta

To serve 4

½ litre	milk	18 fl oz
½ tsp	vanilla extract	½ tsp
125 g	flour, sifted	4 oz
100 g	sugar	3½ oz
	salt	
2	eggs	2
6	egg yolks	6
About 30 g	butter	About 1 oz
2	eggs, beaten	2
100 g	breadcrumbs	3½ oz
	oil or fat for deep frying	
15 g	icing sugar, preferably vanilla flavoured	½ oz

In a saucepan, bring the milk to the boil over a high heat. Remove from the heat, add the vanilla, cover the pan and set aside for 15 minutes. In a large saucepan, mix the flour, sugar, a pinch of salt, the 2 whole eggs and the egg yolks, adding the eggs and yolks one at a time. Mix thoroughly with a wooden spatula. Add the milk a little at a time, stirring

constantly. Over a medium heat, bring this mixture to the boil, continue to boil for 1 minute over a high heat. Remove from the heat and add the butter.

Butter a shallow tray about 3 cm (1¼ inches) deep and pour the cream mixture on to it. It should be about 2 cm (¾ inch) thick. Brush the top with melted butter to prevent hardening and leave to cool. When cool, unmould the cream on to a clean cloth. Cut it into 2.5 cm (1 inch) squares. Dip the squares in the beaten eggs and then in the breadcrumbs; keep them cool until you are ready to fry them.

Deep fry the squares in hot oil or fat: do not turn them, simply shake the frying pan, the squares should move by themselves. When golden, drain them and arrange them on a serving plate. Sprinkle them with icing sugar, and serve.

LUIGI CARNACINA AND LUIGI VERONELLI
LA BUONA VERA CUCINA ITALIANA

Souffléed Fritters
Les Pets-de-Nonne ou Beignets Soufflés

To serve 10

½ litre	water	18 fl oz
100 g	butter	3½ oz
¼ tsp	salt	¼ tsp
60 g	castor sugar	2 oz
325 g	flour, sifted	11 oz
6	eggs	6
	oil for deep frying	
	icing sugar (optional)	

In a saucepan combine the water, butter, salt and sugar. Bring to the boil, then remove the pan from the heat. Pour in the flour all at once, stirring rapidly. Place the saucepan over a medium heat and stir vigorously for a few minutes until the mixture comes away from the sides of the saucepan. Take the pan off the heat, then add the eggs, mixing in each one thoroughly before adding the next.

In a deep frying pan heat the oil to 180°C (350°F). Use a teaspoon to form each fritter, and push each spoonful of the mixture into the hot oil with your fingers. As soon as there are several fritters in the oil, raise the heat so that the oil heats progressively. When the fritters are golden, remove them with a spider or a slotted spoon. Lower the heat, and fry the remaining batches of fritters in the same way. Serve hot or cold on a napkin, sprinkled with icing sugar if desired.

JOSÉPHINE BESSON
LA MÈRE BESSON "MA CUISINE PROVENÇALE"

Magnolia Petal Fritters

Pétales de Magnolia

Other perfumed flowers, such as locust flowers and orange blossoms, can be prepared in the same way.

	To serve 4	
12	magnolia petals	12
	oil for deep frying	
	icing sugar, sifted	
	Batter	
6	egg whites	6
$\frac{1}{4}$ tsp	salt	$\frac{1}{4}$ tsp
30 g	castor sugar	1 oz
30 g	flour, sifted	1 oz

To make the batter, mix the unbeaten egg whites with the salt, castor sugar and flour until smooth. Dip the petals into the batter and drop them into hot oil. The petals will swell up considerably. When the fritters are golden, drain them well, sprinkle them with icing sugar and serve immediately.

H. LECOURT
LA CUISINE CHINOISE

Apricot Fritters

Abrikozen Beignets

	To serve 2	
4	apricots, peeled, halved, stones removed, poached in a medium sugar syrup (*page 8*)	4
4 to 6 tbsp	curaçao	4 to 6 tbsp
	oil for deep frying	
1 to 2 tbsp	icing sugar	1 to 2 tbsp
	Batter	
125 g	flour	4 oz
	salt	
1 tbsp	olive oil	1 tbsp
1	egg yolk, lightly beaten	1
20 cl	tepid milk	7 fl oz
2	egg whites	2

Drain the poached apricot halves and soak them in curaçao for approximately 2 hours.

To make the batter, sift the flour into a bowl, make a well in the centre and add a pinch of salt, the oil and the egg yolk. With a wooden spoon, working from the centre outwards, begin to stir the egg yolk and oil into the flour. Add the milk, progressively, and stir until the batter is smooth and creamy. Do not beat or overmix. Set the batter aside to rest for 1 to 2 hours in a warm place.

Beat the egg whites stiffly, and fold them into the batter. Drain the apricot halves and pat them dry with paper towels. Dip them in the batter and deep fry them in hot oil until golden-brown. Drain the fritters on paper towels. Sprinkle with icing sugar, and serve hot or cold.

HUGH JANS
VRIJ NEDERLAND

Sweet Cheese Fritters

Baignets de Plusieurs Façons

These fritters may be flavoured, according to taste, with 4 tablespoons of ground almonds or ground pistachio nuts, or the grated rind of 1 lemon. The flavouring should be added with the main ingredients. The custard mixture may be cooked and cut up ahead of time, but must be fried immediately before serving.

	To serve 4 to 6	
200 g	cream cheese, *ricotta* or curd cheese	7 oz
5	eggs	5
	salt	
60 g	sugar	2 oz
100 g	flour	$3\frac{1}{2}$ oz
$\frac{1}{2}$ litre	double cream	18 fl oz
	oil for deep frying	
	icing sugar	

In a mixing bowl, mash the cheese until smooth and beat in the eggs. Incorporate a pinch of salt, the sugar and flour. Whisk in the cream, a little at a time, until the mixture is a smooth, fluid custard.

Transfer the mixture to a saucepan and cook over a medium heat, stirring continuously, until it thickens. Pour the mixture on to a lightly floured surface, spreading it to a thickness of about 1 cm ($\frac{1}{2}$ inch). Lightly dust the top with flour and leave the mixture to cool.

Cut the cool fritter mixture into 2.5 cm (1 inch) squares, rectangles or diamond shapes. Heat the oil and deep fry the fritters, a few at a time, until golden-brown, about 1 or 2 minutes on each side. Drain the fritters well, sprinkle them with icing sugar while still hot, and pass them under a hot grill for a few seconds to glaze them before serving.

MENON
LES SOUPERS DE LA COUR

Banana Fritters

Beignets de Bananes

To serve 6 to 8

5 or 6	ripe bananas, peeled and fairly thickly sliced	5 or 6
3 tbsp	castor sugar	3 tbsp
3 tbsp	rum	3 tbsp
	fritter batter *(page 167)*	
	oil for deep frying	
	castor sugar	

Put the banana slices in a shallow dish, sprinkle them with the castor sugar and the rum, and leave them to macerate for 25 minutes. Drain the banana slices, dip them in the batter, and deep fry them in hot oil, a few at a time. Drain the fritters, sprinkle them with sugar and serve.

URBAIN DUBOIS
NOUVELLE CUISINE BOURGEOISE

Spanish Honey Pudding

Torrijas

To serve 6 to 8

6 tbsp	thin honey	6 tbsp
8	slices white bread, crusts removed, cut into 5 cm (2 inch) squares	8
30 cl	milk	½ pint
1	egg, lightly beaten	1
175 g	butter	6 oz
6 tbsp	hot water	6 tbsp

Soak the squares of bread in milk for a few minutes, then drain them. Dip them in the beaten egg and fry them gently in the butter until golden. Put the fried bread pieces in a buttered oven dish and cover with a mixture of equal parts honey and water. Cook slowly in an oven preheated to 180°C (350°F or Mark 4), for about 30 minutes, or until golden-brown.

ELIZABETH CASS
SPANISH COOKING

Poor Knights of Windsor

English cookery books are full of recipes for this dessert—strips of crustless bread, dipped in sweetened milk and egg, fried in butter and served with warm jam or maple syrup. Here is a Spanish variation.

To serve 4

8	slices white bread, crusts removed, and cut into strips	8
2	egg yolks	2
4 tbsp	sweet sherry	4 tbsp
	oil	
	icing sugar	
	ground cinnamon	

Beat the egg yolks and sherry together and dip the bread strips into this mixture. Heat the oil in a pan and fry the bread quickly so that the strips are golden-brown and crisp. Dust with icing sugar and cinnamon and serve immediately.

MARGARET COSTA
MARGARET COSTA'S FOUR SEASONS COOK BOOK

Rich Apple Slices with Sabayon Sauce

Croûte à la Belle Aurore

To serve 6

500 g	stale cake, cut into 8mm (⅓ inch) thick slices	1 lb
8 cl	rum	3 fl oz
250 g	apple purée	8 oz
1 tbsp	double cream	1 tbsp
3 tbsp	chopped mixed glacé fruits	3 tbsp
2	eggs, beaten	2
	plain biscuits, crushed and sieved	
	butter for frying	
	hot *sabayon* sauce *(page 166)*	

Sprinkle the slices of cake generously with the rum. Mix the cream and glacé fruits into the apple purée and spread over half of the cake slices. Place the other slices of cake on the prepared ones, pressing so that they hold together. Dip the slices in the beaten egg, cover with the biscuit crumbs and fry in butter over a medium heat.

Serve the hot *sabayon* sauce separately in a preheated bowl or sauceboat.

ALICE B. TOKLAS
THE ALICE B. TOKLAS COOK BOOK

Frozen Desserts

Claret Granita

Granité au Vin de Saint-Émilion

This dessert must be made a day in advance, because the mixture of syrup, wine and fruit juice takes a long time to set and crystallize into flakes. If desired, the orange juice can be replaced by mandarine orange or tangerine juice.

You can dress up this granita with well-ripened fresh peaches prepared in the following manner. Plunge them in boiling water for 15 seconds to make them easier to peel. Peel them, and cook for 15 minutes in 1 litre (1¾ pints) of boiling water to which 600 g (1¼ lb) of castor sugar and a split vanilla pod have been added. Cool the peaches, and place a whole peach on top of each granita, stuck with 2 mint leaves to look as if it is growing.

	To serve 6	
¾ litre	red wine, preferably Saint-Émilion	1¼ pints
20 cl	water	7 fl oz
200 g	castor sugar	7 oz
1	orange, juice strained	1
1	lemon, juice strained	1
	fresh mint leaves (optional)	

Boil the water and the sugar together for 1 minute in a medium-sized saucepan. Pour the syrup obtained into a bowl and allow to cool. When the syrup is quite cold, add the wine, the orange and lemon juice, and mix together with a small whisk. Pour the mixture into a long, shallow dish or tray, and put it into the freezer or freezing compartment of the refrigerator. The shallow depth of the liquid allows it to set more rapidly. During the course of the day, regularly stir the solidifying liquid with a fork, scraping the crystals from the edges of the dish into the still-liquid central part. Continue until the whole is set into a mass of small, light crystals.

To serve, fill 6 claret glasses with the granita, shaping it into a dome shape with a spoon. Arrange a few mint leaves prettily on top of each sorbet.

MICHEL GUÉRARD
LA CUISINE GOURMANDE

Pear Sherbet

	To serve 8	
1.5 kg	pears	3 lb
300 g	sugar	10 oz
30 cl	water	½ pint
½	lemon	½
3 tbsp	lemon juice	3 tbsp
1	egg white, very lightly beaten	1

In a saucepan, boil the sugar and water together for 10 minutes, covered; this will make a light syrup. Meanwhile, peel, core and quarter the pears and drop them immediately into a bowl of cold water into which you have squeezed the half lemon. The lemon will prevent the pears from turning brown.

Remove the pears from the cold water, drop them into the bubbling syrup and cover. Simmer slowly until they are soft and a sharp knife will pierce their pulp easily. This should take 15 to 20 minutes. Turn the pears once during the cooking and baste them a few times. Let them cool in the syrup.

Drain the fruit, reserving the syrup. Pass the pears through a food mill. There should be about 90 cl (1½ pints) of purée. Add the lemon juice and the egg white and mix well. Taste and add some of the syrup if you want a sweeter flavour. Put the purée into an ice cream freezer or into an ice cube tray. Once the sherbet is hard, remove and beat it until it becomes very fluffy. Then refreeze in a serving mould.

CAROL CUTLER
HAUTE CUISINE FOR YOUR HEART'S DELIGHT

Strawberry Sorbet

	To serve 8	
850 g	fresh strawberries, hulled	1¾ lb
500 g	sugar	1 lb
35 cl	orange juice	12 fl oz
15 to 20 cl	lemon juice	6 fl oz
5 tbsp	Grand Marnier	5 tbsp

Combine in a bowl the strawberries, sugar, the orange juice and lemon juice, and leave to stand at room temperature for 2 to 3 hours. Put the mixture through a sieve or food mill, or purée in an electric blender. Stir in the Grand Marnier and pour the mixture into two large freezing trays. Freeze until about 2.5 cm (1 inch) of the mixture is frozen on all sides of the tray. Remove and beat the mixture until mushy. Return the mixture to the trays and freeze until firm. For a more delicate sorbet, beat the mixture up twice, freezing slightly in between. You may also freeze the sorbet in an ice cream freezer.

JAMES BEARD
HOW TO EAT BETTER FOR LESS MONEY

Lemon Sorbet

Sorbets are half-frozen water ices and generally orange or lemon, though sometimes flavoured with rum or liqueur. They were often served in Victorian and Edwardian days at large dinner parties with long menus, to provide a welcome pause between the roast and the entrée.

To serve 8

8	lemons, rinds finely grated from 2, juice strained	8
250 g	granulated sugar	8 oz
90 cl	water	1½ pints
2	oranges, juice strained	2
2	egg whites	2
60 g	castor sugar	2 oz

In a saucepan, boil the granulated sugar and the water for 5 minutes, skimming off any scum or froth that forms on the surface. Add the lemon rind, lemon juice and orange juice. Bring just to the boil again, then strain and cool. Pour into ice trays and place in the freezing compartment of the refrigerator for about 1 hour. Whisk the whites until they stand in peaks. Transfer the half-frozen sorbet to a bowl and beat in the whites and castor sugar. Return the mixture to the ice trays and freeze until the consistency is as you like it.

ELISABETH AYRTON
THE COOKERY OF ENGLAND

Cherry Ice

Glace de Cerises

The technique of cooking a sugar syrup to the small thread stage is demonstrated on page 8.

To serve 4 to 6

1 kg	very ripe, sound cherries, stalks and stones removed, stones reserved	2 lb
125 g	sugar	4 oz
2	lemons, juice strained	2
½ litre	sugar syrup cooked to the small thread stage	18 fl oz

Put the prepared cherries into a saucepan with the sugar. Crush and stir and bring to the boil. Have ready a fine nylon sieve set over a bowl and press the cherries through this until only the skins remain; pound a handful of the cherry stones in a mortar, and let them infuse for 1 hour with the lemon juice in a tumbler of water. Add the hot sugar syrup to the cherry purée and, just before freezing, pour in the strained infusion of cherry stones, stirring thoroughly with a wooden spoon. Freeze for up to 4 hours, then serve.

VIARD AND FOURET
LE CUISINIER ROYAL

Rhubarb Granité

To serve 4 to 6

750 g	tender rhubarb, washed and cut into 2.5 cm (1 inch) pieces	1½ lb
250 g	sugar	8 oz
¼ litre	water	8 fl oz
2 to 3 tbsp	lemon juice	2 to 3 tbsp
300 g	small strawberries	10 oz

Make a sugar syrup by simmering the sugar and water together in a saucepan for 5 minutes. Add the rhubarb pieces and stew until tender. Add the lemon juice and a few strawberries for colour, and pass the entire lot through a sieve. Cool and taste for sweetness: add more sugar if necessary. Freeze for 3 to 4 hours or until needed. This granité is a particularly lush shade of rose and deserves to be viewed through a transparent dish. Garnish with the remaining unstemmed strawberries before serving.

JUDITH OLNEY
SUMMER FOOD

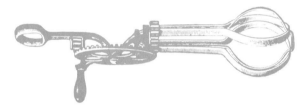

Melon and Champagne Ice

Granité de Melon au Champagne

The technique of making a sugar syrup is shown on page 8.

Buy more melons than you need, and taste them before using them: flavourless melons will make a flavourless ice. If they are of a size that half shells will contain the right quantity for individual servings, cut them in two. Small melons, about 7.5 cm (3 inches) in diameter, are perfect for individual servings.

To serve 4 to 6

2 or 3	medium-sized, or 4 or 6 small Cantaloupe melons	2 or 3
¼ litre	champagne, iced	8 fl oz
60 g	sugar	2 oz
10 cl	water	4 fl oz
2 tbsp	lemon juice	2 tbsp
4 tbsp	cognac	4 tbsp

If using medium-sized melons, halve them, discard the seeds and scoop out the flesh. If using small melons, cut off a lid from each melon, discard the seeds and scoop out the flesh. Purée the melon flesh through a sieve into a bowl. If you have large enough deep-freezing facilities, deep-freeze the melon shells, otherwise chill them thoroughly. Boil the sugar and water together to make a light syrup, and leave to cool before mixing with the melon purée, lemon juice and champagne. Freeze in ice trays, loosening the mixture from the sides and stirring from time to time as it freezes. It is best to start it several hours before it is needed. Just before serving, turn it into an iced bowl, working it a bit with a fork if it is too firm: it should be just slightly mushy. Rinse out the frozen or chilled melon shells with the cognac, pour it into the frozen mixture, mix, and then fill the melon shells with the ice.

RICHARD OLNEY
SIMPLE FRENCH FOOD

◆

Madeira Water Ice

To serve 6 to 8

90 cl	Madeira	1½ pints
2	lemons, rind grated, juice strained	2
30 cl	28 Baumé sugar syrup (page 9)	½ pint

Place the grated lemon rind and the strained juice in a bowl and mix in the Madeira and the syrup. Stir well, turn the mixture into the cylinder of a hand-churn freezer, pack the cylinder in pounded ice and salt, and work the handle vigorously until the mixture is frozen. When sufficiently frozen, transfer the mixture to a 1.25 litre (2 pint) mould. Cover the mould and pack it in pounded ice and salt for 2 hours.

Before serving, dip the mould in warm water, wipe it, then turn the contents carefully out on to a china or glass dish.

OSCAR TSCHIRKY
THE COOK BOOK BY "OSCAR" OF THE WALDORF

◆

Blackberry Water Ice

If sweet-scented geranium leaves are unavailable, a tablespoon or two of rose water makes a fair substitute.

To serve 4 to 6

500 g	blackberries, puréed through a sieve	1 lb
125 g	sugar	4 oz
15 cl	water	¼ pint
3	sweet-scented geranium leaves	3

Make a syrup by boiling the sugar and water together for 5 to 6 minutes, with 2 of the geranium leaves. When cool, remove the geranium leaves, add the syrup to the sieved blackberries, and put into a freezing tray with the remaining geranium leaf on the top. Cover with foil and freeze, at the normal temperature for ice making, for 2½ hours.

ELIZABETH DAVID
SUMMER COOKING

Iced Plum Pudding

If bitter almonds are unavailable, use 30 almonds plus a few drops of almond extract (or substitute kernels from apricot stones for bitter almonds).

To serve 10 to 12

24	sweet almonds, blanched	24
6	bitter almonds, blanched	6
	rose water or lemon juice	
125 g	raisins	4 oz
125g	currants, picked over, washed and dried	4 oz
90 g	candied citron or other candied citrus peel, chopped	3 oz
About 30 g	flour	About 1 oz
¼ litre	creamy milk	8 fl oz
1	vanilla pod, split and cut into 5 cm (2 inch) pieces	1
90 cl	double cream	1½ pints
250 g	sugar	8 oz
1 tsp	grated nutmeg	1 tsp
15 to 20 cl	maraschino, noyau, curaçao or brandy	6 fl oz
8	egg yolks	8
175 g	strawberry or raspberry jam	6 oz
6	preserved apricots or peaches	6
6	preserved green limes	6

Pound the almonds, one at a time, in a mortar till they become a smooth paste free from the smallest lumps; add frequently a few drops of rose water or lemon juice to make them light and prevent "oiling". Mix the raisins, currants and citron; dredge well with flour. Put the milk in a pan with the pieces of vanilla and boil it till the flavour of the vanilla is well extracted, then strain the pieces out and mix the vanilla milk with 45 cl (16 fl oz) of the cream, and stir in gradually the sugar and nutmeg. Add the pounded almonds and liqueur.

In a shallow bowl, beat the egg yolks till very light, thick and smooth, and stir them gradually into the mixture. Simmer over a medium heat (stirring all the time), but take the mixture off the heat just before it boils, otherwise it will curdle. At once stir in the dried fruit, set to cool, and then add the jam and preserved fruit. Whip the remaining cream and add it lightly to the mixture; put the whole into a large 1.75 litre (3 pint) melon-shaped mould that opens in the middle, and freeze for 4 hours. Turn out when wanted and serve the iced pudding in a glass dish.

THE BUCKEYE COOKBOOK TRADITIONAL AMERICAN RECIPES

◆

Mango Parfait

This recipe, based on egg mousse, is a good way of sharing one delectable but very expensive fruit among several people.

To serve 5 or 6

1	very large ripe mango, peeled, halved and stoned	1
3	egg yolks	3
75 g	icing sugar	2½ oz
	sugar	
1 or 2 tsp	lemon juice	1 or 2 tsp
	salt	
15 cl	whipping cream, whipped	¼ pint

Beat the egg yolks lightly with the icing sugar, then, still beating, place the bowl carefully over a pan of barely simmering water. When the mixture is just lukewarm remove it from the pan and go on beating until it is cool.

Sieve the fruit of the mango, sweeten it to taste with sugar, and sharpen it with lemon juice and a pinch of salt. Fold this purée into the mousse and fold in the whipped cream. Freeze. The colour is beautiful.

SUSAN CAMPBELL
THE TIMES

Butterscotch-Rum Parfait

You can make the following variations of this recipe: make the syrup with granulated sugar instead of brown sugar; flavour the egg yolks with 1 tablespoon of vanilla extract instead of rum; and fold in 10 cl (4 fl oz) melted chocolate, or melted chocolate and a coffee-flavoured liqueur; or fresh berries, or peaches, along with the whipped cream.

To serve 6

125 g	brown sugar	4 oz
60 g	butter	2 oz
15 to 20 cl	water	6 fl oz
3	egg yolks	3
1 tbsp	rum	1 tbsp
	salt	
45 cl	double cream	16 fl oz
3 tbsp	crushed, blanched almonds	3 tbsp

In a small saucepan, make a syrup by bringing the sugar, butter and water to the boil, stirring to dissolve the sugar, then boiling hard for 3 minutes. Set the syrup aside to cool.

In the small bowl of an electric mixer, beat the egg yolks at medium speed until light and fluffy. Gradually pour in the reserved syrup, in a thin stream, beating all the while. Beat in the rum and a pinch of salt, then place the mixture in a saucepan and whisk over direct heat until the mixture is as thick as double cream.

Return the mixture to the bowl, set over ice and whisk for about 10 minutes, or until cold. Whip the cream until it is the same consistency as the parfait base, then fold it in. Pour the mixture into parfait glasses and freeze for at least 1 hour. (The longer the parfait stays in the freezer, the more solid it becomes. I like to make it the day before I plan to serve it.)

Three hours before serving, remove the parfaits from the freezer and place them in the refrigerator. When served, the parfaits should be the consistency of frozen custard. Sprinkle the tops with the almonds.

JULIE DANNENBAUM
JULIE DANNENBAUM'S CREATIVE COOKING SCHOOL

Coffee Ice Cream

Some make this coffee ice cream with ground coffee, well strained, but the cream has then a disagreeable brown colour. See that the coffee is not over-roasted. Sometimes half milk and half cream are used instead of all cream; when using the milk and cream, 2 or 3 extra eggs must be mixed in. You boil the milk and the cream and add the eggs and the lemon.

To serve 6 to 8

7 or 8	egg yolks, beaten	7 or 8
60 cl	double cream	1 pint
1	lemon, rind thinly pared	1
1	slice lemon	1
125 g	Mocha coffee beans, roasted	4 oz
175 g	sugar	6 oz

Pour the egg yolks into a copper pan, add the cream and mix together gently. Add the lemon rind and slice to the cream and egg yolks. Put the pan over a medium heat, and stir constantly with a wooden spoon. You must not let the cream boil as it would then curdle and be spoilt. When it gets thick and refuses to obey the motion of stirring, remove it from the heat, for it is done. Put it in a jug or pot. Add the coffee beans to the cream mixture, cover down tight and let it stand for a short time (about 30 minutes) in a warm place. When the cream has become tinctured with the coffee, strain it through a sieve. Sweeten to taste with the sugar. When quite cold, put the coffee cream into a churn freezer, and freeze until it has the consistency of, and is as smooth as, butter.

WILLIAM JEANES
GUNTER'S MODERN CONFECTIONER

Fruit and Almond Ice Cream

Plombières

The technique of pounding almonds is shown on page 12.

To serve 4 to 6

About 125 g	assorted crystallized fruit, diced and macerated in 2 tbsp brandy	About 4 oz
100 g	blanched almonds, pounded to a paste in a mortar with 2 or 3 tbsp water	3½ oz
¼ litre	boiling milk	8 fl oz
6	egg yolks	6
¼ litre	35° Baumé sugar syrup (*page 8*) cooked with a vanilla pod and cooled	8 fl oz
¼ litre	double cream, whipped	8 fl oz

Place the almond paste in a bowl, pour over the boiling milk, cover and infuse for 1 hour. Rub the resulting almond milk through a fine sieve and beat in the egg yolks. Add the cooled sugar syrup and transfer the mixture to a saucepan. Stir continuously over low heat. When the cream thickens, strain it through a sieve into a bowl and beat until cool.

Fold in the whipped cream. Pour the cream mixture into a 1 litre (1¾ pint) mould in layers, separating each of the layers with a thin sprinkling of crystallized fruit, and finishing with a layer of the cream. Freeze for 2 to 3 hours. Unmould and decorate with crystallized fruit.

ROBERT COURTINE
BALZAC À TABLE

Ginger Ice Cream

For the ginger syrup called for in this recipe, use the syrup from the jar of preserved ginger.

To serve 6 to 8

90 to 125 g	preserved ginger, chopped	3 to 4 oz
¼ litre	milk	8 fl oz
2	egg yolks	2
1	egg	1
4 tbsp	ginger syrup	4 tbsp
¼ litre	double cream, whipped	8 fl oz
2 tbsp	icing sugar or soft brown sugar	2 tbsp

Bring the milk to the boil in a saucepan over a high heat, and pour it on to the yolks and the egg very gradually, beating the whole thing together (small wire whisks are the best for this kind of operation). Pour the mixture back into the saucepan and cook slowly over a low heat until the custard thickens: it must not boil or the eggs will curdle. Immediately the thick-

ness seems right, dip the base of the pan into a bowl of very cold water. This prevents the custard continuing to cook in its own heat. Add the ginger syrup immediately after this, to hurry further the cooling process.

When the custard is cool, place the pan in the freezing compartment of the refrigerator, which should be set at the coldest possible temperature. When the custard has set solid round the edges, remove it to a bowl, stir it up well and quickly incorporate the ginger pieces and the whipped cream. Taste and add sugar gradually—ice creams should not be too sickly sweet, mainly on account of the flavour, but also because an oversweetened mixture freezes less well.

Return the mixture to the freezer and leave until hard. If the custard was frozen to the right amount before the ginger and the cream were added, it should not be necessary to stir it at all during the second freezing process. If there was any doubt about this, stir it up gently after 1 hour, so that the ginger pieces do not sink to the bottom.

JANE GRIGSON
ENGLISH FOOD

Tea and Rum Ice Cream

Glace au Thé et Rhum

To serve 4 to 6

15 cl	strong black tea	¼ pint
4 tbsp	rum	4 tbsp
1 litre	milk	1¾ pints
300 g	sugar	10 oz
10	egg yolks	10

Bring the milk and sugar to the boil in a saucepan, then add the rum and tea. Whisk the egg yolks in a bowl, and gradually add the hot milk mixture, whisking all the time. Return the mixture to the saucepan and, over a very low heat, stir constantly until it thickens, but without letting it boil, which would cause the mixture to curdle. Remove from the heat and strain through muslin or a fine sieve. Stir constantly with a wooden spoon until the mixture is quite cold. Freeze in a churn freezer until firm. Transfer the mixture to a bombe mould and freeze for at least 2 hours.

To serve, dip the mould in hot water for a second, and unmould on to a napkin-covered serving dish.

LÉON ISNARD
LA CUISINE FRANÇAISE ET AFRICAINE

Nougat Ice Cream

To serve 6 to 8

¾ litre	single cream	1¼ pints
6	egg yolks	6
¼ litre	honey, preferably orange flower	8 fl oz
2 tbsp	orange flower water	2 tbsp
35 cl	double cream whipped	12 fl oz
3	egg whites, stiffly beaten	3
100g	pistachio nuts, peeled	3½ oz
75 g	almonds, blanched and split	2½ oz

Heat the single cream in a saucepan over a low heat. Stir the egg yolks in another saucepan and add the hot cream. Put over the lowest heat and stir until the spoon is coated. Remove from the heat and, stirring continuously, pour the mixture slowly over the honey in a bowl. Add 1 tablespoon orange flower water. Strain the mixture and leave it to get cold.

Incorporate the whipped cream into the honey mixture, then fold in the beaten egg whites and the nuts. Flavour with the remaining orange flower water and freeze.

ALICE B. TOKLAS
THE ALICE B. TOKLAS COOK BOOK

Almond Crunch Spumone

To serve 8

250 g	sugar	8 oz
5 tbsp	water	5 tbsp
6	egg yolks	6
45 cl	double cream	16 fl oz
½ tsp	almond extract	½ tsp
3 tbsp	kirsch	3 tbsp
	strawberries or raspberries	
	Nut crunch	
60 g	chopped almonds, or filberts	2 oz
15 g	butter	½ oz
2 tbsp	sugar	2 tbsp

To make the nut crunch, heat the butter and sugar in a frying pan; add the nuts and sauté them, stirring until the sugar melts and caramelizes and the nuts are lightly toasted. Turn out the nut crunch on to a sheet of buttered foil and let it cool.

Combine the sugar and water in a saucepan and bring to the boil. Boil until the temperature reaches 114°C (238°F) on a sugar thermometer. Meanwhile, beat the egg yolks until thick and pale yellow. Continue beating the yolks and

immediately pour the hot syrup over them in a fine stream. Beat until the mixture cools to room temperature, about 7 minutes. Then chill until cold.

Whip the cream until stiff and flavour with the almond extract and kirsch. Fold the cream and two-thirds of the nut mixture into the yolks. Pour into a 2 litre (3½ pint) mould, cover and freeze until firm—at least 8 hours.

Unmould by dipping the mould briefly into warm water. Turn out on to a platter and sprinkle with the remaining nut crunch. Decorate with strawberries or raspberries.

LOU SEIBERT PAPPAS
EGG COOKERY

White Ice with Coffee Sauce

To serve 8 to 10

1.25 litres	double cream	2 pints
125 g	sugar	4 oz
1	vanilla pod, grated	1
125 g	plain chocolate, broken into very small pieces, but not grated	4 oz
	Coffee Sauce	
60 cl	freshly made very strong black coffee	1 pint
60 g	sugar	2 oz

Beat the cream with the sugar and the vanilla until it just begins to thicken. Mix in the chocolate pieces. Pour into a 1.5 litre (2½ pint) mould and freeze for 2½ to 3 hours.

To make the coffee sauce, sweeten the coffee with the sugar and serve it in a sauceboat, either hot or cold, with the ice.

RUTH LOWINSKY
MORE LOVELY FOOD

Caledonian Ice (Iced Stapag)

Brown wholemeal breadcrumbs toasted in the oven can be substituted for the coarse oatmeal called for in this recipe.

To serve 4 to 6

1.25 litres	double cream, stiffly whipped	2 pints
125 g	castor sugar	4 oz
2 tsp	vanilla extract	2 tsp
150 g	coarse toasted oatmeal, well dried in the oven without being browned	5 oz

Sweeten the whipped cream with the sugar and flavour it with the vanilla extract; set it to freeze. When nearly frozen, stir in the oatmeal. You may serve the ice cream in a glass dish or in individual glasses.

F. MARIAN McNEILL
THE SCOTS KITCHEN

New York Ice Cream

To serve 8 to 10

Almond ice cream

60 g	blanched almonds	2 oz
40 cl	milk	¾ pint
15 cl	double cream	¼ pint
3	egg yolks	3
125 g	castor sugar	4 oz
1 tsp	kirsch	1 tsp

Chestnut filling

125 g	marrons glacés	4 oz
100 g	castor sugar	3½ oz
5	egg yolks	5
½ tsp	vanilla extract	½ tsp
2 tbsp	curaçao or Benedictine	2 tbsp
30 cl	double cream, whipped	½ pint
350 g	fresh raspberries	12 oz
1 tbsp	kirsch	1 tbsp

Decoration

1	2.5 m (1 inch) square angelica, cut into strips	1
	glacé cherries, halved	
30 g	pistachio nuts, chopped	1 oz
	double cream, whipped	

First make the almond ice cream. Place the almonds in a mortar and pound them to a paste; add the milk and the cream. Mix thoroughly together, then transfer the mixture to a small saucepan; place on the heat and bring to the boil. Remove the almond milk from the heat. Place the egg yolks and the sugar in a bowl and add the kirsch. Mix well for 5 minutes, then gradually add the almond milk, mixing well with a wooden spoon.

Return the mixture to the saucepan and place it over a low heat. Stirring continuously, heat it for 5 minutes without letting it boil. Then allow it to cool. Strain through a sieve into an ice cream freezer, and freeze until the ice cream is firm.

Meanwhile, prepare the filling. Press the marrons glacés through a wire sieve into a basin; add 90 g (3 oz) of the castor sugar and the egg yolks; set the basin over the heat and whisk for 10 minutes; place on ice and stir with a spatula until thoroughly cold; then add the vanilla extract and curaçao or Benedictine. Mix well, then add the whipped cream, and gently mix until well amalgamated.

Line the bottom of a 1.5 litre (2½ pint) mould with a sheet of white paper, then line the bottom and the sides with three-quarters of the almond ice cream. Place the raspberries in a bowl with the remaining castor sugar and the kirsch; mix thoroughly, then arrange three-quarters of the raspberries at the bottom and sides of the mould. Pour in the chestnut preparation; place the remaining raspberries on top, and fill the mould with the remaining almond ice cream. Cover with a sheet of paper, put the lid on the mould and freeze for 1½ hours.

To unmould, remove the lid and the paper and turn the dessert out on to a cold dish. Place the strips of angelica in the centre of the dessert. Arrange glacé cherry halves all round the surface and decorate the base with whipped cream; then sprinkle over the chopped pistachio nuts and serve.

MAY BYRON
MAY BYRON'S PUDDINGS, PASTRIES AND SWEET DISHES

Christmas Ice-Pudding

This dessert is strictly for adults, and is no less rich than the traditional Christmas Pudding.

To serve 4 to 6

175 g	a combination of any of the following: raisins, currants, glacé orange, glacé cherries, marrons glacés, roughly chopped	6 oz
4 tbsp	rum	4 tbsp
30 cl	single cream	½ pint
5	egg yolks, lightly beaten	5
150 g	castor sugar	5 oz
125 g	unsweetened chestnut purée	4 oz
125 g	bitter chocolate	4 oz
30 cl	double cream, whipped	½ pint

Soak the mixed chopped fruits in the rum. In a saucepan, heat the single cream over a medium heat to near the boiling point, pour it on to the egg yolks mixed with the sugar, and return to the pan. Stir over a low heat until the custard thickens, but do not allow it to boil. You may find it easier to do this in a double saucepan. When the custard has thickened, add the chestnut purée and the chocolate, and stir well until they have dissolved and the custard is quite smooth. Taste for sweetness and leave to cool. Mix in the rum-soaked fruits and finally fold in the whipped double cream.

Line a 1 litre (1¾ pint) pudding basin with foil or polythene film. Pour in the mixture, wrap and freeze. If you cannot spare the basin until the pudding is eaten lift the pudding out after 24 hours, wrap it and replace it in the freezer.

Remove the pudding from the freezer about 1 hour before serving. Unwrap the pudding and leave it in the refrigerator until you are ready to eat it.

HELGE RUBINSTEIN AND SHEILA BUSH
A FREEZER FOR ALL SEASONS

Black Forest Bombe

The chocolate ice cream may be prepared well in advance.

To serve 8

Chocolate ice cream

75 g	plain or bitter chocolate, broken into small pieces	2½ oz
20 cl	single cream	7 fl oz
3	egg yolks	3
75 g	sugar	2½ oz
20 cl	double cream	7 fl oz

Bombe mousse

4 tbsp	water	4 tbsp
75 g	sugar	2½ oz
3	egg yolks	3
2 tbsp	kirsch	2 tbsp
15 cl	double or whipping cream	¼ pint
60 g	stale pumpernickel, finely grated	2 oz
400 g	stoneless black cherries in syrup, drained and roughly chopped	14 oz
1	egg white	1

To prepare the chocolate ice cream, rinse out a saucepan in cold water and in it heat the chocolate in the single cream, stirring from time to time, until the chocolate has melted and the mixture is hot but not boiling. In a heatproof bowl or the top of a double saucepan, beat the yolks and the sugar until they are thick and creamy, and slowly add the chocolate mixture, stirring well. Place over a pan of simmering water and stir or gently beat the mixture until it begins to thicken. Cool. Whip the double cream lightly and fold it into the chocolate mixture. Freeze in an ice cream freezer.

If the ice cream has been prepared in advance, transfer it from the freezer to the refrigerator 1 hour before use to allow the ice cream to soften. Line a chilled 1 litre (2 pint) bombe mould with the softened ice cream and freeze.

To prepare the bombe mousse, boil the water and sugar until a thick syrup forms, but do not allow the syrup to change colour. The time this takes depends on the quantity of syrup in relation to the size of the saucepan, but 3 minutes' steady boiling should be about right. In a heatproof bowl or double-saucepan top, whisk the egg yolks until they are pale and fluffy, and pour in the hot but not boiling syrup in a thin stream, still whisking. Place the bowl over a pan of simmering water, and continue to beat until the mixture has thickened and doubled in volume. Remove from the heat, place in a bowl of iced water and beat until the mixture has cooled.

Blend in the kirsch. Whip the cream lightly and fold it in, together with the pumpernickel and the cherries. Whisk the egg whites stiffly and fold them into the mixture. Fill the

centre of the bombe and freeze for about 4 hours. Remove from the freezer about 45 minutes before serving, turn out on to a plate and leave in the refrigerator, until ready to serve.

HELGE RUBINSTEIN AND SHEILA BUSH
ICES GALORE

Chocolate Chestnut Bombe

The technique of making a chestnut purée is shown on page 30.

To serve 8

Chocolate ice cream

140 g	plain chocolate, broken into small pieces	4½ oz
3	egg yolks	3
90 g	castor sugar	3 oz
	salt	
30 cl	single cream	½ pint
4 to 5 tbsp	milk	4 to 5 tbsp
20 cl	double cream, whipped	7 fl oz

Filling

500 g	sweetened chestnut purée	1 lb
1	egg white	1
30 cl	double cream	½ pint

Decoration

1	egg white	1
15 cl	double cream	¼ pint
About 15 g	icing sugar	About ½ oz
¼ tsp	vanilla extract	¼ tsp
	Marrons glacés, crystallized violets, and angelica	

First prepare the chocolate ice cream. Beat the egg yolks with the sugar and a pinch of salt until light and lemon-coloured. Scald the single cream, and add it to the egg mixture, beating vigorously until well blended. Pour the mixture into the top of a double saucepan and cook over hot water for about 10 minutes, stirring, until the mixture coats the back of the spoon. Melt the chocolate in the milk and add it to the custard. Mix well; strain and cool. When the chocolate custard is cool, fold in the whipped double cream. Pour the mixture into a freezing tray and freeze until quite firm, 2 to 3 hours.

Chill a 1.5 litre (2½ pint) bombe mould thoroughly in the deep freeze. Soften the chocolate ice cream slightly and, with a spatula, spread it smoothly over the base and sides of the mould to make a layer about 2.5 cm (1 inch) thick. Return the mould to the freezer until the ice cream is firm again.

Meanwhile, turn the chestnut purée into a bowl. If necessary, beat it with a spoon or spatula to eliminate lumpiness. Whisk the egg white until stiff but not dry. Whisk the double cream until it just leaves a trail on the surface when the beaters are lifted. Fold the chestnut purée gently into the whipped cream until the mixture is no longer streaky. Fold in the beaten egg white. Pour the chestnut mixture into the chocolate-lined mould. Cover the mould with a lid or a sheet of foil. Freeze until firm, preferably overnight.

Transfer the bombe to the main compartment of the refrigerator about 1 hour before you intend to serve it. To unmould, remove the lid or foil and invert the mould on to a serving dish. Wrap a cloth wrung out in hot water around it for about 30 seconds, re-dipping the cloth in hot water and wringing it out again when it cools. If the surface of the ice cream melts slightly as you unmould it, smooth it over with a knife and return the ice cream to the freezer for 15 to 30 minutes.

Just before serving, make a *crème Chantilly* as follows: whisk the egg white until stiff but not dry. Whisk the cream until it holds its shape in stiff peaks, adding a little icing sugar and a few drops of vanilla extract to taste—the cream should be only faintly sweet. Fold enough beaten egg white into the cream to lighten its texture without making it flow. Pipe the *crème Chantilly* over and around the bombe, and finish decoration with a few marrons glacés, crystallized violets and angelica cut into diamond-shaped "leaves".

ROBERT CARRIER
THE ROBERT CARRIER COOKERY COURSE

Apricot and Chablis Bombe

Bombe Marquise

To serve 8

	Apricot ice	
1 kg	apricots, stoned	2 lb
$\frac{1}{4}$ litre	water	8 fl oz
300 g	sugar	10 oz
$\frac{1}{4}$ tsp	ground cinnamon	$\frac{1}{4}$ tsp
1	lemon, rind finely grated, juice strained	1

	Chablis ice	
20 cl	Chablis wine	7 fl oz
$\frac{3}{4}$ litre	28° Baumé sugar syrup (*page 8*)	1$\frac{1}{4}$ pints
$\frac{1}{2}$	vanilla pod	$\frac{1}{2}$
1	lemon or orange, rind finely peeled	1
4 tbsp	strained lemon juice	4 tbsp

First prepare the apricot ice. In a saucepan cook the apricots, water, sugar, cinnamon and lemon rind over medium heat until the mixture thickens like jam. Rub through a fine sieve

and add the lemon juice. Reheat the mixture until it reaches 22° on the hydrometer. Leave to cool, then freeze in an ice-cream churn or in the deep freeze.

Meanwhile prepare the Chablis ice. In a saucepan gently simmer the sugar syrup with the vanilla and lemon or orange rind for 15 minutes. Leave this flavoured syrup to cool, remove the vanilla pod and rind, and add the wine and lemon juice. Freeze as above.

To assemble the bombe, line a 2 litre (3$\frac{1}{2}$ pint) bombe mould with apricot ice and fill the inside with Chablis ice. Refreeze the ices for at least 1 hour before unmoulding and serving.

JOSEPH FAVRE
DICTIONNAIRE UNIVERSEL DE CUISINE PRATIQUE

Frozen Pistachio Soufflé

The technique of blanching pistachio nuts is shown on page 12.

To serve 4

60 g	pistachio nuts, blanched and very finely chopped	2 oz
12	egg yolks	12
4	egg whites	4
90 g	castor sugar	3 oz
1 tsp	vanilla extract	1 tsp
1 tbsp	orange flower water	1 tbsp
$\frac{1}{8}$ tsp	green food colouring	$\frac{1}{8}$ tsp
30 cl	double cream, stiffly whipped with 15 g ($\frac{1}{2}$ oz) sugar	$\frac{1}{2}$ pint

Put in a basin the egg yolks, egg whites, sugar, vanilla extract, orange flower water, a few drops of food colouring and the pistachio nuts; whisk this over boiling water until the mixture is warm, then take it off the heat and continue to whisk it until cold and thick. Add to the mixture the slightly sweetened, stiffly whipped double cream, folding it in carefully. Then pour the whole into a 90 cl (1$\frac{1}{2}$ pint) soufflé case around which a band of kitchen paper has been folded and fastened, standing 12 to 15 cm (4 to 5 inches) above the top of the case. Freeze for 3$\frac{1}{2}$ to 4 hours. When sufficiently frozen remove the paper. Dish up on a napkin and serve.

MRS. A. B. MARSHALL
FANCY ICES

Frozen Blackcurrant Liqueur Soufflé

Soufflé alla Crème de Cassis

To serve 6

10 cl	*crème de Cassis*	4 fl oz
3	eggs, yolks separated from whites	3
	salt	
100 g	castor sugar	3½ oz
30 cl	whipping cream	½ pint

Whisk the egg whites with a pinch of salt. Beat the egg yolks with the sugar until white and creamy. Add the *crème de Cassis* to the beaten egg yolk mixture, and mix well. Fold in the cream, then gently fold in the egg whites.

Surround a 60 cl (1 pint) soufflé dish with an aluminium collar that stands about 7.5 cm (3 inches) above the rim of the dish. Pour the soufflé mixture into the dish, and freeze for 3 to 4 hours. Remove the foil collar just before serving.

ELENA SPAGNOL
I GELATI FATTÌ IN CASA CON O SENZA MACCHINA

Rainbow Iced Soufflé

Soufflé Glacé Arc-en-Ciel

A recipe from La Réserve restaurant, at Beaulieu-sur-Mer.

Rainbow iced soufflé is composed of layers of four different colours and flavours: pistachio, vanilla with roasted hazelnuts and almonds, raspberry and coffee.

To serve 8

8	egg yolks	8
250 g	vanilla sugar	8 oz
¾ litre	double cream, whipped	1¼ pints
400 g	raspberries, puréed through a nylon sieve and sweetened to taste	14 oz
10 cl	strong black coffee	4 fl oz
1 tsp	vanilla extract	1 tsp
3 tbsp each	finely chopped roasted hazelnuts and almonds	3 tbsp each
60 g	shelled pistachio nuts, pounded to a paste with 3 tbsp light sugar syrup (*page 8*) and 2 tbsp boiling water	2 oz
60 g	raspberries	2 oz
30 g	plain chocolate shavings (*page 11*)	1 oz
	icing sugar	

Mix the egg yolks and the vanilla sugar in a copper bowl and place over a very low heat, or over hot water in a water bath, and whisk until the mixture reaches the consistency of a lightly beaten cream. Take the bowl off the heat, set over ice

and continue to whisk the mixture until it is cool; then fold in the whipped cream, incorporating it thoroughly.

Divide the mixture into four parts. Flavour one part with all but 2 or 3 tablespoons of the raspberry purée, one with all of the coffee, one with the vanilla extract and chopped nuts, and one with the pistachio paste.

In an 18 cm (7 inch) diameter soufflé dish, with a paper collar three times the height of the dish, make a layer of about half of the raspberry-flavoured mixture. Leave to set in the freezer. Add a layer of the coffee-flavoured mixture, freeze, then repeat the process with a vanilla and nut layer, then a pistachio layer. Continue layering in this way, then put the dessert in the freezer for 3 to 6 hours.

Remove the paper collar, spoon the remaining raspberry purée on top and decorate with whole raspberries, chocolate shavings and a sprinkling of icing sugar.

LES PRINCES DE LA GASTRONOMIE

Frozen Macaroon Soufflé

Soufflé all'Amaretto

As a variation, you may, if you wish, dip some additional macaroons in sherry and put them in the bottom of the dish before pouring in the soufflé mixture.

To serve 6

6	macaroons, coarsely crumbled	6
3	eggs, separated, whites stiffly beaten with a pinch of salt	3
About 60 g	castor sugar	About 2 oz
4 tbsp	sweet sherry	4 tbsp
35 cl	double cream, whipped	12 fl oz

Beat the egg yolks with the sugar until white and creamy. Add the crumbled macaroons and the sherry, and mix well. Fold in the whipped cream, then gently fold in the egg whites.

Surround a 60 cl (1 pint) soufflé dish with an aluminium foil collar, cut to stand 2 to 3 cm (about 1 inch) above the rim of the soufflé dish. Pour the soufflé mixture into the dish, and freeze in the deep-freeze for at least 4 hours. Remove the aluminium foil collar at the last minute before serving.

ELENA SPAGNOL
I GELATI FATTI IN CASA CON O SENSA MACCHINA

Assemblies

Vanilla Charlotte Russe

Charlotte à la Russe

To make a raspberry charlotte russe, add 10 cl (4 fl oz) of puréed raspberries to the custard before adding the whipped cream. Surround the unmoulded pudding with raspberries macerated in kirsch and heavily sugared.

To serve 6		
20	sponge finger biscuits (*page 167*), sides and ends neatly cut, trimmings crumbled	20
20 cl	milk, or half milk and half double cream	7 fl oz
1	vanilla pod	1
100 g	castor sugar	$3\frac{1}{2}$ oz
4	egg yolks	4
7 g	leaf gelatine, softened in a little cold water	$\frac{1}{4}$ oz
30 cl	whipped double cream, flavoured with 2 tbsp sugar and $\frac{1}{2}$ tsp vanilla sugar	$\frac{1}{2}$ pint

Cover the bottom and sides of a 1.5 litre ($2\frac{1}{2}$ pint) charlotte mould with greaseproof paper, a round piece for the bottom and a long strip for the sides. Cover the paper in the bottom of the mould with some sponge fingers cut into triangles to form a rosette. Line the sides with sponge fingers cut 1 to 2 cm ($\frac{1}{2}$ to $\frac{3}{4}$ inch) higher than the mould and all the same length, so that the charlotte balances when unmoulded. The sponge fingers should be placed side by side, very close together, with the curved sides against the mould where they will show when the charlotte is unmoulded.

Prepare a *crème anglaise*; bring the milk or milk and cream to the boil, remove the saucepan from the heat, add the vanilla pod and leave to steep, covered. In a bowl mix the sugar and the egg yolks; beat this mixture with a wooden spoon until it is frothy, thick and nearly white. Then remove the vanilla pod from the milk and slowly add the milk to the egg mixture. Pour the egg and milk mixture back into the saucepan, and cook over low heat; stir continuously with the wooden spoon, moving it all around the bottom of the pan to prevent the egg yolks from scrambling into tiny particles. As the sauce heats, the egg yolks will thicken the mixture. As soon as the mixture starts to coat the spoon, remove the pan from the heat, and add the softened gelatine. Stir until dissolved. Strain the mixture through a fine sieve into a bowl.

Let the custard cool on ice or refrigerate, stirring often. As soon as it starts to set, carefully fold in the whipped cream. Pour the mixture into the lined mould, filling it to the top. Smooth the surface with a knife blade and sprinkle with sponge finger crumbs; refrigerate for at least 2 hours.

To serve, unmould the charlotte russe on to a round platter covered with a doily.

PAUL BOCUSE
THE NEW CUISINE

Charlotte Russe

Noyau is a bitter almond-flavoured liqueur. Kirsch or another fruit liqueur may be substituted.

Almost any cream mixture stiffened with gelatine may be used as a filling for this dessert (*see recipes pages 115-116*).

To serve 5 or 6		
16 to 20	sponge finger biscuits (*page 167*), sides and ends trimmed	16 to 20
1	egg white (optional)	1
40 cl	double cream	$\frac{3}{4}$ pint
About 2 tsp	castor sugar	About 2 tsp
About $\frac{1}{2}$ tsp	vanilla extract or about 1 tbsp noyau or other liqueur	About $\frac{1}{2}$ tsp
15 g	powdered gelatine	$\frac{1}{2}$ oz
5 tbsp	water	5 tbsp

A plain 1 litre ($1\frac{1}{2}$ pint) mould is required, with straight sides and a flat bottom like a soufflé tin. First place at the bottom of the tin a round of oiled greaseproof paper, oiled side down, cut to fit it exactly. Then arrange sponge finger biscuits evenly round the sides of the tin. They should be long enough to reach to the top of the tin, and must be packed very closely together. The joins may be brushed over with a little white of egg to seal them. The bottom of the tin may also be lined with sponge fingers, cut into triangular pieces and fitted in evenly.

Whip the cream to a stiff froth, and add sugar to taste. Flavour to taste with vanilla extract or liqueur. Dissolve the gelatine in the water, and strain it slowly into the cream, stirring all the time. When the mixture begins to stiffen, turn it into the prepared mould.

When the cream is set, turn out the charlotte russe on a glass or silver dish covered with a lace-edged paper.

FLORENCE B. JACK
COOKERY FOR EVERY HOUSEHOLD

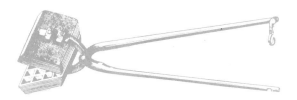

Malakoff Pudding

Pouding à la Malakoff

The sponge finger biscuits may be soaked in any orange-flavoured liqueur or in rum.

To serve 4 to 6

60 cl	pouring custard (*page 166*) to which 15 g (½ oz) softened gelatine has been added	1 pint
12	sponge finger biscuits (*page 167*), soaked in liqueur	12
30 cl	apple purée	½ pint
30 cl	pear purée	½ pint
60 g	finely sliced blanched almonds	2 oz
1 tbsp	finely diced orange rind	1 tbsp
40 g	raisins, soaked in medium/light sugar syrup (*page 8*)	1½ oz
60 cl	*sabayon* sauce (*page 166*)	1 pint

Lightly oil a 1.5 litre (2½ pint) charlotte mould. Put in a layer of custard about 1 cm (½ inch) thick, cover with a layer of sponge fingers, spread with a layer of apple purée, and sprinkle with the almonds, orange rind and raisins. Add another layer of custard, more sponge fingers, pear purée and more almonds, orange rind and raisins. Continue layering, alternating layers of apple and pear purée, until the mould is full, finishing with a layer of custard. Refrigerate until needed. Unmould and serve with cold *sabayon* sauce.

COUNTESS MORPHY
SWEETS AND PUDDINGS

Charlotte Malakoff

This is an extravagant pudding, but luckily it is so rich that no one can eat much of it. It is particularly delicious served with a tart fruit purée, such as raspberry or redcurrant.

You can make the following variations of this pudding. For a raspberry charlotte malakoff, add 250 g (8 oz) raspberries to the list of ingredients. Pour one-third of the malakoff mixture into the prepared mould, cover with a layer of raspberries, repeat the process and finish with a layer of the malakoff mixture. For a walnut charlotte malakoff, follow the recipe below, substituting ground walnuts for the ground almonds. (This is only for those with a passion for walnuts, as the taste is very strong.) For a chocolate charlotte malakoff, add 125 g (4 oz) plain chocolate and 2 tablespoons of strong black coffee to the basic ingredients. You can also substitute Tia Maria for the Grand Marnier. Dip the sponge fingers in a mixture of the liqueur and 1 tablespoon of the coffee. Melt the chocolate with the other tablespoon of the coffee over a gentle heat or in a double saucepan, and add it to the well-beaten butter and sugar mixture.

To serve 12

2 tbsp	Grand Marnier	2 tbsp
1 tbsp	water	1 tbsp
About 24	sponge finger biscuits (*page 167*)	About 24
250 g	unsalted butter	8 oz
250 g	castor sugar	8 oz
250 g	ground almonds	8 oz
30 cl	double cream	½ pint

Mix 1 tablespoon of the Grand Marnier with the water in a plate and dip the smooth sides of the sponge fingers briefly in the liquid. Line the bottoms and sides of two ½ litre (1 pint) charlotte moulds or pudding basins with the sponge finger biscuits, standing them round the sides, the sugar side outwards, and trim them to size.

Cream the butter and the sugar until they are white and fluffy and add the rest of the Grand Marnier and the ground almonds. Whip the cream lightly and fold it in also. Pour this mixture into the lined moulds and tap them sharply on the table two or three times to get rid of any air bubbles.

Chill for 3 to 4 hours, turn out of the moulds and serve.

HELGE RUBINSTEIN AND SHEILA BUSH
A FREEZER FOR ALL SEASONS

Moulded Fruit Pudding

Diplomate aux Fruits

To serve 6 to 8

500 g	strawberries and redcurrants or raspberries, mashed	1 lb
250 g	sponge finger biscuits (*page 167*), soaked in 4 tbsp each of water and kirsch or rum	8 oz
60 cl	pouring custard (*recipe page 166*)	1 pint

Place the soaked sponge fingers in a 1 litre (1¾ pint) mould in layers with the strawberries and redcurrants or raspberries between each. Cover the mould and leave it in the refrigerator overnight, with a weight of about 1 kg (2 lb) over it.

Turn out the mould and serve it very cold accompanied by the cold pouring custard.

X. MARCEL BOULESTIN
THE FINER COOKING

Strawberry and Raspberry Charlotte

Fraisalia

	To serve 6	
250 g	strawberries, hulled	8 oz
250 g	raspberries	8 oz
About 30	sponge finger biscuits (*page 167*)	About 30
100 g	castor sugar	3½ oz
4 tbsp	rum	4 tbsp
	vanilla pouring custard (*page 166*)	

Place a layer of sponge fingers in the bottom of a lightly oiled 1 litre (1¾ pint) charlotte mould; then add a layer of strawberries followed by a layer of raspberries. Sprinkle with sugar and rum. Continue to layer the sponge fingers and fruit in the same order until the mould is full, pressing each layer down well and sprinkling it with sugar and rum. Finish with a layer of sponge fingers. Cover the contents of the mould with a round of cardboard wrapped in foil; put a weight on top to press the pudding down lightly. Chill in the refrigerator for 5 to 6 hours, or overnight. To serve, unmould into a serving dish and pour over the custard.

MME. JEANNE SAVARIN (EDITOR)
LA CUISINE DES FAMILLES (MAGAZINE)

Prune Charlotte with Sabayon Sauce

Charlotte aux Pruneaux, Crème Sabayon

	To serve 6	
750 g	prunes, soaked for 2 to 3 hours in hot water	1½ lb
	strip lemon rind	
¼ litre	double cream	8 fl oz
100 g	castor sugar	3½ oz
25	sponge finger biscuits (*page 167*), dipped in sherry	25
	sabayon sauce (*page 166*)	

Drain the prunes and simmer for 15 minutes in fresh water with the lemon rind. Drain, remove the stones, and mash the prunes. Whip the cream and add the sugar. Fold the prunes into the whipped cream. Line the sides of a lightly oiled 1.75 litre (3 pint) charlotte mould with sponge fingers. Fill the mould to halfway with the prune and cream mixture, then add a layer of sponge fingers, then the rest of the mixture and another layer of sponge fingers. Cover with a plate and place in the refrigerator for 3 hours.

Make the *sabayon* sauce, and when quite cold, unmould the charlotte and pour the sauce over it.

ELIZABETH W. ESTERLING (EDITOR)
LE COOKBOOK

Normandy-Style Chocolate Mousse

Mousse au Chocolat Normandie

	To serve 6 to 8	
250 g	plain chocolate, broken into small pieces	8 oz
24	sponge finger biscuits (*page 167*), or other crisp sweet finger-length biscuits	24
5 tbsp	water	5 tbsp
250 g	unsalted butter, softened	8 oz
About 125g	granulated sugar	About 4 oz
3	eggs, yolks separated from whites, whites stiffly beaten	3
125 g	salted, blanched almonds, ground	4 oz
¼ litre	double cream, whipped	8 fl oz
¼ litre	double cream, whipped with 1 tbsp icing sugar and ½ tsp vanilla extract	8 fl oz

Have ready a 1.25 litre (2 pint) charlotte mould and 60 cm (2 feet) of 5mm (¼ inch) satin ribbon. Cut a round of greaseproof paper to fit the bottom of the mould, and put the paper into the mould. Line the sides of the mould with the sponge fingers or other biscuits.

Put the pieces of chocolate in a pan with the water, and stir over a low heat until the chocolate melts. Immediately, take the pan off the heat and let the chocolate cool a little. Put the butter in a mixing bowl and beat with the sugar until light and fluffy. One at a time beat in the egg yolks. Add the ground almonds to the butter and egg mixture. Mix in the cool melted chocolate, then fold in the beaten egg whites. Last, carefully and smoothly fold in the plain whipped cream.

Fill the mould, cover it with plastic wrap, and put it in the freezer to set for about 1½ hours.

When the mousse is well set, carefully turn it on to a flat serving plate and remove the paper. Put the flavoured whipped cream in an icing tube, fitted with a star nozzle, and pipe rosettes and scallops on top of the mousse. Tie the ribbon round the middle of the mousse with a little bow, and serve.

DIONE LUCAS AND MARION GORMAN
THE DIONE LUCAS BOOK OF FRENCH COOKING

Lemon Icebox Cake

This dessert freezes beautifully. I always keep one on hand.

To serve 6

250 g	butter	8 oz
250 g	sugar	8 oz
3	eggs, yolks separated from whites	3
1½	oranges, rind grated and juice strained	1½
1	lemon, rind grated and juice strained	1
350 g	sponge cake, cut into fingers, or 15 sponge finger biscuits (*page 167*)	12 oz

Cream the butter and sugar together and add the egg yolks, grated rind and fruit juices. Beat the egg whites until stiff and fold into the butter mixture. Line the bottom of a 90 cl (1½ pint) mould or cake tin with the sponge cake fingers and cover with a layer of the mixture. Repeat for as many layers as you wish, ending with the cake on top. Refrigerate overnight, or deep freeze for at least 2 hours.

HELEN CORBITT
HELEN CORBITT'S COOKBOOK

Coffee and Cream Assembly

Biskuit Fanny

To serve 4 to 6

175 g	butter, softened	6 oz
3	egg yolks	3
4 tbsp	icing sugar, sifted	4 tbsp
4 tbsp	freshly made strong black coffee, chilled	4 tbsp
20	sponge finger biscuits (*page 167*)	20
60 cl	double cream, whipped	1 pint
60 g	toasted almonds	2 oz

Beat the butter until it is creamy. Add the egg yolks and icing sugar alternately. Add the cold coffee drop by drop and beat until the mixture is thick and creamy. On a glass platter heap the coffee mixture and the sponge fingers in alternate layers. Cover the whole with the whipped cream, and sprinkle with the toasted almonds.

ELIZABETH SCHULER
MEIN KOCHBUCH

Dirty Face

During the Second World War, the author of this recipe joined the United Seamen's Service for the merchant marine. USS clubs, which still exist, were formed to provide merchant seamen with recreational and welfare facilities in ports of call. It was at the club in Rio de Janeiro that he discovered this popular Brazilian dessert—called, in translation, Dirty Face. The technique of caramelizing sugar is shown on page 8.

To serve 4

300 g	sugar	10 oz
6	ripe bananas, peeled	6
2	egg whites	2
¼ tsp	cream of tartar	¼ tsp
	salt	
125 g	sugar	4 oz
	double cream, whipped	

Caramelize 200 g (7 oz) of the sugar in a heavy saucepan. Use some of the caramel to line a shallow 22 × 22 cm (9 × 9 inch) baking pan. Cover the surface with the bananas and brush them with the remaining caramel. Beat the egg whites until very stiff, add the cream of tartar and a pinch of salt, and gradually beat in the remaining sugar, adding it a tablespoon at a time. Beat well after each addition. Cover the bananas with this meringue, and bake in an oven preheated to 180°C (350°F or Mark 4) for 15 minutes. Then bake for another 30 minutes, gradually reducing the heat to 130°C (200°F or Mark ½). Turn off the heat, and leave the bananas in the oven with the door open for 1 hour. Cool the dessert before eating. Whipped cream is excellent with this.

JAMES BEARD
DELIGHTS AND PREJUDICES

Apple Hedgehog

To serve 8 to 12

36	small cooking apples, 12 left whole, peeled and cored; the rest peeled, cored and sliced	36
250 g	sugar	8 oz
60 cl	water	1 pint
½ tsp	finely grated lemon rind	½ tsp
2	egg whites, stiffly beaten	2
3 tbsp	castor sugar	3 tbsp
125 g	blanched almonds, cut into strips	4 oz

Stew the whole apples in a covered tin-lined saucepan with the sugar and water, and when tender lift them carefully on to a dish. Take the sliced apples, put them into the sugar and water syrup with the lemon rind, and boil gently until reduced to a pulp; keep stirring to prevent burning. Cover the bottom of an ovenproof dish with some of this apple marmalade, then a layer of the whole apples, and fill up the cavities with the marmalade, then another layer and so on, forming the whole in a raised oval shape. Beat the egg whites to a stiff froth and gradually add the castor sugar. Cover the apples smoothly with the egg whites. Stick the strips of almond in upright at equal distances over the egg whites like hedgehog spines, and place the dish in a slow oven, 150°C (300°F or Mark 2), for a few minutes, or until a light golden colour, before serving.

HILDAGONDA J. DUCKITT
HILDA'S "WHERE IS IT?" OF RECIPES

Hungarian Bread Pudding

Máglyarakás

To serve 6 to 8

200 g	croissants or light milk bread, 1 or 2 days old, cut into small slices	7 oz
3	eggs, yolks separated from whites	3
100 g	sugar	3½ oz
30 g	butter, melted	1 oz
60 cl	milk	1 pint
100 g	sultanas or preserved sour cherries macerated in about 4 tbsp rum	3½ oz
100 g	walnuts, ground	3½ oz
500 g	apples, peeled, cored and thinly sliced	1 lb
3 tbsp	puréed apricot jam	3 tbsp

Cream the egg yolks with the sugar and mix in the melted butter. Add the milk and pour the mixture over the sliced croissants or bread. Set aside until the slices become thoroughly soaked in the mixture.

Butter a shallow ovenproof dish and place half of the soaked croissant or bread mixture in the bottom. Sprinkle over the sultanas or sour cherries and the ground walnuts. Cover with the remaining croissant or bread mixture. Then

top with the apple slices, sticking them vertically into the dough. Bake for 30 minutes in an oven preheated to 190°C (375°F or Mark 5).

Meanwhile, beat the egg whites until they are stiff, fold the whites into the puréed apricot jam and pour them over the baked mixture. Smooth the surface with a knife. Return the pudding to the oven, reducing the heat to 170°C (325°F or Mark 3), and bake for 10 to 15 minutes or until the meringue rises well and browns a little. To serve, cut into large blocks.

FRED MACNICOL
HUNGARIAN COOKERY

Baked Alaska

For the base, you may use any other sponge cake that you like, but this is a very quick, easy recipe.

To serve 6 to 8

150 g	sifted flour	5 oz
125 g	sugar	4 oz
1½ tsp	baking powder	1½ tsp
½ tsp	salt	½ tsp
60 g	shortening	2 oz
10 cl	milk	4 fl oz
1	egg	1
1 tsp	vanilla extract	1 tsp
About 1 litre	brick vanilla ice cream (*page 166*)	About 1¾ pints
3	egg whites	3
100 g	granulated sugar	3½ oz

Butter and flour a 22 cm (9 inch) square cake tin. Sift the flour with the sugar, baking powder and salt into a mixing bowl. Add the shortening and milk. Beat for 1½ minutes with an electric mixer on a slow speed, or with a spoon, until well blended and thick. Add the egg and the vanilla. Beat for 1½ minutes more. Pour the mixture into the cake tin and bake in an oven preheated to 180°C (350°F or Mark 4) for 20 to 25 minutes, or until the cake springs back when lightly touched in the centre. Cool.

Place the cake on a cutting board; cut strips 5 cm (2 inches) wide from each side of the cake, and discard them. Make a meringue by beating the egg whites until they form soft peaks, then beat in the sugar, a tablespoon at a time, until the whites are thick and glossy. Place the ice cream brick on top of the cake. Completely cover it and the cake with the meringue. Bake in the oven at 230°C (450°F or Mark 8) for 5 minutes, or until delicately brown. Serve at once.

JAMES BEARD
JAMES BEARD'S AMERICAN COOKERY

Queen's Pudding
Pouding à la Reine

To serve 6

500 g	breadcrumbs	1 lb
1.25 litres	milk	2 pints
125 g	sugar	4 oz
1 tsp	grated lemon rind, or 2 sugar cubes rubbed on all sides against a lemon, then crushed	1 tsp
60 g	butter, softened	2 oz
4	eggs, lightly beaten	4
125 g	apricot jam	4 oz
6	egg whites	6
350 g	castor sugar	12 oz
	double cream, whipped	

Mix the breadcrumbs with milk, sugar, lemon rind, butter and beaten eggs. Transfer the mixture to a buttered pie dish and cook in a preheated, 180°C (350°F or Mark 4) oven for about 40 minutes or until set. When done, spread the top of the pudding with apricot jam. Beat the egg whites until very firm and lightly stir in the castor sugar. Mask the pudding with this meringue, and return it to the oven turned down to 150°C (300°F or Mark 2) for a further 10 to 15 minutes, or until the top is coloured. Serve cold with whipped cream.

MASSEY AND SON'S COMPREHENSIVE PUDDING BOOK

Meringue of Pears

Cherries, bullaces and damsons stewed or baked with sugar, answer as well as pears for this dish. Apples, peaches, apricots or common plums may also be used, if boiled down to a marmalade, with sufficient sugar to sweeten them moderately. The skins and stones of these last should be removed, but a few of the kernels may be blanched and added to the fruit.

To serve 6

1 kg	pears, peeled, cored and stewed in water to cover for 20 minutes	2 to 2½ lb
5	egg whites	5
5 tbsp	sugar	5 tbsp

Fill a deep tart dish nearly to the brim with the stewed pears, and let them be something more than half covered with their juice. Whisk to a froth the whites of the eggs, and stir the sugar into them. Lay the egg whites lightly and evenly over the fruit. Put immediately into a moderate oven, preheated to 180°C (350°F or Gas Mark 4), and bake for 30 minutes.

ELIZABETH RAY (EDITOR)
THE BEST OF ELIZA ACTON

Meringues
Meringues Ordinaires

These meringues may be flavoured to taste with either coffee extract or cocoa powder.

To make 3 to 4 dozen meringues, depending on size

8	egg whites	8
500 g	icing sugar	1 lb

Whisk the egg whites until very stiff, then sift in the icing sugar, whisking all the time. Continue whisking for about 10 minutes longer. Put spoonfuls of the meringue mixture on to an oiled baking tray and put into a very slow oven, 50°C (150°F or Mark ¼), to dry for several hours or overnight.

LA MÈRE BRAZIER
LES SECRETS DE LA MÈRE BRAZIER

Pistachio Meringues
Meringues aux Pistaches

To make about 20 meringues

125 g	pistachio nuts, blanched and dried in a 170°C (325°F or Mark 3) oven for 10 minutes	4 oz
6	egg whites	6
125 g	castor sugar	4 oz

Pound the pistachio nuts in a mortar, adding a little egg white from time to time, until a fine paste is formed. In a heatproof bowl, beat the remaining egg whites until stiff; set the bowl over a saucepan of simmering water and gradually add 90 g (3 oz) of the sugar, beating continuously. When the meringue mixture is stiff and shiny, fold in the pistachio paste.

Line tin baking sheets with buttered or oiled greaseproof paper and, using a sifter, sprinkle the paper with sugar. Place spoonfuls of meringue 1 cm (½ inch) apart on the paper and bake in a very cool oven, 50°C (150°F or Mark ¼), for several hours or until the meringues are thoroughly dried but not coloured. With a spatula, remove the meringues from the baking tins and place them on a wire rack. Place the rack in the oven until the bottoms of the meringues are thoroughly dried. Store them in a dry place until ready to use.

VIARD AND FOURET
LE CUISINIER ROYAL

Iced Meringue Sandwich

Le Vacherin Glacé

In order to assemble the vacherin—*a dessert typical of Alsace—the ice creams should be soft enough to handle. But the* vacherin *must be returned to the freezer whenever necessary to keep its form. The technique of making meringue cases is demonstrated on page 86.*

To make the strawberry or raspberry ice cream, purée 125 g (4 oz) strawberries or raspberries through a nylon sieve, and sweeten to taste with about 60 g (2 oz) castor or icing sugar. Whip 15 cl (¼ pint) double cream until it forms soft peaks, fold the cream into the puréed fruit, and freeze for about 2 hours.

To serve 6 to 8

2	shallow meringue cases, 20 cm (8 inch) diameter	2
60 cl	vanilla ice cream (*page 166*)	1 pint
2 tbsp	kirsch	2 tbsp
60 g	preserved strawberries or whole strawberry jam	2 oz
60 g	fresh pineapple, cut into small cubes	2 oz
6	macaroons, crushed	6
30 cl	strawberry or raspberry ice cream	½ pint
125 g	strawberries or raspberries	4 oz
30 cl	double cream, chilled	½ pint
2 tbsp	vanilla sugar	2 tbsp

Soften the vanilla ice cream just enough to blend in the kirsch, preserved strawberries or strawberry jam, pineapple cubes and macaroons. Sandwich the meringue cases together with this ice cream mixture and put the assembly in the freezer for 30 minutes. Then coat the sides of the *vacherin* with the strawberry or raspberry ice cream, and decorate the sides with whole berries of the same sort as those in the ice cream. Return to the freezer.

Whip the cream until stiff, adding the vanilla sugar at the last. Decorate the top of the *vacherin* with the cream, so that the assembly is pink around the sides with a white topping.

AUSTIN DE CROZE
LES PLATS RÉGIONAUX DE FRANCE

Meringue Baskets

Buttered and floured greaseproof paper may be used instead of rice-paper to line the baking sheet.

To make 4 or 5 small baskets or 1 large basket

4	egg whites	4
250 g	icing sugar, sifted	8½ oz
1 tsp	vanilla extract	1 tsp

Place the egg whites in a heatproof bowl, set over a saucepan of simmering water, and whisk, gradually adding the sugar, until the meringue mixture is very thick. Flavour the mixture with the vanilla extract.

Using a piping bag with a rosette nozzle, pipe swirls of meringue on to rice-paper laid on a baking sheet, to form 4 or 5 small baskets or 1 large basket. Set in a preheated, 130°C (250°F or Mark ½) oven for 1 to 1½ hours, or until the meringue is firm and dry to the touch.

CONSTANCE SPRY AND ROSEMARY HUME
THE CONSTANCE SPRY COOKERY BOOK

Ice Cream Pudding

Pudding Mère Brazier

The technique of caramelizing sugar is shown on page 8. To use up stale or broken sweet biscuits and uneaten ice cream, Mère Brazier made this pudding all the year round for her staff. It was delicious enough to serve in the restaurant.

To serve 6 to 8

1 litre	ice cream (*page 166*)	1¾ pints
500 g	stale and broken sweet biscuits of any kind	1 lb
	Caramel	
250 g	sugar	8 oz
2 tbsp	water	2 tbsp

Boil the sugar and water in a 1.5 litre (2½ pint) charlotte mould, over moderate heat, swirling the mould frequently until the syrup caramelizes. Dip the mould immediately into cold water to cool it slightly, then tilt it in all directions to coat the base and sides with caramel.

Mix the ice cream with the crumbled biscuits and fill the charlotte mould. Place the mould in a shallow oven pan half-filled with hot water and bake in an oven preheated to 180°C (350°F or Mark 4), for 45 minutes. Leave to cool and refrigerate overnight before serving.

LA MÈRE BRAZIER
LES SECRETS DE LA MÈRE BRAZIER

Peach Melba

Pêche Melba

The white peaches may be replaced by yellow peaches. If the peaches are perfectly ripe and unblemished, they need not be poached: simply peel them, rub them with the cut side of half a lemon, remove the stones, and sprinkle the peaches with castor sugar. If preferred, the peaches can be coated with puréed raspberries, sweetened to taste, instead of the cooked raspberry sauce.

	To serve 6	
6	fresh white peaches, peeled and rubbed with lemon	6
250 g	sugar	8 oz
35 cl	water	12 fl oz
1	vanilla pod	1
1 litre	vanilla ice cream (*page 166*)	1¾ pints
250 g	fresh almonds, hulled, peeled and thinly sliced lengthwise, or about 40 g (1½ oz) blanched, slivered almonds	8 oz
	Raspberry sauce	
500 g	fresh raspberries, puréed through a nylon sieve	1 lb
3 tbsp	castor sugar	3 tbsp
1 tsp	lemon juice	1 tsp

Place 6 sorbet glasses in the refrigerator to chill.

In a heavy pan, bring the sugar and water to the boil with the vanilla pod. Reduce the heat, add the peaches to the syrup, cover, and poach for 5 to 6 minutes. Allow the peaches to cool in their syrup. Drain the peaches thoroughly, halve them and remove the stones.

To make the raspberry sauce, put the puréed raspberries into a small, preferably enamelled, saucepan, and add the sugar. Taste for sweetness, and add more sugar if desired. Simmer for 5 to 6 minutes, stirring with a wooden spoon, then add the lemon juice, which will enhance the flavour of the raspberries. Set the sauce aside to cool.

To serve, place spoonfuls of the vanilla ice cream in the bottom of each champagne glass. Cover the ice cream in each glass with two peach halves. Pour the raspberry sauce over the peaches, sprinkle them with the almonds, and serve.

LOUISETTE BERTHOLLE
UNE GRANDE CUISINE POUR TOUS

Macaroon Mould

Le Délicieux

The technique of caramelizing a mould is shown on page 42.

	To serve 8	
600 g	good macaroons, dried out in the oven, finely pounded in a mortar, and sieved	1¼ lb
8	egg whites	8
About 4 tbsp	castor sugar	About 4 tbsp
125 g	plain chocolate, melted with 1 to 2 tbsp water over a low heat	About 4 oz
About 125 g	caramel (*page 8*) for lining mould	About 4 oz
½ litre	cold *sabayon* sauce (*page 166*), flavoured with kirsch	1 pint

Beat the egg whites until they are stiff, then whisk in castor sugar to taste, the melted chocolate and the sieved macaroons. Caramelize a 2 litre (3½ pint) charlotte mould, and turn the macaroon mixture into the mould.

Cook in a preheated, 180°C (350°F or Mark 4) oven for 25 minutes. Remove from the oven and allow to cool, then unmould on to a round of rich sponge cake. Just before serving, pour over the cold *sabayon* sauce.

ÉDOUARD NIGNON
LES PLAISIRS DE LA TABLE

Chestnut Gateau

Gâteau de Chataignes

This gateau must be made the day before it is to be served.

	To serve 4	
1 kg	chestnuts, shells slit	2 to 2½ lb
100 g	castor sugar, dissolved in about 10 cl (4 fl oz) water	3½ oz
300 g	plain chocolate, broken into pieces	10 oz
About 1 tbsp	water	About 1 tbsp
3	eggs	3
15 g	butter	½ oz
10 cl	rum	4 fl oz

Boil the chestnuts for 20 to 40 minutes, or until tender. When they are cooked, take them from the water one by one with a spoon, squeezing them between two fingers over a mixing bowl so that the pulp is released, free of skin and shell. Mix this with the sugared water. Crush and knead the mixture for 10 minutes, using a wooden pestle. The sugared water and the chestnut pulp should form an extremely fine paste.

Over a low heat, melt the chocolate in a very small quantity of water to make a very thick cream. Remove from the heat.

When it is almost cold, mix in the eggs, butter and rum. Put alternate layers of the chestnut paste and the chocolate cream in a glass fruit dish. Shape the gateau to your taste and cover the whole with the rest of the chocolate cream.

CLARISSE OU LA VIEILLE CUISINIÈRE

Chocolate Pye

One of the many varieties of pastry used by the Georgians was crackling crust, made from almonds and egg whites. This crisp crust, with a very delectable filling of chocolate and cream, they chose to call quite simply "chocolate pye".

To serve 8 to 10

250 g	plain chocolate, broken into small pieces	8 oz
30 cl	single cream	$\frac{1}{2}$ pint
1 tbsp	icing sugar	1 tbsp
1 tbsp	rum	1 tbsp
30 cl	double cream, chilled	$\frac{1}{2}$ pint
60 g	almonds, toasted	2 oz
60 g	chocolate flakes	2 oz
	Crackling crust	
175 g	ground almonds	6 oz
60 g	castor sugar	2 oz
1	egg white, beaten	1

First make the crackling crust flan shell. Work the ground almonds, castor sugar and beaten egg white into a stiff paste and leave in the refrigerator for 30 minutes. Form the paste into a ball and roll it out to line a buttered 20 cm (8 inch) flan ring. Dredge the paste with flour if it gets too sticky.

If you find the paste very soft, it is quite all right to press it into the ring, where it may have broken. Trim and decorate the edge with your finger and thumb, or the prongs of a fork. There is no need to employ the usual lining of paper and dried beans to bake "blind": just cut a strip of foil and fit that round the inside edge to prevent it from collapsing.

Bake the flan shell in an oven preheated to 180°C (350°F or Mark 4), for 20 to 25 minutes. Take care that the paste does not scorch, as almonds tend to burn quickly. Allow the crust to cool before removing the foil and flan ring. Stand the shell on a wire rack to cool.

Now make the filling. Put the pieces of chocolate into a basin and cover them with the single cream. Stand the basin in a pan of boiling water and stir until all the chocolate has melted. Allow the filling to cool, stirring it from time to time to ensure even cooling. As it starts to set add the icing sugar and gently beat it into a light foam, taking care to note if it starts to separate: if it does, stop beating. The chocolate mixture will have become lighter in colour and will have increased in volume.

Pour the mixture into the flan shell. Add the rum to the double cream and whip. Decorate the flan with swirls of piped whipped cream. Stick the toasted almonds and chocolate flakes into the whipped cream. This "pye" should be as exotic as it must have been when the Georgians decorated it with real gold-leafed almonds and crystallized rose petals, and all the frills and furbelows that they could think up.

MICHAEL SMITH
FINE ENGLISH COOKERY

Pears with Chocolate Sauce
Poires Belle-Hélène

To serve 6

6	eating pears, peeled but left whole	6
150 g	castor sugar	5 oz
20 cl	water	7 fl oz
1 litre	vanilla ice cream (*page 166*)	$1\frac{3}{4}$ pints
60 g	toasted, slivered almonds	2 oz
	Chocolate sauce	
200 g	plain chocolate, broken into pieces	7 oz
20 cl	water	7 fl oz
90 g	unsalted butter, cut into small pieces	3 oz

Simmer the pears in the sugar and water for 10 to 25 minutes, or until tender. (The cooking time depends on the type, size and ripeness of the pears.) Allow the pears to cool in the syrup in which they were cooked.

To make the chocolate sauce, put the chocolate and the water into a heavy pan and stir over a low heat until the chocolate melts and the mixture is smooth. Off the heat, stir in the butter, a few pieces at a time, until the butter melts and the sauce is glossy.

To serve, put the vanilla ice cream in a bowl, place the pears on top, and sprinkle them with the almonds. Serve the hot chocolate sauce separately.

GINETTE MATHIOT
JE SAIS FAIRE LA PÂTISSERIE

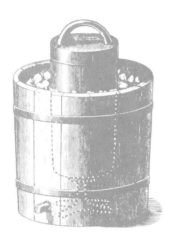

Floating Island

This was very often served as a side dish at feasts and great dinners in the 17th century and was still made for Victorian dinner parties, though it is scarcely ever seen today. It is a kind of floating trifle. Many variants exist; most recipes build one large island to float in its lake of cream, but some suggest small individual islands. In either case, the dish used must be large and fairly flat. A pouring custard (*page 166*) can be used instead of the fruit purée.

To serve 4

40 cl	purée raspberries or strawberries	¾ pint
60 cl	double cream	1 pint
500 g	round sponge cake, sliced across into 3 thin layers	1 lb
125 g	apricot jam	4 oz
90 g	almonds, blanched and finely chopped	3 oz
2 tbsp	sherry	2 tbsp
125 g	castor sugar	4 oz
½ tsp	vanilla extract	½ tsp

Mix the fruit purée with half of the cream, beat well together or blend, and pour on to a large rather flat dish. Spread each of the three slices of sponge cake with a little apricot jam, and sprinkle with almonds. Lay the first layer lightly on the purée in the centre. Put the other layers, always lightly, one above the other. It should be floating, supported on the purée. Pour into the cake a little sherry. Whip the remaining cream with the sugar and vanilla and pile high on the island cake.

Chill in the refrigerator for an hour if possible, and serve. If the island does not float the dish is still delicious, but it should move freely on its purée.

ELISABETH AYRTON
THE COOKERY OF ENGLAND

An Excellent Trifle

If possible, the syllabub should be made a day ahead. The wine in the trifle may be replaced by ¼ litre (8 fl oz) of sherry or Madeira, in which case use only 10 cl (4 fl oz) of brandy.

To serve 8

15 to 20 cl	wine	6 fl oz
15 to 20 cl	brandy	6 fl oz
8	sponge finger biscuits (*page 167*)	8
250 g	mixed macaroons and ratafias	8 oz
¼ litre	whipping cream, flavoured with about 2 tbsp wine	8 fl oz

Whipped syllabub

2	large lemons	2
200 g	castor sugar	7 oz
35 cl	sherry	12 fl oz
35 cl	brandy	12 fl oz
60 cl	double cream	1 pint

Custard

½	lemon, rind only, very thinly pared	½
20 cl to ¼ litre	milk	7 to 8 fl oz
40 g	castor sugar	1¼ oz
6	egg yolks, thoroughly beaten	6
20 cl to ¼ litre	cream	7 to 8 fl oz
8 cl	brandy (optional)	3 fl oz
30 g	blanched almonds, cut into slivers (optional)	1 oz

To make the syllabub: pare the rind of the lemons very thinly and infuse it for some hours in the juice from the lemons. Put the sugar into a bowl with the strained lemon juice, sherry and brandy; when the sugar has dissolved add the cream and whisk the mixture well; when it has become a solid froth, turn the mixture into a muslin-lined sieve to drain.

To make the custard: add the lemon rind to the milk and let it infuse for 30 minutes, then simmer them together for a few minutes and add the castor sugar. Mix the beaten egg yolks with the cream, stir the boiling milk quickly into them, take out the lemon rind, and turn the custard into a deep, heatproof jug; set this over the heat in a pan of boiling water, and keep the custard stirred gently, but without ceasing, until it begins to thicken; then move the spoon rather more quickly, making it always touch the bottom of the jug, until the mixture is brought to the point of boiling, when it must be instantly taken from the heat, or it will curdle in a moment. Pour the custard into a bowl, and keep it stirred until it is nearly cold, then add to it by degrees the brandy and blanched almonds; or omit these, if you prefer.

To make the trifle: mix the wine and brandy and soak the

sponge finger biscuits, macaroons and ratafias in this mixture; cover the bottom of a dish with half of these, pour the custard over them, lay the remainder of the soaked biscuits upon the custard, and pile over the whole the syllabub. Now whip the wine-flavoured cream to the lightest possible froth: skim it off and heap it gently over the trifle.

ELIZABETH RAY (EDITOR)
THE BEST OF ELIZA ACTON

To Make a Trifle

The whip to lay over the top of the trifle should be made the day before it is required for table, as the flavour is better, and it is much more solid than when prepared the same day.

To serve 8

6	small sponge cakes, or slices of sponge cake	6
12	macaroons	12
24	ratafia biscuits	24
30 cl	sherry or sweet wine	$\frac{1}{2}$ pint
6 tbsp	brandy	6 tbsp
1	lemon, rind grated	1
60 g	blanched almonds, cut into strips	2 oz
	raspberry or strawberry jam	
60 cl	custard, made with 8 egg yolks, cooled (*page 166*)	1 pint
	Whip	
90 g	castor sugar	3 oz
2	egg whites, stiffly beaten	2
2 to 3 tbsp	sherry or sweet wine	2 to 3 tbsp
60 cl	double cream	1 pint

To make the whip, put into a large bowl the sugar, beaten egg whites, sherry or sweet wine and the cream. Whisk these ingredients well in a cool place, and take off the froth with a skimmer as fast as it rises, and put it on a sieve to drain; continue the whisking till there is sufficient of the whip, cover, and put away in a cool place to drain overnight.

The next day, place the sponge cakes, macaroons and ratafias at the bottom of a 1.5 litre (2$\frac{1}{2}$ pint) dish. Mix the sherry or wine with the brandy and pour over the cakes; should this proportion of wine not be found quite sufficient, add a little more as the cakes should be well soaked. Over the cakes put the grated lemon rind, the almonds and a layer of raspberry or strawberry jam. Pour the custard over all and heap the whip lightly over the top: this should stand as high as possible, and it may be garnished with bright currant jelly, crystallized fruits or flowers.

MRS. ISABELLA BEETON
THE BOOK OF HOUSEHOLD MANAGEMENT

Gooseberry Trifle

To serve 6 to 8

1 kg	gooseberries, topped and tailed	2 to 2$\frac{1}{2}$ lb
15 cl	water	$\frac{1}{4}$ pint
About 350 g	soft brown sugar	About 12 oz
60 cl	pouring custard (*page 166*)	1 pint
30 cl	double cream, whipped	$\frac{1}{2}$ pint
	preserved or crystallized fruit	

Boil the gooseberries with the water, and sugar to taste, for 15 to 25 minutes over a medium heat. When the gooseberries are sufficiently soft to pulp, put them at the bottom of a glass trifle dish, and pour the custard over them. Set the trifle in a cool place. When the custard has set, pile the whipped cream over the trifle and decorate with rings of preserved or crystallized fruit, and serve.

MARY JEWRY (EDITOR)
WARNE'S MODEL COOKERY AND HOUSEKEEPING BOOK

Trifle

This recipe is from a book published anonymously in 1747, but which is generally attributed to the English cookery writer, Hannah Glasse. The author suggests garnishing the trifle with ratafia biscuits, currant jelly and flowers if desired. For instructions on making syllabub, see page 89.

To serve 4

3	sponge finger biscuits (*page 167*)	3
90 g	macaroons, halved	3 oz
90 g	ratafia biscuits	3 oz
10 cl	sherry	4 fl oz
40 cl	pouring custard (*page 166*)	$\frac{3}{4}$ pint
40 cl	syllabub	$\frac{3}{4}$ pint

Cover the bottom of a dish or bowl with the sponge fingers, halved macaroons and ratafias. Soak them through with the sherry, then pour over the custard. Finish the trifle by pouring syllabub over all.

THE ART OF COOKERY, MADE PLAIN AND EASY

Standard Preparations

Calf's Foot Jelly

This basic jelly will set up to 40 cl (¾ pint) wine or fruit juice. Start preparing the jelly the day before it is required. The technique of splitting calf's feet is demonstrated on page 16.

To make about 60 cl (1 pint) jelly

2	small calf's feet, or 1 large calf's foot, split	2
1.25 litres	water	2 pints
175 g	sugar	6 oz
	ground cinnamon	
	thin strips orange or lemon rind	
1 each	orange and lemon, juice strained	1 each
2	egg whites	2
8 cl	white wine	3 fl oz
2	egg shells, crushed	2

Soak the pieces of calf's foot in cold water for several hours to draw out any traces of blood. Drain the calf's foot pieces, place them in a pan, and cover them generously with cold water. Bring to the boil, and simmer for 8 to 10 minutes. Drain the calf's foot pieces, rinse them well, and return them to a clean, deep saucepan. Add the water, which should amply cover the pieces, bring to the boil, skim, cover with the lid slightly ajar, and cook at a bare simmer for about 7 hours. The calf's foot should remain immersed throughout the cooking: if necessary, add a little boiling water from time to time. Strain the liquid through a sieve into a bowl, and refrigerate overnight.

The next day, cleanse the surface of the jelly of all traces of fat by scraping with a spoon; then wipe the surface with a cloth that has been dipped in hot water and wrung out.

In a large saucepan, heat the jelly enough to melt it, and add the sugar, a pinch of ground cinnamon, several strips of orange and lemon rind and the orange and lemon juice. Beat the egg whites and the white wine together in a large mixing bowl, then add the mixture to the liquid jelly, along with the crushed egg shells, whisking all the while. Bring to the boil, still whisking, until a thick head of froth forms. Reduce the heat to very low, and simmer gently for about 15 minutes. Strain the liquid into a bowl through a jelly bag, or a sieve lined with a tightly woven cloth or a tea towel. The liquid should be quite clear: if necessary, strain it again. Covered and refrigerated the jelly will keep for up to 5 days.

Sabayon

To make about 60 cl (1 pint) sabayon

6	egg yolks	6
200 g	castor sugar	7 oz
30 cl	dry white wine, sauternes, champagne, marsala or sherry	½ pint
6	thinly pared strips lemon rind, cut into a fine *julienne* (optional)	6

In a saucepan large enough to hold triple their volume, beat together the egg yolks and sugar until the mixture is creamy. Partially immerse the pan in a large pan of water heated to just below boiling point. Continue to whisk the mixture. Pour in the wine, add the lemon rind if desired, and whisk until the mixture froths up into an abundant mousse. Remove the pan from the water bath, and keep whisking for a minute or so.

As a dessert, *sabayon* is usually eaten hot: pour it into individual glasses and serve it immediately. As a sauce, *sabayon* may be used hot or cold. For a cold sauce, set the pan in a bowl of ice cubes and whisk the *sabayon* until sufficiently chilled. Whipped cream may be added if desired.

Basic Custard Ice Cream

To flavour this ice cream with vanilla, follow the instructions for vanilla-flavoured custard (*below*).

To make about 60 cl (1 pint) ice cream

8	egg yolks	8
125 to 150 g	sugar	4 to 5 oz
60 cl	milk, scalded	1 pint

With a whisk, beat the egg yolks and sugar together in a bowl until the mixture is thick and pale and forms a slowly dissolving "ribbon" when it is dribbled from the whisk. Gradually add the hot scalded milk, stirring constantly. Transfer the mixture to a heavy saucepan. Over a water bath or over direct, very low heat, stir and cook the mixture, without allowing it to boil, until it coats the spoon. Strain the custard through a sieve into a bowl, and stir occasionally until cool. Freeze, preferably in an ice cream churn.

Basic Pouring Custard

Crème Anglaise

To make about 60 cl (1 pint) custard

6	egg yolks	6
60 to 125 g	castor sugar	2 to 4 oz
60 cl	milk, scalded	1 pint

In a bowl, beat the eggs and sugar with a wire whisk until the mixture turns pale and forms a "ribbon" when dribbled on the surface. Slowly add hot scalded milk, stirring all the time.

Transfer the mixture to a heavy saucepan. Cook the custard over a low heat and, using a wooden spoon, stir continuously in a figure-of-eight pattern. Do not let the custard boil. When the custard coats the spoon, remove the pan from the heat immediately and stand the pan in a bowl of ice cubes, to which a little water has been added, in order to arrest the cooking and prevent the custard from curdling. To ensure an even consistency, continue to stir for 5 minutes until the custard cools a little. Strain the custard to remove any lumps. To keep the custard warm, transfer it to a hot water bath and stir occasionally. For a cold custard, continue to stir occasionally over ice until the custard is sufficiently chilled.

Vanilla custard. Place a vanilla pod in the pan of scalded milk, cover the pan and leave to infuse for 20 minutes before removing the pod. The pod can be rinsed and used once more.

Coffee custard. Mix 30 g (1 oz) of freshly ground coffee with 8 to 10 cl (3 to 4 fl oz) of boiling water—just enough to make a smooth paste. Strain the paste through several thicknesses of muslin before adding to the scalded milk.

Caramel custard. Caramelize 90 g (3 oz) of sugar with 1 tablespoon of water in a heavy pan (*see page 8*). Remove the pan from the heat, and pour the scalded milk on to the caramel. Return the pan to a low heat and stir until the caramel dissolves into the milk.

Rum custard. Stir about 1 tablespoon rum into the prepared pouring custard.

Sponge Finger Biscuits

Sponge finger biscuits will keep for 2 to 3 weeks in an airtight container. To flavour the fingers with chocolate, sift ½ to 1 tablespoon of cocoa with the flour. To flavour the fingers with orange, add 1 tablespoon of finely grated orange rind to the egg yolk and sugar mixture, along with the flour.

To make about 30 sponge finger biscuits

3	large eggs, yolks separated from whites	3
90 g	castor sugar	3 oz
75 g	flour, sifted with a pinch of salt	2½ oz

Butter 3 baking sheets, line them with buttered greaseproof paper, and dust them with flour. Preheat the oven to 220°C (425°F or Mark 7).

Put the egg yolks and sugar into a bowl and whisk together until very thick: this should take about 5 minutes using an electric hand whisk. Carefully fold in the sifted flour. Whisk the egg whites until they form stiff peaks. Fold a quarter of the egg whites into the egg yolk mixture to lighten it, then very carefully fold in the remaining egg whites.

Fit a large piping bag with a 1 cm (½ inch) plain nozzle. Fill the bag with the sponge finger mixture, and pipe 10 cm (4 inch) long strips of the mixture on to the prepared baking sheets, allowing about 5 cm (2 inches) space between each strip. Dust the piped strips lightly with castor sugar, and bake in the oven for 8 to 10 minutes, or until the sponge fingers are very lightly browned. Carefully remove the sponge fingers from the paper and place them on a cooling rack.

Crêpe Batter

To make enough batter for about 15 crêpes, each 15 to 17 cm (6 to 7 inches) across

125 g	flour	4 oz
	salt	
2	eggs	2
30 cl	milk	½ pint
30 g	butter, melted	1 oz
1 tbsp	brandy or Grand Marnier (optional)	1 tbsp

Sift the flour with a pinch of salt into a mixing bowl. Make a well in the centre of the flour and break the eggs into the well. Gradually whisk the eggs into the flour, working from the centre outwards and adding the milk at the same time. Whisk only until smooth, then stir in the melted butter, and the brandy or Grand Marnier if desired. The crêpe batter should have the consistency of single cream: if necessary, add a little more milk. Use the batter immediately.

Fritter Batter

The consistency of this batter may be varied by increasing or decreasing the ratio of liquid to flour. A thin batter will cook crisper and lighter but some of it will be lost in the oil during frying; a thicker batter clings better, but is more stodgy.

To coat about 8 bananas, halved lengthwise

125 g	flour	4 oz
	salt	
1 tsp	castor sugar (optional)	1 tsp
30 g	butter, melted	1 oz
4 tbsp	beer	4 tbsp
15 cl	tepid water	¼ pint
1 tbsp	brandy (optional)	1 tbsp
1	large egg white, stiffly beaten	1

Sift the flour with a pinch of salt, and the sugar if desired, into a large mixing bowl. Form a well in the centre of the flour, and add the melted butter, beer and water. Whisk the mixture, working from the centre outwards, for as long as it takes to produce a smooth batter. If you wish, whisk in the brandy. Let the batter rest, covered, in a warm place, for about 1 hour. Just before using the batter, fold in the beaten egg white.

Recipe Index

English recipe titles are listed by categories such as "Apple", "Dried Fruit", "Crêpe", "Ice Cream" or "Pudding" and within those categories alphabetically. Foreign recipe titles are listed alphabetically without regard to category.

General Index/Glossary

Included in this index are definitions of many of the culinary terms used in this book: definitions are in italics. The recipes in the Anthology are listed in the Recipe Index on page 168.

Recipe Credits

The sources for the recipes in this volume are shown below. Page references in brackets indicate where the recipes appear in the Anthology.

The Art of Cookery, Made Plain and Easy By a Lady. The Sixth Edition, 1758 (*pages 115, 165*).
Audot, L. E., *La Cuisinière de la Campagne et de la Ville ou la Nouvelle Cuisine Économique.* Published by Librairie Audot, 1881 edition (*pages 108, 111*).
Ayrton, Elisabeth, *The Cookery of England.* Copyright © Elisabeth Ayrton, 1974. Published by Penguin Books Ltd., London. By permission of Penguin Books Ltd. (*pages 120, 146 and 164*).
Barberousse, Michel, *Cuisine Normande.* Published by Éditions Barberousse, Paris. Translated by permission of Michel Barberousse (*page 96*).
Beard, James, *James Beard's American Cookery.* Copyright © 1972 by James A. Beard. Published by Hart-Davis, Mac-Gibbon Ltd. Granada Publishing Ltd., Hertfordshire and Little, Brown and Co., Boston. Reproduced with the permission of Granada Publishing Ltd., and Little, Brown and Co.(*page 159*).
Beard, James, *Delights and Prejudices.* Copyright © 1964 by James Beard. Published by Atheneum Publishers, New York. By permission of A. M. Heath & Company Ltd. and Atheneum Publishers (*page 158*).
Beard, James, *How to Eat Better for Less Money.* Copyright © 1954, 1970 by James A. Beard and Sam Aaron. Published by Simon and Schuster, New York. By permission of John Schaffner Literary Agent (*page 145*).
Beeton, Mrs. Isabella, *The Book of Household Management* (1861). Reproduced in facsimile by Jonathan Cape Ltd., London (*pages 124, 165*).
Bergeron, Victor J., *Trader Vic's Rum Cookery and Drinkery.* Copyright © 1974 by Victor J. Bergeron. Published by Doubleday & Company, Inc., New York. By permission of Harold Matson Co., Inc. (Authors' Agent) (*page 94*).
Bertholle, Louisette, *Une Grande Cuisine pour Tous.* © Opera Mundi, Paris. Published by Éditions Albin Michel, Paris. Translated by permission of Éditions Albin Michel (*page 162*).
Besson, Joséphine, *La Mère Besson "Ma Cuisine Provençale".* © Éditions Albin Michel, 1977. Published by Éditions Albin Michel, Paris. Translated by permission of Éditions Albin Michel (*page 142*).
Bobinet, Adrien-Jean, *Gastronomie.* Copyright by Adrien-Jean Bobinet, Lyon, 1949. Published by Éditions Adrien-Jean Bobinet, Lyon (*pages 101, 133*).
Bocuse, Paul, *The New Cuisine.* Copyright © Flammarion 1976. This translation Copyright © 1977 by Random House, Inc. Published by Hart-Davis, MacGibbon Ltd./Granada Publishing Ltd., Hertfordshire. By permission of Granada Publishing Ltd. (*pages 131, 155*).
Bouillard, Paul, *La Cuisine au Coin du Feu.* Copyright 1928 by Albin Michel. Published by Éditions Albin Michel, Paris. Translated by permission of Éditions Albin Michel (*pages 125, 132 and 139*).
Boulestin, X. Marcel, *The Finer Cooking.* Published by Cassell & Company Limited, London 1937. By permission of A. D. Peters and Co., Ltd. (*pages 98, 156*).
Boulestin, X. Marcel, *Recipes of Boulestin.* © The Estate of X. M. Boulestin 1971. Published by William Heinemann Ltd., London. By permission of William Heinemann Ltd. (*page 94*).
Boulestin, X. Marcel, *Simple French Cooking for English Homes.* Published by William Heinemann, Ltd., London 1923. By permission of A. D. Peters and Co., Ltd. (*page 93*).

Brazier, Eugénie, *Les Secrets de la Mère Brazier.* © Solar 1977. Published by Solar, Paris. Translated by permission of Solar (*pages 126, 160 and 161*).
Breteuil, Jules, *Le Cuisinier Européen.* Published by Garnier Frères Libraires-Éditeurs c.1860 (*page 109*).
Brown, Helen, *Helen Brown's West Coast Cook Book.* Copyright 1952, by Helen Evans Brown. Published by Little, Brown and Company, Boston. By permission of Little, Brown and Company (*page 112*).
The Buckeye Cookbook: Traditional American Recipes. As published by the Buckeye Publishing Co. 1883. Published by Dover Publications Inc., New York 1975 (*page 147*).
Bugialli, Giuliano. *The Fine Art of Italian Cooking.* Copyright © 1977 by Giuliano Bugialli. Published by Times Books, A Division of Quadrangle/The New York Times Book Co. Inc., New York. Reprinted by permission of Times Books, A Division of Quadrangle/The New York Times Book Co. Inc. (*page 113*).
Byron, May, *May Byron's Puddings, Pastries and Sweet Dishes.* Published by Hodder and Stoughton Limited, London 1929. By permission of Hodder and Stoughton Limited (*pages 97, 127, 133 and 151*).
Campbell, Susan, *The Times Newspaper, 5th July, 1978.* By permission of Susan Campbell (*page 148*).
Carnacina, Luigi and Veronelli, Luigi, *La Buona Vera Cucina Italiana.* © 1966 by Rizzoli Editore, Milano. Published by Rizzoli Editore, Milan. Translated by permission of Rizzoli Editore (*pages 126, 142*).
Carrier, Robert, *The Robert Carrier Cookery Course.* © Robert Carrier, 1974. Published by W. H. Allen and Co. Ltd. By permission of W. H. Allen and Co. Ltd. (*pages 117, 152*).
Cass, Elizabeth, *Spanish Cooking.* Copyright © Elizabeth Cass, 1957. First published by André Deutsch Ltd., 1957. Also published by Mayflower Books, 1970. By permission of André Deutsch Ltd., London (*page 144*).
Clarisse ou la Vieille Cuisinière. Copyright © 1922 by Éditions de l'Abeille d'Or. Published by Éditions de l'Abeille d'Or, Paris. Translated by permission of Éditions Rombaldi, Paris (*page 162*).
Corbitt, Helen, *Helen Corbitt's Cookbook.* Copyright © 1957 by Helen Corbitt. Published by Houghton Mifflin Company, Boston. Reprinted by permission of Houghton Mifflin Company (*page 147*).
Costa, Margaret, *Margaret Costa's Four Seasons Cookery Book.* Copyright © Margaret Costa. First published in Great Britain by Thomas Nelson & Sons Ltd., 1970, also by Sphere Books Ltd., London, 1976. By permission of Margaret Costa (*pages 99, 144*).
Couffignal, Huguette, *J'Aime les Noix.* Published by Robert Morel Éditeur, Apt. Translated by permission of Robert Morel Éditeur (*page 140*).
Courtine, Robert, *Balzac à Table.* © Éditions Robert Laffont, S.A., Paris 1976. Published by Éditions Robert Laffont, Paris. Translated by permission of Robert Courtine (*page 149*).
Courtine, Robert, *Mes Repas les Plus Étonnants.* © 1973 Éditions Robert Laffont, S.A. Published by Éditions Robert Laffont, Paris. Translated by permission of Robert Courtine (*page 100*).
Cox, J. Stevens (Editor), *Dorset Dishes of the Seventeenth Century.* © J. Stevens Cox, 1967. Published by The Toucan Press, Guernsey. Reprinted by permission of J. Stevens Cox (*page 95*).
Craig, Elizabeth, *The Art of Irish Cooking.* Published by Ward Lock & Co. Limited, London. By permission of John Farquharson Ltd. (Authors' agent) (*page 135*).
Croze, Austin de, *Les Plats Régionaux de France.* Published by Éditions Daniel Morcrette, B.P.26,95270 Luzarches, France. Translated by permission of Éditions Daniel Morcrette (*pages 119, 161*).
Cuisinier Gascon, Le—1740. Reprinted by Éditions Daniel Morcrette, B.P.26,95270, Luzarches, France. Translated by permission of Éditions Daniel Morcrette (*page 100*).
Cutler, Carol, *Haute Cuisine for your Heart's Delight.* Carol Cutler © 1973. Published by Clarkson N. Potter. Inc/Publisher New York and Crown Publishers Inc., New York. By permission of Crown Publishers Inc. (*page 145*).
Dannenbaum, Julie, *Julie Dannenbaum's Creative Cooking School.* Copyright © 1971 by Julie Dannenbaum. Published by E. P. Dutton & Co. Inc., New York. By permission of John Schaffner, Literary Agent (*pages 97, 148*).

David, Elizabeth, *Summer Cooking.* Copyright © Elizabeth David, 1955, 1965. Published by Penguin Books Ltd., London. By permission of Penguin Books Ltd. (*pages 98, 147*).
David, Elizabeth, *Syllabubs and Fruit Fools.* Copyright © Elizabeth David, 1969. By permission of Elizabeth David (*pages 96, 119*).
David, Josephine, *Every-Day Cookery for Families of Moderate Income.* Published by Frederick Warne and Co. Ltd., London. By permission of Frederick Warne and Co. Ltd. (*page 95*).
Derys, Gaston, *L'Art d'Être Gourmand.* Copyright by Albin Michel, 1929. Published by Éditions Albin Michel, Paris. Translated by permission of Éditions Albin Michel (*page 141*).
Douglas, Joyce, *Old Pendle Recipes.* Copyright © Joyce Douglas, 1976. Published by Hendon Publishing Co. Ltd., Nelson, Lancaster. By permission of Hendon Publishing Co., Ltd. (*page 120*).
Dubois, Urbain, *Nouvelle Cuisine Bourgeoise.* Published by Paul Bernardin, Librairie-Éditeur, Paris, 1888 (*page 144*).
Dubois, Urbain, *Cuisine de Tous les Pays,* 4th Édition 1882 (*page 129*).
Duckitt, Hildagonda J., *Hilda's "Where is it?" of Recipes.* Published by Chapman and Hall, Ltd., London. By permission of Associated Book Publishers Ltd. (*page 158*).
Dumont, Émile, *La Bonne Cuisine.* Published by Degorce-Cadot, Paris 1873 (*page 103*).
D'Ermo, Dominique, *The Chef's Dessert Cookbook.* © 1976 Dominique D'Ermo. Published by Atheneum Publishers, New York. By permission of Atheneum Publishers (*page 115*).
Escudier, Jean Noel, *La Véritable Cuisine Provençale et Niçoise.* Published by U.N.I.D.E., Paris. Translated by permission of U.N.I.D.E. (*page 93*).
Esterling, Elizabeth W. (Editor), *Le Cookbook.* © The American Hospital of Paris, 1976. Published by The American Hospital of Paris. Translated by permission of The American Hospital of Paris (*page 157*).
Fairclough, M. A., *The Ideal Cookery Book.* Published by George Routledge & Sons Ltd., London. By permission of George Routledge & Sons Ltd. (*page 127*).
Favre, Joseph, *Dictionnaire Universel de Cuisine Pratique.* Published by Laffitte Reprints, Marseille 1978. Translated by permission of Laffitte Reprints (*page 153*).
Firuski, Elvia and Maurice (Editors), *The Best of Boulestin.* Published by William Heinemann Ltd., London 1932. By permission of William Heinemann Ltd. (*page 93*).
Flower, Barbara and Rosenbaum, Elisabeth, *The Roman Cookery Book.* A critical translation of "The Art of Cooking by Apicius". © E. Rosenbaum, 1958. Published by George G. Harrap and Co. Ltd., London. By permission of George G. Harrap and Co. Ltd. (*page 110*).
Foods of the World, *African Cooking.* © 1970 Time Inc. Published by Time-Life Books, Alexandria (*page 95*).
Francatelli, Charles Elmé, *The Modern Cook.* A Practical Guide to the Culinary Art in all its branches. Published by Richard Bentley, London 1862 (*page 93*).
Francatelli, Charles Elmé, *The Royal English and Foreign Confectioner.* Published by Chapman and Hall, London 1862 (*page 93*).
Frank, Kato, *Cooking the Hungarian Way.* © Paul Hamlyn Ltd. 1963. Published by Paul Hamlyn, London. By permission of The Hamlyn Group (*page 138*).
Gilbert, Philéas, *La Cuisine de Tous les Mois.* Published by Abel Goubaud, Éditeur, Paris 1893 (*page 134*).
Gouy, Jean de, *La Cuisine et la Pâtisserie Bourgeoises à la Portée de Tous.* Published by J. Lebègue & Cie. Libraires-Éditeurs, Paris 1896 (*pages 120, 121*).
Grigson, Jane, *English Food.* Copyright © Jane Grigson, 1974. First published by Macmillan 1974. Published by Penguin Books Ltd., London 1977. By permission of Macmillan London Ltd. (*pages 106, 119, 135 and 149*).
Guérard, Michel, *Michel Guérard's Cuisine Gourmande.* © Macmillan London Ltd. 1977, 1978. Originally published in French as "La Cuisine Gourmande". © Éditions Robert Laffont S.A., Paris 1978. Published by Macmillan London Ltd. By permission of Macmillan London Ltd. (*page 145*).
Hellermann, Dorothee V., *Das Kochbuch aus Hamburg.* © Copyright 1975 by Verlagsteam Wolfgang Hölker. Published by Wolfgang Hölker. Translated by permission of Wolfgang Hölker (*page 128*).
Hewitt, Jean, *The New York Times Weekend Cookbook.*

Copyright © 1975 by Jean Hewitt. Published by Times Books, A Division of Quadrangle/The New York Times Book Co. By permission of Times Books, A Division of Quadrangle/The New York Times Book Co. (page 95).

Meyraud, H., La Cuisine à Nice. Privately published, Nice, 1922 (page 92).

Isnard, Léon, La Cuisine Française et Africaine. Copyright 1949, by Éditions Albin Michel. Published by Éditions Albin Michel, Paris. Translated by permission of Éditions Albin Michel (page 149).

Jack, Florence B., Cookery for Every Household. Published by Thomas Nelson and Sons, Ltd., London 1934. By permission of Thomas Nelson and Sons, Ltd. (pages 112, 155).

Jans, Hugh, Vrij Nederland (Dutch Magazine). Published by Vrij Nederland, Amsterdam, December 1970 (pages 93, 143).

Jarrin, G. A., The Italian Confectioner. Published by E. S. Ebers and Co., London 1841 (page 100).

Jeanes, William, Gunter's Modern Confectioner. Published by Dean & Son, Publishers and Factors, London 1861 (page 148).

Jewry, Mary (Editor), Warne's Model Cookery and House-keeping Book. © Copyright F. Warne (Publishers) Ltd. Published by Frederick Warne & Co. Ltd., London. By permission of Frederick Warne & Co. Ltd. (pages 106, 118 and 165).

Kahn, Odette (Editor), Cuisine et Vins de France (Magazine). Published by Société Française d'Éditions Vinicoles. Translated by permission of Odette Kahn (page 137).

Kenney-Herbert, Col. A. F. (Wyvern), Fifty Dinners. Published by Edward Arnold, London 1895 (page 115).

Kenney-Herbert, Col. A. F. (Wyvern), Sweet Dishes. Published by Higginbotham & Co., Madras 1900 (page 136).

King, Susan, Susan King's Cook Book. © Copyright Woman's Realm 1967. Published by Paul Hamlyn Limited, London. By permission of Woman's Realm (page 99).

King, Susan, Woman's Realm (Magazine). By permission of Woman's Realm, London (page 136).

Kiehnle, Hermine and Hädecke, Maria, Das Neue Kiehnle Kochbuch. © Walter Hädecke Verlag. (Vorm Süddeutsches Verlagshaus). Published by Walter Hädecke Verlag. Translated by permission of Walter Hädecke Verlag (pages 99, 121).

Lang, George, The Cuisine of Hungary. Copyright © 1971 by George Lang. Published by Atheneum Publishers, New York. By permission of Atheneum Publishers (page 140).

Lecourt, H., La Cuisine Chinoise. Copyright Éditions Robert Laffont S.A. 1968. Published by Éditions Robert Laffont, Paris. Translated by permission of Éditions Robert Laffont (page 143).

Leyel, Mrs C. F., Puddings. Published by George Routledge & Sons Ltd., London (pages 105,131).

Lin, Florence, Florence Lin's Chinese Vegetarian Cookbook. Copyright © 1976 Florence S. Lin. Published by Hawthorn Books, Inc., New York. By permission of Hawthorn Books, Inc. (page 106).

Lowinsky, Ruth, More Lovely Food. Published by the Nonesuch Press, London 1935 (pages 105,150).

Lucas, Dione, and Gorman, Marion, The Dione Lucas Book of French Cooking. Copyright 1947 by Dione Lucas. Copyright © 1973 by Mark Lucas and Marion F. Gorman. Published by Little, Brown and Company, Boston. By permission of Little, Brown and Company (page 157).

Lune, Pierre de, Le Nouveau Cuisinier 1656 (pages 111,112).

Macnicol, Fred, Hungarian Cookery. Copyright © Fred Macnicol, 1978. Published by Penguin Books Ltd., London. By permission of Penguin Books Ltd. (page 159).

Marshall, Mrs. A. B., Fancy Ices. Published by Simpkin, Marshall, Hamilton, Kent and Co. Ltd. c. 1890 (page 153).

Massey and Son's Comprehensive Pudding Book. Published by Massey and Son's, London 1865 (page 160).

Mathiot, Ginette, Je Sais Faire la Pâtisserie. Published by Éditions Albin Michel. Translated by permission of Éditions Albin Michel (page 163).

McInerny, Claire and Roche, Dorothy, Savour—A New Cookery Book. Published by Oxford University Press, London 1939. By permission of Claire McInerny (page 101).

McNeill, F. Marian, The Scots Kitchen. Published by Blackie and Son Limited, London. By permission of Blackie and Son Limited (pages 129, 150).

70 Médecins de France. Le Trésor de la Cuisine du Bassin Méditerranéen (page 127).

Menon, La Cuisinière Bourgeoise, 1745 (page 99).

Menon, Les Soupers de la Cour, 1746 (pages 110,143).

Molchanova, O. P., et al., Kniga O Vkusnoi i Zdorovoi Pishche. Published by Pishchepromizdat Publishing House, Moscow, 1952 (pages 95,137).

Molokhovets, Elena, Podarok Molodým Khozyaĭkam. Published in St. Petersburg, 1892 (pages 102, 122, and 130).

Montagné, Prosper, Larousse Gastronomique. © Copyright The Hamlyn Publishing Group Limited, 1961. Published by The Hamlyn Publishing Group Limited, London. By permission of The Hamlyn Publishing Group Limited (pages 118, 130).

Montagné, Prosper and Gottschalk, A., Mon Menu—Guide d'Hygiène Alimentaire. Published by Société d'Applications Scientifiques, Paris (page 124).

Morphy, Countess, Sweets and Puddings.. Published by Herbert Joseph Limited, London 1936. By permission of Herbert Joseph (page 156).

Nignon, Edouard, Les Plaisirs de la Table. Published by the author c.1920. Reprinted by Éditions Daniel Morcrette, B.P.26, 95270 Luzarches, France 1979. Translated by permission of Éditions Daniel Morcrette (pages 108, 116 and 162).

Norberg, Inga, Good Food from Sweden. Published by Chatto & Windus, London 1935. By permission of Curtis Brown Ltd. (pages 108, 123).

Oliver, Raymond, La Cuisine—Sa Technique, Ses Secrets. Published by Éditions Bordas, Paris. Translated by permission of Leon Amiel Publishers, New York (page 120).

Olney, Judith, Summer Food. Copyright © 1978 by Judith Olney. Published by Atheneum Publishers, New York. By permission of Atheneum Publishers (pages 101, 105 and 146).

Olney, Richard, The French Menu Cookbook. Copyright © 1970 by Richard Olney. Published by Simon and Schuster, New York. By permission of John Schaffner, Literary Agent (page 125).

Olney, Richard, Simple French Food. Copyright © 1974 by Richard Olney. Published by Atheneum Publishers, New York. By permission of Penguin Books Ltd. (pages 102, 126 and 146).

Orga, Irfan, Cooking the Middle East Way. © Paul Hamlyn Limited, 1962. Published by The Hamlyn Publishing Group Limited, London. By permission of The Hamlyn Publishing Group Limited (pages 130,132).

Orosa del Rosario, Helen (Editor), Maria Y. Orosa—Her Life and Work. Copyright 1970 by Helen Orosa del Rosario. Published by Helen Orosa del Rosario, Philippines 1970. By permission of Helen Orosa del Rosario (page 113).

Owen, Sri, The Home Book of Indonesian Cookery. © Sri Owen 1976. Published by Faber and Faber, Ltd., London. By permission of Faber and Faber (page 141).

Pappas, Lou Seibert, Egg Cookery. Copyright © 1976 Lou Seibert Pappas. Published by 101 Productions, California. By permission of 101 Productions (page 150).

Peck, Paula, Paula Peck's Art of Good Cooking. Copyright © 1961, 1966 by Paula Peck. Published by Simon & Schuster, A Division of Gulf and Western Corporation, New York. By permission of John Schaffner Literary Agent (page 94).

Petit, A., La Gastronomie en Russie. Published by Émile Mellier, Libraire-Éditeur, Paris 1860 (page 140).

Les Petits Plats et Les Grands. © 1977, by Éditions Denoël, Paris. Published by Éditions Denoël Sarl, Paris. Translated by permission of Éditions Denoël Sarl (pages 114, 139).

Petrov, Dr L., Djelepov, Dr N., Iordanov, Dr E., Uzunova, S., Bulgarska Nazionalna Kuchniya. Copyright © by the four authors. Published by Zemizdat, Sofia 1978. Translated by permission of Jusautor (Bulgarian Copyright Agency) (pages 96, 102).

Philpot, Rosl, Viennese Cookery. Published by Hodder and Stoughton Limited, London. By permission of Hodder and Stoughton Limited (page 128).

Pomiane, Édouard de, Le Code de la Bonne Chère. Published by Éditions Albin Michel, Paris. Translated by permission of Éditions Albin Michel (page 96).

Portinari, Laura Gras, Cucina e Vini del Piemonte e della Valle d'Aosta. © Copyright 1971 Ugo Mursia Editore—Milan. Published by Ugo Mursia Editore S.p.A. Milano. Translated by permission of Ugo Mursia Editore (pages 97, 100 and 113).

Les Princes de la Gastronomie. © 1.2.1975—Les Éditions Mondiales. Published by Modes de Paris. Translated by permission of Les Éditions Mondiales (pages 125, 138 and 154).

Quillet, Aristide, La Cuisine Moderne. Copyright Librairie Aristide Quillet 1946. Published by Librairie Aristide Quillet. Translated by permission of Librairie Aristide Quillet (page 104).

Ray, Elizabeth (Editor), The Best of Eliza Acton. Copyright © Longmans, Green & Co. Ltd., 1968. Introduction Copyright © Elizabeth David 1968. Published by Penguin Books Ltd., London. By permission of Penguin Books Ltd. (pages 103, 160 and 164).

Reboul, J. B., La Cuisinière Provençale. Published by Tacussel, Marseilles. Translated by permission of Tacussel, Éditeur (page 114).

Roden, Claudia, A Book of Middle Eastern Food. Copyright © Claudia Roden, 1968. Published by Penguin Books Ltd., London and Alfred A. Knopf, New York. By permission of Claudia Roden (page 92).

Rubinstein, Helge and Bush, Sheila, A Freezer for All Seasons. Published by André Deutsch Limited, London. By permission of André Deutsch Limited (pages 151, 156).

Rubinstein, Helge and Bush, Sheila, Ices Galore. Copyright © 1977 by Helge Rubinstein & Sheila Bush. Published by André Deutsch Limited, London. By permission of André Deutsch Limited (page 152).

Rundell, Mrs., Modern Domestic Cookery. Published by Milner and Company, Limited, London (page 127).

Saint-Ange, Madame, La Cuisine de Madame Saint-Ange. © Éditions Chaix. Published by Éditions Chaix, Grenoble. Translated by permission of Éditions Chaix (page 108).

Salvatori de Zuliani, Mariú, La Cucina di Versilia e Garfagnana. Published by Franco Angeli Editore, Milan. Translated by permission of Franco Angeli Editore (page 121).

Savarin, Mme Jeanne (Editor), La Cuisine des Familles, (Magazine). No. 107 July 7 1907 (page 157).

Schuler, Elizabeth, Mein Kochbuch. © Copyright 1948 by Schuler-Verlag, Stuttgart-N, Lenzhalde 28. Published by Schuler Verlagsgesellschaft, Stuttgart. Translated by permission of Schuler-Verlag (page 158).

Singh, Dharamjit, Indian Cookery. Copyright © Dharamjit Singh, 1970. Published by Penguin Books Ltd., London. By permission of Penguin Books Ltd. (page 133).

Skipwith, Sofka, Eat Russian. © Sofka Skipwith 1973. Published by David & Charles (Holdings) Ltd., Newton Abbot. By permission of David & Charles (Holdings) Ltd. (page 122).

Smith, Michael, Fine English Cookery. © Michael Smith 1973. Published by Faber and Faber, London. By permission of David Higham Associates Limited, London (Authors' Agent) (pages 106, 116 and 163).

Sorbiatti, Giuseppe, La Gastronomia Moderna. Published by Tip, Boniardi-Pogliani Di Ermenegildo Besozzi, Milano 1866 (page 104).

Spagnol, Elena, I Gelati Fatti in Casa con o Senza Macchina. © 1975 Rizzoli Editore, Milano. Published by Rizzoli Editore, Milano. By permission of Rizzoli Editore (page 154).

Spry, Constance and Hume, Rosemary, The Constance Spry Cookery Book. First published 1956 by J. M. Dent & Sons Ltd. Published by Pan Books Ltd., London 1972. By permission of J. M. Dent & Sons Ltd. (page 161).

Tibbott, S. Minwel, Welsh Fare. © National Museum of Wales (Welsh Folk Museum). Published by the National Museum of Wales (Welsh Folk Museum) 1976. By permission of the National Museum of Wales (Welsh Folk Museum) (page 134).

Toklas, Alice B., The Alice B. Toklas Cook Book. Copyright 1954, by Alice B. Toklas. Published by Harper & Row, Publishers, Inc., New York. By permission of Harper & Row, Publishers, Inc. (pages 107, 116, 144 and 150).

Tschirky, Oscar, The Cook Book by "Oscar" of the Waldorf. Published by The Werner Company, New York (pages 114, 141 and 147).

Turgeon, C., Tante Marie's French Kitchen. Copyright 1950 by Cartes Taride, Éditeurs Libraires, Paris. Published by S.A.R.L. Cartes Taride, Paris. By permission of S.A.R.L. Cartes Taride & Kaye and Ward Ltd. (pages 109, 128).

Viard and Fouret, Le Cuisinier Royal, 1828 (pages 110, 123, 146 and 160).

Waldo, Myra, The Complete Round-the-World Cookbook. Copyright 1954 by Myra Waldo. Published by Doubleday & Company, Inc., New York. By permission of Doubleday & Company, Inc. (page 110).

Wason, Betty, *The Art of German Cooking.* © Elizabeth Wason Hall 1967. First published in Great Britain by Allen & Unwin 1971. By permission of George Allen & Unwin (Publishers) Ltd., Hemel Hempstead (*page 132*).

Weber, J. M. Erich, *Theory and Practice of the Confectioner.* Published by Internationaler Fachverlag, Dresden c.1927 (*page 104*).

Willan, Anne, *Great Cooks and their Recipes from Taillevent to Escoffier.* Copyright © 1977 by McGraw-Hill Book Company (UK) Limited, Maidenhead. First published in Great Britain in 1977 by Elm Tree Books/ Hamish Hamilton Ltd., London. By permission of Hamish Hamilton & McGraw-Hill Book Company (*page 123*).

Willinsky, Grete, *Kochbuch der Büchergilde.* © Büchergilde Gutenberg, Frankfurt am Main 1958. Published by Büchergilde Gutenberg, Frankfurt. Translated by permission of Büchergilde Gutenberg (*page 115*).

Wilson, Jose (Editor), *House and Garden's New Cookbook.* Copyright © 1967 by The Condé Nast Publications Inc. Published by Simon and Schuster, New York. By permission of Condé Nast Publications Inc. (*page 117*).

Witwicka, H. and Soskine, S., *La Cuisine Russe Classique.* © Éditions Albin Michel, 1968 et 1978. Published by Éditions Albin Michel, Paris. Translated by permission of Éditions Albin Michel (*pages 139, 142*).

Wren, Jenny, *Modern Domestic Cookery.* Published by Alexander Gardner, Paisley 1880 (*page 134*).

Acknowledgements and Picture Credits

The Editors of this book are particularly indebted to Pat Alburey, Royston, Hertfordshire; and A. R. Huelin, Westminster College, London.

They also wish to thank the following: Skeffington Ardron, London; Robert Bruce, London; Sarah Bunney, London; The Chelmer Institute of Higher Education, Chelmsford, Essex; R. C. Coates, London; Jennifer Davidson, London; Pamela Davidson, London; Fiona Duncan, London; Diana Grant, London; Fayal Greene, London; Maggie Heinz, London; Shirley King, London; Marion Hunter, Sutton, Surrey; Brenda Jayes, London; John Leslie, London; Elizabeth Moreau, Langley Park, Bucks; Maria Mosby, London; Dilys Naylor, Kingston upon Thames, Surrey; Jo Oxley, Morden, Surrey; Joanna Roberts, London; David Simpson, London; Anne Stephenson, London; Stephanie Thompson, Hampton Court, Surrey; J. M. Turnell & Co., New Covent Garden, London; Eileen Turner, Brighton, Sussex.

Photographs by Tom Belshaw: Cover, 4, 8, 10—top, 11, 12—top right, 13—top right and bottom, 14 to 15, 16—bottom, 32, 39—bottom, 40 to 41, 44—bottom, 45—bottom, 46 to 47, 51—bottom, 52, 53—top, 58 to 59, 62—bottom, 63—bottom, 64 to 65, 68, 70, 71—bottom, 72 to 77, 80 to 83, 87—box, 89.

Photographs by Alan Duns: 9, 10—bottom, 18, 20 to 31, 33 to 36, 38, 39—top, 42 to 43, 56 to 57, 60, 62—bottom, 63—bottom, 66 to 67, 71—top, 84 to 86, 87—top and bottom, 90.

Other photographs (alphabetical): Gina Harris, 16—17—top and bottom left, 44—top, 45—top, 48, 50, 51—top, 53—bottom, 78, 88. Louis Klein, 2. David Levin, 12—left and centre, 13—top left and centre, 54 to 55.

All line cuts from Mary Evans Picture Library and private sources.

Colour separations by Gilchrist Ltd.—Leeds, England
Typesetting by Camden Typesetters—London, England
Printed and bound by Brepols S.A.—Turnhout, Belgium.